Transforming International Institutions

Erin R. Graham is Associate Professor of Global Affairs and Faculty Fellow at the Kellogg Institute for International Studies and the Pulte Institute for Global Development at the University of Notre Dame, USA. She received her PhD from The Ohio State University and held positions at Perry World House at the University of Pennsylvania and the Niehaus Center for Globalization and Governance at Princeton University. Her research focuses on international institutions and is published in *International Organization*, the *Journal of Politics*, *International Studies Quarterly*, the *European Journal of International Relations*, and other outlets.

T0369568

Praise for *Transforming International Institutions*

'*Transforming International Institutions* is a tour de force that cements Erin Graham as one of the most important and innovative voices in International Relations. In this timely, well-researched, and theoretically innovative study of the United Nations, Graham revisits traditional understandings of how change takes place in the world's leading organization. With deep anchors in historical institutionalism, Graham meticulously documents a quiet revolution in the UN from an organization that was multilateral in theory and practice to an organization where a small number of states control agendas by means of earmarked budgets. This is a must-read for global governance scholars and practitioners who will benefit equally from Graham's historical research and analysis of the contemporary period.'

Orfeo Fioretos, Temple University

'*Transforming International Institutions* masterfully demonstrates how minor changes in United Nations funding rules had major unanticipated consequences; ultimately granting individual donor states substantial policy influence over UN agencies. Professor Graham's book makes important contributions to international relations theory and it is deeply grounded in history. But the book will also appeal to students and policymakers who are interested in better understanding how donor money has gradually become such an important determinant of what UN agencies do and don't do.'

Erik Voeten, Georgetown University

'The United Nations has significantly transformed since its founding, as the practice of earmarked funding progressively took over the mandatory state contributions provided by the Charter. Based on extensive longitudinal research, this excellent book not only throws light on this crucial, troublesome and yet partly belowground change in multilateral politics—it also develops an insightful theory of incremental institutional design that further illuminates the plasticity of international rules and the continued efforts of decision makers to remold them. A great scholarly accomplishment, both analytically and empirically.'

Vincent Pouliot, McGill University

Transforming International Institutions

How Money Quietly Sidelined Multilateralism at The United Nations

ERIN R. GRAHAM

Associate Professor of Global Affairs
Keough School of Global Affairs
University of Notre Dame

OXFORD
UNIVERSITY PRESS

Great Clarendon Street, Oxford, OX2 6DP,
United Kingdom

Oxford University Press is a department of the University of Oxford.
It furthers the University's objective of excellence in research, scholarship,
and education by publishing worldwide. Oxford is a registered trade mark of
Oxford University Press in the UK and in certain other countries

Published in the United States of America by Oxford University Press
198 Madison Avenue, New York, NY 10016, United States of America

British Library Cataloguing in Publication Data
Data available

Library of Congress Control Number: 2023935220

ISBN 978–0–19–887793–6
ISBN 978–0–19–887794–3 (pbk.)

DOI: 10.1093/oso/9780198877936.001.0001

Printed and bound by
CPI Group (UK) Ltd, Croydon, CR0 4YY

Acknowledgments

This book is the product of around ten years of thinking about the relationship between multilateralism and international organizations' financing, especially in the United Nations system. I started thinking about these issues during my post-doc year at the Niehaus Center for Globalization and Governance at Princeton and received early encouragement from Bob Keohane and Andy Moravcsik. My tremendous respect for these two scholars meant that I took their interest as sufficient reason to pursue what was then a nascent but relatively clear idea: that earmarked funding to IOs did not meet the standard of multilateralism and, as a result, its use was altering IO governance. Without their encouragement, I might not have moved forward, since a major departure from my dissertation felt risky at the time.

In the years that followed, my thinking on funding and multilateralism evolved through engagement with a number of generous, sharp scholars, especially Bentley Allan, Burcu Bayram, Sarah Bush, Xinyuan Dai, Julia Gray, Alex Grigorescu, Tammi Gutner, Anne Holthoefer, Simon Hug, Ayse Kaya, David Lake, Ron Mitchell, Mark Pollack, Vincent Pouliot, Bernhard Reinsberg, Duncan Snidal, Alex Thompson, Mike Tierney, and Erik Voeten. My work was facilitated by a modest teaching load at Drexel University, an outstanding research assistant in Allie Serdaru, and a tenure bar that allowed space to pursue projects I found interesting without fear of losing my job.

The emergence of historical institutionalism in IR and its resonance with my own thinking about the UN's evolution in financing and governance altered the trajectory of this book and informs its theory. On this front I thank Gerry Berk for teaching American political development in such a compelling way that it always lurked in the back of my mind: how can we do this in IR? I was further educated by the work of three giants of comparative and American political development, none of whom I have met: Kathleen Thelen, Jacob Hacker, and Paul Pierson. Enter another bit of contingency: I moved down the street from Orfeo Fioretos, who was already "doing this in IR." Orfeo's generous guidance facilitated my entrée into HI's burgeoning IR scene.

Helping further, Bill Burke-White invited me to spend a semester at Perry World House at Penn as a visitor in 2018 during which time I wrote an early but recognizable version of the book's theory chapter for an APSA panel. Orfeo, Abe Newman, Tonya Putnam, and Taylor St. John provided invaluable feedback. Further instructive comments came from Jessica Stanton, and Mark Pollack (again). I benefited immensely from their engagement. An ample research award, the Moody Research Grant from the Lyndon Baines Johnson Foundation and Moody Foundation of Galveston, Texas, supported my archival work at the LBJ Library in Austin.

I am extremely grateful to have a supportive and responsive editor in Dominic Byatt at Oxford University Press who facilitated a remarkably smooth process. Three insightful reviewers helped me to sharpen the book's contributions and improve it in ways large and small. I am further grateful to Scott Appleby, the Dean of the Keough School at Notre Dame, for ensuring I had time to finish the book despite a move and transition to a new university.

I must also thank my family and friends. I begin with my Mom and Dad, Connie and Dave Graham. I am thankful for so many things they gave me, but perhaps most relevant here, I am thankful they encouraged me to pursue whatever path I wanted without much input or restriction, expecting only that I try my best. I am thankful to my sister, Ashley, for her friendship and perspective. I am thankful to Ron Mitchell for his steady, thoughtful support since 2004. I am thankful for a few really good friends in the discipline: Phil Ayoub, Ayse Kaya, Eleonora Mattiacci, and Sarah Bush. I can confirm that these people are there when you need them. That my arrival in Philly coincided with Sarah's such that we learned to be assistant professors together was especially fortunate.

I thank my daughter, Stella Ruth, whose welcome arrival was quickly followed by my first publications in *IO* and *ISQ*, such that the line from Brandi Carlile's song Mother, "I'll never hit the big time without you" is especially apt in my case. When I shared with Stella that my book would be published, she asked if she could have her own copy. When I replied that she could, she remarked, "then we can read it together, and I can learn something new." Although the prose pales in comparison to Harry Potter & the Goblet of Fire and the figures cannot compete with the illustrations in Patricia Pollacco's Ginger and Petunia, my heart swelled with appreciation at my favorite five-year-old's suggestion.

That leaves Zoltán. To have a second-to-none IR theorist living in my home is an unfair advantage that I readily acknowledge. He is my sounding board and testing ground for all ideas, including but not limited to those about processes of institutional development and multilateralism that lie at the center of this book. He read every page; most more than once. Zoltán is dogged in his belief in me and in the support and encouragement he provides. His efforts—especially in moments when I do not excel as a recipient of encouragement—undoubtedly facilitated forward movement on this project in hard times. To have met him and have him by my side will forever be the great stroke of luck in my life.

Notre Dame, Indiana
2022

Contents

List of Figures

List of Tables

List of Abbreviations

ACABQ	Advisory Committee on Administrative and Budgetary Questions
ATS	Antarctic Treaty System
DAC	Development Assistance Committee (OECD)
DANIDA	Danish International Development Agency
ECHR	European Convention on Human Rights
ECtHR	European Court of Human Rights
ECOSOC	Economic and Social Council
EPTA	Expanded Program for Technical Assistance
FAO	Food and Agriculture Organization
FRUS	Foreign Relations of the United States
GATT	General Agreement on Tariffs and Trade
IBRD	International Bank for Reconstruction and Development
ICJ	International Court of Justice
IDA	International Development Agency
IHL	International Humanitarian Law
ILO	International Labor Organization
IMF	International Monetary Fund
IRS	Internal Revenue Service (US)
JIU	Joint Inspections Unit
MDTF	Multi-Donor Trust Fund
NIEO	New International Economic Order
NORAD	Norwegian Agency for Development Cooperation
OCHA	Office for the Coordination of Humanitarian Affairs
ODI	Overseas Development Institute
OECD	Organization for Economic Co-operation and Development
ONUC	United Nations Operation in the Congo
RAF	Royal Air Force (UK)
SADCC	Southern African Development Cooperation Conference
SDGs	Sustainable Development Goals
SF	Special Fund
SIDA	Swedish International Development Agency
SUNFED	Special UN Fund for Economic Development
TA	Technical Assistance
TAA	Technical Assistance Administration
TAB	Technical Assistance Board
TAC	Technical Assistance Committee
UNCDF	United Nations Capital Development Fund
UNCTAD	United Nations Conference on Trade and Development

UNDP	United Nations Development Program
UNDS	United Nations Development System
UNEF	United Nations Emergency Force
UNEP	United Nations Environment Program
UNESCO	United Nations Educational, Scientific, and Cultural Organization
UNFPA	United Nations Population Fund
UNFSSTD	UN Financing System in Science and Technology Development
UNGA	United Nations General Assembly
UN-HABITAT	United Nations Human Settlement Program
UNHCR	United Nations High Commissioner for Refugees
UNICEF	United Nations Children's Fund
UNIDO	United Nations Industrial Development Organization
UNODC	United Nations Office on Drugs and Crime
UNOPS	United Nations Office for Project Services
UNRRA	United Nations Relief and Rehabilitation Administration
UNSC	United Nations Security Council
UN-WOMEN	UN Entity for Gender Equality and the Empowerment of Women
USAF	United States Air Force
USAID	United States Agency for International Development
USUN	United States Mission to the United Nations
VCLT	Vienna Convention on the Law of the Treaties
WFP	World Food Program
WHO	World Health Organization
WTO	World Trade Organization

1

Introduction

Among the documents included in the United Nations Quadrennial Comprehensive Policy Review in 2016 was a report from Romesh Muttukumaru, a veteran of the United Nations Development System (UNDS). The report's aim was to propose how United Nations entities might encourage member states to reduce the conditions they placed on financial contributions to the United Nations system. Expansive use of these "conditions" led, for example, to 75 percent of the US contributions to the UN Development Program being used in two countries, Iraq and Afghanistan.[1] It led, for example, to contributions from the French Government skewing toward its former colonial possessions (the Central African Republic, Vietnam, and Haiti).[2] In short, it often led the United Nations to look like a contract agency for bilateral aid. Among the purposes of the Muttukumaru Report was to develop a set of strategies that would encourage member states to provide a larger share of their contributions in the form of "core" resources, without strings attached.

The topic was a familiar one; by 2016, 75 percent of the money flowing through UNDS came in the form of "non-core" resources that were earmarked by the donor for a specific use. For the most part, these were not large pots of money with multiple donors. Nearly 90 percent of earmarked contributions to UNDS were single-donor or single-project contributions.[3] Disproportionate reliance on earmarked funding had become a source of concern across the UN system. Often expressed with an audience of donors in mind, these concerns were typically couched in the language of effectiveness. The Joint Inspections Unit, the main evaluation arm of the United Nations system, had concluded nine years earlier in 2007 that earmarked contributions "inhibited secretariats of the organizations in their efforts to deliver mandated programs."[4] In 2012, the Economic and Social Council released a report stating that earmarked funding "is often seen as potentially distorting program priorities."[5] The World Food Program reported that earmarked aid prevented the organization from complying with its mandate to prioritize

---

[1] UNDP, "The United States and UNDP: A Partnership that Advances US Interests." See https://www.undp.org/funding/core-donors/UnitedStates (accessed July 11, 2022).
[2] See United Nations Multi-donor Trust Fund Office, available at http://mptf.undp.org/factsheet/donor/00112 (accessed April 7, 2020).
[3] United Nations Multi-donor Trust Fund Office 2016, 30.
[4] Yusef et al. 2007, ii.
[5] UN General Assembly and ECOSOC 2012, 12.

Transforming International Institutions. Erin R. Graham, Oxford University Press. © Erin R. Graham (2023).
DOI: 10.1093/oso/9780198877936.003.0001

least-developed and low-income food-deficit countries.[6] At the Office for the Coordination of Humanitarian Affairs (OCHA), earmarks led some emergencies to be overfunded while others were left without resources.[7] And the UN Development Program itself—the centerpiece of UNDS—identified "the earmarked nature of funds" as "a major reason for non-delivery of planned outputs."[8] Each statement aimed to communicate, explicitly or implicitly, that earmarked funding caused a divergence between the agreed-upon priorities of UN programs, whether thematic or geographic, and the work that UN entities supported in practice.

The source of this divergence between multilateral priorities and resource allocation lay in the governance of earmarked funds, which the various reports also sometimes mentioned, but often in technical, bureaucratic language. Earmarked funds are "designed and implemented outside the organisations' formal governing systems (...),"[9] they are "not subject to direct programmatic control by the governing bodies of United Nations entities,"[10] and they are "not directly regulated by intergovernmental bodies and processes."[11] Reports like these tended not to ruminate on what it meant that 75 percent of UNDS resources were not subject to control by intergovernmental bodies. It was here that the 2016 Muttukumaru Report was distinct. Drawing a direct line between earmarked contributions and UN governance, the report conveyed the reality in clear terms: "the continuing erosion of UNDS core funding and the resulting dependence on noncore resources to finance even its basic mandated activities *may undermine the multilateral character and democratic nature of the system as per its Charter.*"[12]

The Muttukumaru Report was not the first to suggest the effects of earmarked contributions extended to fundamental principles of UN governance. In 2010, Timo Mahn of the German Development Institute authored a briefing paper that began: "Changes in the financing of United Nations development cooperation are gradually eroding the multilateral character of UN development aid."[13] Later, in 2019, the UN system would speak more clearly when adopting its Funding Compact aimed at addressing earmarked funds, about which the Compact states: "Ultimately, they undermine the multilateral nature of United Nations'" support for development.[14] But the 2016 Report was among the first emanating from inside Turtle Bay to propose that what, for many, remained a technical issue of funding modalities was altering the fundamental nature of the UN system. If the UN was reluctant to acknowledge the link, it is understandable. The multilateral

---

[6] Executive Board of the World Food Program 2000.
[7] Yusef et al. 2007, 13. JIU/REP/20071.
[8] Executive Board of the UNDP 2013, 4.
[9] DANIDA 2013, iii.
[10] UN Secretary-General 2012, 20.
[11] UN General Assembly and ECOSOC 2012, 12.
[12] Muttukumaru 2016. Emphasis added.
[13] Mahn 2012.
[14] UN General Assembly 2019, 3 (A/74/73/Add.1-E/2019/4/Add.1).

character of the UN is fundamental to its identity, to how the world sees the institution and how the institution sees itself. More than that, the UN is identified with a particularly egalitarian variety of multilateralism. Outside the Security Council, where rules reflect power asymmetries, the egalitarian multilateralism of the General Assembly—one-country-one-vote—is carved in stone in the United Nations Charter. It is replicated across UN programs like the UN Development Program (UNDP), the UN Environment Program (UNEP), the UN Children's Fund (UNICEF), and the World Food Program (WFP). Egalitarian multilateralism distinguishes the UNDS from its Bretton Woods counterpart, the World Bank, where votes are distributed based on economic might. It also makes the UN the preferred institutional home for developing states, who enjoy strong majorities, and is often a forum to be avoided by its wealthiest member states, who do not.

These conceptions of the United Nations system have not changed significantly in past decades in either the popular imagination or scholarly research, yet the system has quietly undergone a remarkable transformation. The egalitarian multilateralism so fundamental to the Charter, and to basic understandings of what the UN *is* and how it operates, is still present on the rule books and in the decision-making processes of various UN governing bodies. But it does not govern the vast majority of money that flows through the system. Multilateral bodies do not exercise direct authority over earmarked contributions. As the proportion of earmarked funding grows, the egalitarian multilateralism of UN governing bodies controls an ever-shrinking portion of the UN's operational work. Bilateral contracts negotiated between donors and UN entities govern earmarked funds and sidestep egalitarian multilateralism.

The nature of the UN's transformation poses a series of questions for international relations (IR) scholars. The UN is often depicted as rigid and incapable of change.[15] The Charter was last amended in 1971. The legal barriers to change, which require two-thirds of the General Assembly to approve and ratify amendments, including all permanent members of the Security Council, are prohibitively high. The impression that the UN has not changed, and cannot change, is reflected and reinforced by routine criticism from the United States and others calling for reforms to improve efficiency and coordination year after year without ever conveying satisfaction with the results. Expressing a widely shared view, one commentator quipped that the Charter "bears little more resemblance to the modern world than does a Magellan map."[16] Yet today UN financing bears little resemblance to Charter rules that remain on the books. How did UN financing change so

---

[15] E.g., Idris and Bartolo 2000, 85–86; Lipscy 2017, 18; Hosli and Dörfler 2019. Howard LaFranchi, "The United Nations: Indispensable or Irrelevant?" *Christian Science Monitor*, September 18, 2020.
[16] Cited in Buga 2018, 298–299. For an exception, see Schlesinger (1997, 50) who calls the standard critique, that the UN "is an inflexible institution set in its ways and unwilling to change," a "myth worth exploding."

radically? Equally important, how was egalitarian multilateralism—a fundamental principle of UN governance—compromised and sidelined almost without notice?

These questions motivate the book. I offer a framework to understand transformational change in international institutions where transformation is defined as the reorganization of relationships among key actors and principles of governance. To explain the UN's transformation from an institution designed with rules that produce egalitarian multilateralism to one that operates a system of governance by bilateral contract, I develop a theoretical framework that emphasizes the gradual, subterranean, and uncoordinated nature of transformation. In the UN case, I argue that incremental changes in financing rules made in the late 1940s, and most important, in the 1960s, made possible a transformation in UN governance in the 2000s. Often, those who acted in earlier decades did not foresee or intend their actions to enable this transformation.

Despite an extensive literature on international organizations (IOs) in political science, scholarly inquiry into questions of financing is relatively new. There are exceptions. The UN funding crisis of the 1960s, with the proximate cause being the Soviet Union's refusal to pay dues for two peacekeeping missions, provoked scholarly interest. Prominent UN scholar Chadwick Alger persuasively argued in 1973 that the US preferred voluntary contributions to enhance its influence over UN programs.[17] Driven in large part by the growth in earmarked funding across IOs, sometimes referred to as multi-bi aid, non-core, or restricted funding, IO financing scholarship reemerged in the 2010s.[18] This research illuminates the breadth of earmarking trends across IOs, and tackles questions about why earmarked funding is so often the preferred modality of states and private actors. For the most part, this literature focuses on explaining variation in the contemporary moment rather than change over time. But consistent with Alger's early work, many studies that explain variation in earmarking behavior in a given snapshot imply an intuitive hypothesis about change: Donors want more control over their contributions to IOs and earmarks are a way to achieve this.

On the surface, the timing of the shift to increased earmarking appears favorable to this hypothesis. Most studies identify the 1990s or early 2000s as the decades earmarks took off.[19] This came on the heels of waning Western support during the 1980s when the Geneva Group—a group of UN member states that each contribute more than 1 percent of the UN regular budget—enforced a policy of zero real growth across the UN system for most of the decade. Earmarks appear to answer wealthy states' frustration with what they perceived as insufficient control

---

[17] Alger 1973.

[18] E.g., Sridhar and Woods 2013; Graham 2015; Bayram and Graham 2017; Eichenauer and Reinsberg 2017; Graham 2017; Michaelowa et al. 2017; Reinsberg 2017; Reinsberg et al. 2017; Eichenauer and Hug 2018; Baumann 2021; Graham and Serdaru 2020; Schmid et al. 2021; Thorvaldsdottir et al. 2022.

[19] E.g., Sridhar and Woods 2013, 328–329; Jenks and Topping 2016; Eichenauer and Reinsberg 2017, 172; Schmid et al. 2021, 435.

over their contributions. In this telling, the uptick in wealthy states' behavior would reflect their desire to exert control. But upon further interrogation the hypothesis is unsatisfying in two ways. Its first oversight is to ignore the importance of rules in enabling wealthy states' behavior. The historical record demonstrates that rule change preceded significant behavioral change—by decades. Voluntary funding rules were layered alongside mandatory ones. Mandatory rules were interpreted in more restrictive ways. Voluntary rules initially prohibited earmarks, but later came to permit them. In short, the hypothesis that powerful donors sought to reassert control in the 1990s makes sense as far as it goes, but why were rules altered decades earlier to permit donor earmarks? Did the same states push for rule change at that time, only to wait decades to take advantage? This points to the second shortcoming of the hypothesis: the UN's most powerful member states and largest suppliers of mandatory dues during the twentieth century, like the United States, United Kingdom, Japan, and others, did not advocate for rule changes that would permit earmarks. Rather, these changes came at the behest of other member states and non-state actors, often those associated with a pro-UN orientation like Sweden, the Netherlands, and the UN Office of Legal Affairs. These are not the actors we would typically suspect of conspiring to upend egalitarian multilateralism at the UN. In fact, they did not conspire to do so, but their actions substantially contributed to that outcome.

Focusing on powerful states' assertion of control through earmarking in the 1990s mistakes the end of the UN's transformation for its beginning. I argue that the UN's transformation was gradual, taking place over decades. In contrast to the conventional narrative that traces the rise of earmarked funding to the 1990s, I identify incremental changes to funding policy in 1949, reinforced in 1958 as the beginning of a gradual change process. I locate the decade of the 1960s as the critical period when institutional groundwork that enabled donors' behavioral changes was laid. These changes in the middle of the twentieth century contributed to the transformation of UN financing that gathered steam in the 1990s. I further argue that the transformative process was uncoordinated over time with a subterranean dynamic. By uncoordinated, I mean that actors who made decisions early in the process that proved critical to transformation, did not foresee or anticipate a transformative outcome, or actively work with actors who would carry the process forward at subsequent moments. The process is subterranean from the perspective of those key actors. In retrospect, those who are identified as enacting pivotal change in the transformation process, can, at the moment they enact change, genuinely intend the act to be *only* incremental. A gradual, uncoordinated change process allows that those who set transformation in motion can do so unknowingly, and can do so even if they would oppose the downstream, transformative effects of the changes they enact.

This argument rests on a particular set of assumptions about institutional design, rules, and agents. In contrast to prominent approaches in IR that focus on the design challenges posed by risk, the framework assumes that institutional architects operate in decision-making environments that are *also* characterized by genuine uncertainty. This assumption is important conceptually because it renders passable unintentional change pathways that would otherwise be closed off or confined to the error term. But the assumption also squares with empirical reality. As international institutions age, it becomes more difficult to maintain an assumption that actors who initially designed the rules could be reasonably expected to anticipate all relevant future states of the world and assign probabilities to the likelihood they would occur. Most of the international organizations designed in the period between 1945 and 1949 persist in the twenty-first century, but few would maintain that institutional architects of that era could *see* twenty-first-century states of the world from their immediate postwar perch. As early as 1965, Rupert Emerson wrote that "The United Nations two decades after San Francisco is a very different body from the one its creators fashioned, and it is a reasonable presumption that there were none or virtually none who presided over its creation who foresaw even dimly what it would become in the span of twenty years."[20] When even a medium-term metric of two or three decades is used, institutional designers often cannot anticipate the effects of their choices, let alone design institutions for future states of the world they cannot anticipate.

The downstream effects of institutional rules are subject to genuine uncertainty but they also contribute to it. In addition to their standard function as constraints that regulate behavior, the framework offered here treats rules as inherently permissive. This permissiveness is not only the product of intentional design as accounts of strategic ambiguity suggest, but is rooted in an unavoidable linguistic indeterminacy.[21] It is also aided by the passage of time; interpretations and purposes that were not conjured initially can be inspired by later contexts. Armed with rule permissiveness, motivated agents are capable of unpredictable action. They forward reinterpretations and redeploy rules in ways that serve their contemporary ends but were not anticipated by those who designed the rules and may even be at odds with the purposes they intended.

This set of assumptions opens space for rethinking how international rules change. In many international organizations, negotiating the revision, amendment or outright replacement of formal rules is extremely difficult, and not infrequently prohibitively so. The same is often true for bodies of international law. Yet interstate negotiation in which member states debate, persuade, coerce, or bribe one another to enact multilateral agreement remains the default method for thinking about how change occurs in IOs or international treaties. In this traditional conception, when the rules on the books are not revised, amended, or removed, it is easy to conclude that the rules have not changed. Scholars of international law

---

[20] Emerson 1965, 484.
[21] Greenstone 1986; Schauer 1991; Putnam 2020, 32.

point out that empirically this is simply not the case.[22] The law changes more often through evolutive treaty interpretation, and subsequent practice than through multilateral (re)negotiation.[23] If we exclude these mechanisms of change from our conceptual toolbox we may miss not only incremental change, but transformation.

In chapter two, I integrate mechanisms of change from international law with historical institutionalist thinking on gradual change. I contribute to the historical institutionalist research program in IR by articulating why and how change of this sort often has an under-the-radar, subterranean dynamic. Drawing on multiple archives across six decades of the postwar twentieth century, the book tracks how financing rules were added and reinterpreted at different moments in time and for distinct purposes in ways that ultimately facilitated a shift from egalitarian multilateralism to governance by bilateral contract, all without any renegotiation of Charter rules that govern UN funding.

Why Funding Matters for Multilateralism

Pressed for which rules are most important for the operation of multilateralism at international organizations, most would reply by focusing on representation or decision rules.[24] In conventional terms, multilateralism involves collective decision-making among a group of actors. Representation rules determine which states or other actors are represented in governing bodies and allocate votes across represented parties. Decision rules determine the threshold that resolutions or other decisions require for passage (e.g., majority, supermajority, unanimity) and in doing so facilitate collective decision-making. It is worth noting that the two pieces—a group of actors and collective decision-making—go together. Whether one thinks 20 actors engaged in collective decision-making is *more* multilateral than 10 actors doing so is open for debate, but neither the 10 nor the 20 is "doing" multilateralism if they make independent decisions rather than collective ones.

Multilateralism is widely understood to operate as a "leveling principle" that, while not eliminating power politics, has a restraining effect.[25] In contrast to ad hoc bargaining, voting and representation rules ensure voice opportunities and influence to weaker actors.[26] These rules also signal egalitarian and inegalitarian "varieties" of multilateralism.[27] Egalitarian rules allocate votes equally across member states, regardless of economic might or other factors. Inegalitarian rules, like those at the International Monetary Fund, or international development

---

[22] See Nolte 2013, 3; Buga 2018.

[23] Buga 2018, 4.

[24] E.g., This view is present in prominent IR scholarship on institutional design, including Koremenos et al. 2001, 772; Blake and Payton 2015; Kaya 2015, 9; Lipscy 2017, 49.

[25] Ikenberry 2003; Finnemore 2005.

[26] Kahler 1992, 681–682.

[27] Bayer et al. 2015; Graham 2015; Iannantuoni et al. 2021.

banks, allocate greater voice to larger economies and less to smaller ones. Outside the Security Council, the UN system is a model of egalitarian multilateralism. Governing bodies across its programs and specialized agencies make collective decisions based on the one-country-one-vote principle.

If representation and voting rules are so obviously central to the production of multilateralism at IOs, why do funding rules require attention? The answer is that funding rules determine whether multilateral governing bodies control the resource allocation process. No funding rule denies that governing bodies operate in ways consistent with multilateralism, but while some funding rules ensure that those governing bodies control resource allocation, others do not. In particular, funding rules that permit earmarks allow for resource allocation to be detached from multilateral control. That control shifts from the multilateral body to the individual donor, who can dictate how its contribution is used. Put differently, funding rules determine (and can limit) the reach of multilateral governance. Basic limits on donor discretion remain. In the UN system, all financial contributions must be used for purposes consistent with those of the relevant organization or program, but this leaves a wide berth for donors to fund bilateral priorities, whether programmatic, geostrategic, or both. As later chapters in the book will demonstrate, rules that permit earmarks do not ensure that earmarking itself will be a common practice. It remained relatively infrequent for most member states until the 1990s. But while permission does not ensure the popularity of the practice, it also does not limit its use. Rules that permit earmarks generally do not restrict the portion of IO funds that *can* be subject to earmarks. In short, they make possible a situation in which control over resource allocation is transferred entirely from multilateral governing bodies to individual donors. Such an outcome would be extreme, but most UN programs receive more than half of their contributions in the form of earmarked funding, and for a few the portion exceeds 80 percent. Earmarked funding levels at United Nations agencies and programs exceed the levels of other IOs, including the World Bank Group.[28]

Figure 1.1 depicts funding at four major UN voluntary programs: UNDP, the United Nations Children's Fund (UNICEF), the UN Population Fund (UNFPA), and the WFP.[29] None of these programs receives money under the mandatory assessments regime governed by Article 17 of the UN Charter. All contributions from member states (or from other actors) are voluntary. Although the portion varies, earmarked funding far exceeds any other funding type across the programs. It represents 93 percent of all funding to WFP, 82 percent to UNDP, 73 percent to UNICEF, and 65 percent of all funding to UNFPA. It is only the remaining portion of funds, a combination of voluntary core resources and fees (7 percent at WFP,

---

[28] Weinlich et al. 2020, 30.
[29] Data for Figures 1.1 and 1.2 are found in Topping and Jenks 2021, 31.

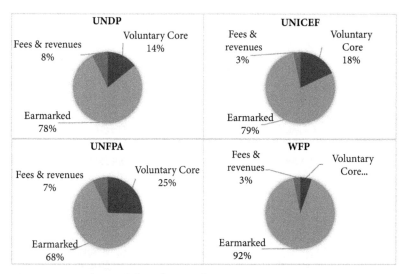

Figure 1.1 Funding at Selected UN Voluntary Programs.
Source: Topping and Jenks 2021, 31.

18 percent at UNDP, 27 percent at UNICEF, and 35 percent at UNFPA) that is governed directly by multilateral bodies.

Other UN programs receive money from the mandatory assessments system governed by Article 17 of the UN Charter but this generally represents a small portion of their funds (see Figure 1.2). For instance, earmarked funding represents 86 percent of all contributions to the UN Office on Drugs and Crime (UNODC), and 83 percent of the contributions to the UN High Commissioner for Refugees (UNHCR). When UN programs like UNODC and UNHCR are eligible for mandatory contributions, their use is typically confined to administrative costs rather than operational activities. The UN Environment Program stands out; its proportion of earmarked funds stands at just 57 percent alongside 33 percent in mandatory dues, and 9 percent from voluntary core contributions.[30] Remarkably, even at the UN Secretariat, the primary recipient of mandatory funds from the regular budget, earmarked contributions account for nearly half (48 percent) of all funding.

These figures make clear that earmarked funding is a prevalent, and even dominant funding modality across the UN system. They also clarify that the UN's multilateralism governs a relatively small portion of the money that flows through

---

[30] UNEP remains a small program relative to its development counterparts ($742 million versus $5517 million at UNDP); it also benefits from an agreement between the General Assembly and the UNEP Governing Council in 2012 to reverse the rise of earmarks and "shift towards unearmarked funding." Since that time, UNEP's regular budget allocation has grown from $12.1 million in 2012–13 to $247 million in 2018–19.

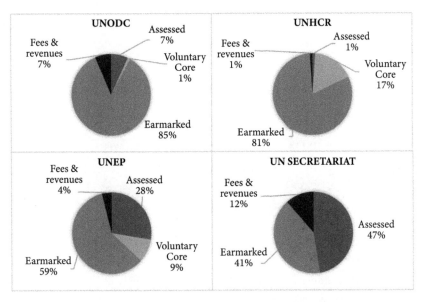

Figure 1.2 Funding at Selected UN Programs That Receive Mandatory Contributions.

Source: Topping and Jenks 2021, 31.

that system. Most funds are governed by contracts designed not by multilateral governing bodies, but by donors in negotiation with UN officials. These are customized to fit the preferences of the donor (or donors) regarding not only the purpose and project, but also terms of support, reporting requirements, and evaluation metrics. Of the same type of earmarked trust funds at the World Bank, Reinsberg explains that, "donors have great leverage in the design stage (...) donors can negotiate indicative preferences into the administrative agreement that Bank staff try to (and usually do) satisfy."[31] Many compare the governance of earmarked funding to bilateral aid, essentially making the UN a contract agency for the donor government. This is reflected in the language used by UN programs and donor governments to refer to earmarked funds. Denmark's aid agency (DANIDA) distinguishes between "assistance to multilateral organizations (core funding)" and "bilateral assistance through multilateral organizations (earmarked funding)."[32] The World Food Program refers to its earmarked food aid as "restricted for use in specific provinces supported bilaterally by the donor concerned."[33] In contrast to multilateral aid where resources are pooled and the identity of individual donors disappears, earmarked funding "preserves the national identity of a grant or

---

[31] Reinsberg 2017, 91.
[32] DANIDA 2013, emphasis added.
[33] Executive Board of the World Food Programme, 2000, 36.

concessionary loan. The 'light of sight' from source to results ensures that contributions can at all times be connected to the donor through planning frameworks, accountability mechanisms, and visibility (...)"[34]

Permissive funding rules are a feature of the contemporary UN's institutional design. Those rules make possible the status quo: that a mass of individualized contracts govern the work of UN operational programs. This was not always the case. Technical assistance programs, the predecessors of "social and economic development" work at the UN, were initially funded by mandatory assessments under the regular budget. When early UN development programs, like the Expanded Program for Technical Assistance (EPTA) and the UN Special Fund were established to rely on voluntary contributions, rules prohibited donors from placing earmarks on their contributions, ensuring that multilateral bodies controlled resource allocation.[35] Earmark prohibitions began to disappear only in the mid-1960s. The transition to disproportionate reliance on earmarked contributions came decades later. This shift occurred despite no change whatsoever in the voting and representation rules that are so closely associated with the production of multilateralism at the UN and other international organizations. That the change occurred through funding rules meant that it was subterranean, occurring below the surface, while decision-making in UN governing bodies—those bastions of egalitarian multilateralism—continued undisturbed.

Rethinking How International Rules Change

This book is interested in two types of change: change in formal international rules, and the transformation of fundamental principles embedded in international organizations. In conventional accounts in IR, international rules change through negotiation, followed by amendment or replacement. For instance, De Bruyne et al. articulate and operationalize rule change in the conventional way: "While the majority of treaties tend to remain unchanged, others are renegotiated over time, either gradually by treaty amendment or abruptly by treaty replacement."[36] Haftel and Thompson similarly equate renegotiation with change: "While some agreements have remained intact after their initial conclusion, others are amended, updated, or replaced. Why are some international agreements renegotiated while others remain stable?"[37] In this conception, change is synonymous with amendment or replacement and rules remain unchanged, "stable,"

---

[34] Weinlich et al. 2020, 27.

[35] ECOSOC 1949. Resolution 222(IX), pp. 7–8. August 14–15, 1949. ECOSOC resolution adopted by the General Assembly establishing EPTA in Resolution 304 (IV) November 16, 1949. See also: UN Yearbook 1948–49, 444. https://www.un.org/en/yearbook

[36] De Bruyne et al. 2020, 321. The conventional conception of how change occurs is often implicit and taken for granted rather than explicitly stated.

[37] Haftel and Thompson 2018, 25.

when these acts do not occur. The change process is further characterized by two features, often taken for granted rather than explicitly stated. First, it is understood to be intentional, that is, actors design and redesign rules in response to problems, with the aim of solving or mitigating those problems. Second, the process and outcome are relatively transparent. By this I do not mean that the public is privy to private conversations of diplomats that may make or break negotiations, but rather that rule change itself is visible on the page. Put another way, when we treat rules as ontologically closed, rule meaning remains static absent a literal rewriting of the rules through revision or amendment.

If rules are instead treated as inherently permissive—ontologically open—then meaning can change even if the written words do not. Deciphering rule meaning requires interpretation and cannot be deduced from words alone.[38] This means both that a single written rule can support multiple interpretations at any given moment, and that meaning may change over time. Equating change with renegotiation and identifying change as amendment or revision is likely to miss much of the action. This treatment of international rules as permissive is consistent with a new body of work at the intersection of IR and international law that understands international law as unsettled, "momentary achievements," that can "remain subject to contestation" after they are codified.[39] It similarly allows that the same rule might be used for multiple purposes, a premise of historical institutionalist scholarship on transformational change.[40]

How do meaning and purpose change absent renegotiation? International legal scholarship illuminates how rules often change through reinterpretation rather than negotiation. These interpretive tools include evolutive treaty interpretation, subsequent practice, and reading one body of law through another. The United Nations Charter includes just one Article, Article 17, that pertains explicitly to funding. It governs the mandatory assessments system, obligating member states to pay "the expenses of the Organization." Subsequent practice has been particularly important to reinterpreting Article 17 to limit the expansion of the mandatory system. The Vienna Convention on the Law of the Treaties (VCLT) codified subsequent state practice, that is, state behavior related to the law in question, as an interpretive tool. Subsequent practice is used to infer states parties' understanding of treaty obligations. If subsequent practice evolves over time, so too can treaty obligations evolve to reflect states' understandings, as inferred from their behavior. Subsequent practice squares with the framework's assumptions. As an interpretive tool, it is intended to be used when states parties intend their behavior to reflect their understanding of the law. In practice, of course, whether a state intended its behavior to signal its understanding of the law is difficult to evaluate.

---

[38] Putnam 2020.
[39] Mantilla 2020, 9.
[40] Hacker 2002; Pierson 2003; Thelen 2003, 2004; Mahoney and Thelen 2010; St. John 2018.

Legal analysis reveals that rule interpreters, whether international courts, or states parties forwarding interpretations, make arguments and render decisions based on subsequent practice even when states engaged in the practice did not explicitly intend their behavior to signal their interpretation.[41] Legal arguments to justify withholding dues to the UN, made to considerable success in the 1970s and 1980s as Western support for the UN declined, relied on subsequent practice to reinterpret the Charter to restrict the reach of Article 17. This constrained the UN's trajectory. Arguments in favor of legal withholding effectively sealed off the mandatory assessments system as a source of growth for the UN, making any future growth reliant on voluntary contributions by default.

Permissive earmark rules also changed over time, but repurposing rather than reinterpretation served as the relevant mechanism. Underlining the importance of genuine uncertainty in making change possible, repurposing involves using existing rules to achieve ends that are new and distinct from those imagined by their original designers. A first step in this process occurred when the UN Office of Legal Affairs repurposed rules designed to provide the Secretary-General with discretion to accept contributions for specific purposes from private actors, and redeployed them to allow the UNDP to accept earmarked resources from a member state. The second step occurred when the United States repurposed earmark rules originally designed to provide additional, supplementary funding to UN programs, to constrain those programs and limit multilateral control. The book makes the case that reinterpretation and repurposing are as important to understanding change in international rules as renegotiation and revision. They do not involve changes in written text, rendering them less visible, but are no less important to institutional development.

Ultimately, the book is interested not only in changes in individual rules but in how those changes transformed UN governance. Its central argument is that the UN's transformation was made possible by the relative invisibility of the process. Unlike representation and voting rules, funding rules were not widely perceived to have a direct relationship to multilateralism. In part because of this, and in part because changes to funding rules—whether reinterpretations of Article 17, the introduction of voluntary rules, or the disappearance of earmark prohibitions— were initially made for reasons unrelated to multilateralism, the transformation had a subterranean dynamic. It was not foreseen until it was well underway. Low visibility meant that changes to funding rules did not immediately mobilize opposition from those with a stake in the persistence of egalitarian multilateralism at the UN—a group that includes most developing countries and makes up

[41] For the general argument see Nolte 2013; Buga 2018. For specific cases: *Hassan v. United Kingdom* (European Court of Human Rights); *Certain Expenses Advisory Opinion* (International Court of Justice).

the majority of UN member states. Transformation occurred in part because it was unforeseen by those who set it in motion.

This process builds on theories of gradual transformation, first developed in American and comparative political development that are now emerging in IR.[42] For instance, in explaining the rise of investor-state arbitration, Taylor St. John argues that the groundwork for the twenty-first-century investor-state dispute settlement was laid decades earlier in the 1960s by actors who "did not intend to create" the system as it exists today and in fact would likely be "horrified" by it.[43] Like St. John's argument, the framework offered here is distinct from conventional understandings of institutional transformation that emphasize punctuated change, often at moments of historic critical juncture. In those moments, bold, radical revision is possible. Gradual transformation does not require such moments but the change it ushers in is no less radical.

Contributions

Theoretically, this book contributes to a growing literature that emphasizes timing and sequence, contingency, and creativity in explaining international institutional origins and change. Various strands of this work wear the labels of historical institutionalism (HI), practice theory, and ideas scholarship, but together they share a commitment to the study of the process through which outcomes are produced.[44] HI has gained traction in IR in the past decade,[44] and this project aims to move it forward. IR scholars have integrated useful insights from the HI tradition, especially drawing on arguments about path dependence, illuminating why international institutions so often resist change. HI insights into how institutions transform have received less attention.[45] I emphasize the subterranean, uncoordinated nature of transformation. The transformative process does not exist as such for those who participate in its early phases. Genuine uncertainty makes possible actors' participation in such a process. Permissive rules and actors' ability to exploit them in unpredictable ways makes possible unexpected turns in rule-use and interpretation, and feeds genuine uncertainty.

Empirical accounts of gradual transformation often eschew a thorough discussion of theoretical foundations that make transformational change possible. Convincing empirical accounts of gradual transformation are essential, but the decision not to elaborate the associated theoretical foundations undercuts the

---

[42] IR scholars have more often utilized HI's concept of path dependence to explain persistence rather than importing HI arguments about gradual change. For examples that utilize elements of gradual change arguments from HI, see St. John 2018 and Pouliot 2020.

[43] St. John 2018, 4.

[44] E.g., Fioretos 2011; Rixen et al. 2016; Fioretos 2017.

[45] Exceptions include Posner 2009; Chwieroth 2014; Farrell and Newman 2015; St. John 2018.

challenge that these empirical stories pose to rationalist theories of design and change that remain predominant in the discipline. This book answers the call from numerous scholars[46] to forward a coherent theoretical framework. Genuine uncertainty, permissive rules, and creative agents make possible gradual, subterranean transformation, and provide an alternative to rationalist accounts in the field.

The book also contributes by integrating legal interpretive strategies elaborated in International Law (IL) scholarship into HI and IR accounts of institutional change. IR has benefited from cross-fertilization with IL research generally, and IR scholarship on international courts recognizes the importance of interpretation. But the interpretive tools that international lawyers know to facilitate change have received scant attention.[47] These interpretive tools, especially subsequent practice as outlined in the Vienna Convention on the Law of the Treaties, render behaviors we think of as non-legal (i.e., not having legal implications) relevant to what international rules mean. Equally important, interpretive arguments that rely on these tools are regularly made by actors other than international courts, including states seeking to legitimate their positions through legal arguments.[48] Learning about interpretive tools enriches IR scholarship on change theoretically and also helps to clarify that rule meaning often changes, sometimes radically, without the negotiation and revision process envisioned by IR scholars.

Empirically, this is a book about the United Nations, about what it *is* and how it works. In the immediate postwar period political scientists paid ample attention to the UN, but as decolonization progressed, UN membership expanded, and its place in US foreign policy diminished, its popularity as a subject of IR scholars declined. This is particularly true for the UN system outside the UN Security Council (UNSC), where an interest in Council decisions and peacekeeping kept the UN name both in the headlines and in scholarly journals.[49] Books that do focus primarily on the UN system outside the UNSC are often primarily normative enterprises, often with a policy focus.[50] And many of these focus on individual UN programs rather than the system writ large. By contrast, this book analyzes the governance trajectory of the UN from its establishment to the contemporary period and tracks system-wide trends in its financing and their effects. Based on archival research, it sheds new light on the UN Charter, and on how decolonization shaped the UNDS. It also offers a compelling solution to a long-standing puzzle of the post-1980s United Nations. Wealthy states, fed up with ever-increasing regular budgets, implemented stringent austerity measures on the UN in the 1980s,

---

[46] See Fioretos 2011; Moschella and Tsingou 2013; Pouliot 2020, 745.

[47] For exceptions, see Dunoff and Pollack 2018; Búzás and Graham 2020.

[48] Murphy 2013, 83.

[49] Important exceptions include works that study (re)alignments in international politics by analyzing General Assembly voting patterns and rhetoric (e.g., Voeten 2000; Kentikelenis and Voeten 2021) and studies focused on vote buying (e.g., Dreher et al., 2008; Carter and Stone 2015).

[50] E.g., Murphy 2006; Browne 2012; Ivanova 2021.

with some member states suggesting they might leave the institution altogether.[51] But instead of shriveling up, the UNDS expanded rapidly. The book's emphasis on financing demonstrates how nearly all post-Cold War growth in the UN system is powered by earmarked funds. Wealthy states did not leave the UN, but many radically altered their engagement by changing how they provide funding.

These changes render the UN larger and stronger in many ways, but governance is also qualitatively different than the egalitarian multilateralism so closely associated with the UN. Earmarked funding and governance through bilateral contract affect far more than resource distribution. Within UN bureaucracies they necessitate capable resource mobilization departments to attract funding and support donor relations. They implicate the legitimacy of UN funds and programs. The legitimacy of IOs is premised on both outcomes and procedural components, including whether procedures are "fair" and "democratic."[52] Pouliot emphasizes the "processual advantages" of multilateralism as an institutional practice that lend legitimacy to policy outcomes of the process.[53] Governance through bilateral contract raises these concerns about fairness and participation and, more pointedly, about developing states losing influence, and these concerns have grown as earmarking practices become more widespread.[54] The concluding chapter, Chapter 7, lays out two models—one donor driven and one driven by agency staff—for thinking about UN programs and agencies as actors in world politics today.

Plan for the Book

Chapter 2 introduces international relations literature on institutional change and identifies its limits: its reluctance to address the shortcomings of functionalism and its emphasis on punctuated equilibrium models in understanding major change. I define transformation and offer a distinct theoretical framework for explaining how it occurs built on the assumptions of uncertainty, permissive rules, and creative agents. I integrate interpretive mechanisms from international law into an HI framework to illuminate how incremental rule change can produce transformation. I articulate a set of observable implications that follow from the framework's assumptions and mechanisms of change.

The next four chapters illustrate how transformational change occurred at the UN and demonstrate the framework's empirical purchase. Chapter 3 centers on negotiations over the design of the UN Charter during and following World War II. It provides an account of the core rules in the Charter that produce egalitarian

---

[51] On leaving IOs, see von Borzyskowski and Vabulas 2019.
[52] Scholte and Tallberg 2018, 7–9.
[53] Pouliot 2011, 23.
[54] See Graham and Serdaru 2020, 694; Weinlich et al. 2020.

multilateralism. I address not merely what the rules say, but also their intended meaning based on the archival record, and memoirs and diaries of the principal negotiators. This provides an important basis for evaluating any subsequent reinterpretation of Charter rules. Chapter 3 also provides the first opportunity to evaluate the framework's observable implications regarding the decision-making environment. If designers operate in a world of risk, they can identify potential downstream states of the world that are associated with their rule choices. We see, by contrast, that the future was opaque to UN architects in important ways; they did not foresee a world in which General Assembly control over financial matters would be problematic.

Chapter 4 covers the period between the UN's founding and its first major budget crisis in 1960. Two critical developments occur during this period. The first involved the introduction of voluntary funding rules for economic development activity. In retrospect, these rules provide a clear, first step away from egalitarian multilateralism embedded in the Charter. But I demonstrate how, at the time, their introduction was not intended to drive such a shift. Instead, voluntary rules were introduced to expand UN activity despite opposition from critical states, especially the Soviet Union. This speaks directly to the theory's emphasis on the importance of small, technical changes in gradual processes of transformation.

Chapter 5 covers the crucial period in which permissive earmark rules were adopted at the United Nations Development Program. As with the introduction of voluntary rules, permissive earmark rules were not intended to transform UN governance and were pursued by actors perceived to be benign to the system (e.g., the Netherlands and Sweden). But the chapter also usefully demonstrates how, faced with constraints, creative actors access rule permissiveness to create something new. Faced with the predicament of how to make the Netherlands' contribution compliant with UNDP rules, the UN Office of Legal Affairs repurposed a financial rule that existed elsewhere on the UN books. The creative repurposing was consolidated into UNDP rules in an unremarkable resolution in 1967. The chapter demonstrates both that permissive earmark rules set the stage for the UN's transformation and that at the time, transformation was not intended.

Chapter 6, which covers the 1980s, illustrates processes of reinterpretation and repurposing, the latter with an emphasis on subsequent state practice, articulated in the theoretical framework. As the UN's transformation is pursued in earnest by the Reagan administration, the chapter illustrates how that transformation emerged gradually through *uncoordinated actions* by various actors over time. Change is uncoordinated in the sense that, for example, the Netherlands or the UN Office of Legal Affairs hardly had the Reagan administration's strategy in mind when they "found" a way for UNDP to legally accept an earmarked contribution. Nevertheless, US Ambassador to the UN Jeane Kirkpatrick utilized opportunities created by these actions two decades later. The 1980s end with the mandatory assessments system effectively capped and earmarked funding on the rise.

Chapter 7 concludes with an overview of the state of the United Nations today. It covers the late-breaking realization that earmarked funds had reached levels that threatened the UN's fundamental principle of multilateralism, as well as recent efforts to reverse the trend. I outline the book's implications for institutional change, and how we conceive of and understand the UN system today. Finally, I consider the prospects of the United Nations Funding Compact that treats earmarked funding as an obstacle to achieving the Sustainable Development Goals and reflect on the obstacles to its successful implementation.

References

Alger, Chadwick. 1973. "The United States and the United Nations." *International Organization* 27: 1–23.

Baumann, Max-Otto. 2021. "How Earmarking Has Become Self-perpetuating in United Nations Development Cooperation." *Development Policy Review* 39: 343–359.

Bayer, Patrick, Christopher Marcoux, and Johannes Urpelainen. 2015. "When International Organizations Bargain: Evidence from the Global Environment Facility." *Journal of Conflict Resolution* 59(6): 1074–1100.

Bayram, A. Burcu, and Erin R. Graham. 2017. "Financing the United Nations: Explaining Variation in How Donors Provide Funding to the UN." *The Review of International Organizations* 12(3): 421–459.

Blake, Daniel, and Autumn Payton. 2015. "Balancing Design Objectives: Analyzing New Data on Voting Rules in Intergovernmental Organizations." *Review of International Organizations* 10(3): 377–402.

Browne, Stephen. 2012. *United Nations Development Programme and System* (UNDP). New York: Routledge.

Buga, Irina. 2018. *The Modification of Treaties by Subsequent Practice*. Oxford: Oxford University Press.

Búzás, Zoltán I., and Erin R. Graham. 2020. "Emergent Flexibility in Institutional Development: How International Rules Really Change." *International Studies Quarterly* 64(4): 821–833.

Carter, David, and Randall Stone. 2015. "Democracy and Multilateralism: The Case of Vote Buying in the UN General Assembly." *International Organization* 69(1): 1–33.

Chwieroth, Jeffrey. 2014. "Controlling Capital: The International Monetary Fund and Transformative Incremental Change from Within International Organizations." *New Political Economy* 19(3): 445–469

DANIDA. 2013. "Danish Multilateral Development Cooperation Analysis." Ministry of Foreign Affairs of Denmark. DANIDA, International Development Cooperation, April.

De Bruyne, Charlotte, Itay Fischendler, and Yoram Haftel. 2020. "Design and Change in Transboundary Freshwater Agreements." *Climatic Change* 162: 321–341.

Dreher, Axel, Peter Nunnekam, and Rainier Thiele. 2008. "Does US Aid Buy UN General Assembly Votes? A Disaggregated Analysis." *Public Choice* 136: 139–164.

Dunoff, Jeffrey, and Mark Pollack. 2018. "Practice Theory and International Law." In *Research Handbook on the Sociology of International Law*. Edited by Moshe Hirsch and Andrew Lang. Cheltenham: Edward Elgar, 252–272.

Eichenauer, Vera, and Simon Hug. 2018. "The Politics of Special Purpose Trust Funds." *Economics and Politics* 30(2): 211–255.

Eichenauer, Vera, and Bernhard Reinsberg. 2017. "What Determines Earmarked Funding to International Development Organizations? Evidence from the New Multi-bi Aid Data." *Review of International Organizations* 12(2): 171–197.

Emerson, Rupert. 1965. "Colonialism, Political Development, and the UN." *International Organization* 19(3): 484–503.

Executive Board of the United Nations Development Program (UNDP). 2013. "Evaluation of the UNDP Strategic Plan, 2008–2013." Executive Summary, Annual Session 2013, April 5, DP/2013/17.

Executive Board of the World Food Program. 2000. "A Resource Mobilization Strategy for the World Food Programme." Third Regular Session, Rome, October 23–26, WFP/EB.3/2000/3-B.

Farrell, Henry, and Abraham Newman. 2015. "The New Politics of Interdependence: Cross National Layering in Trans-Atlantic Regulatory Disputes." *Comparative Political Studies* 48(4): 497–526.

Finnemore, Martha. 2005. "Fights about Rules: The Role of Efficacy and Power in Changing Multilateralism." *Review of International Studies* 31: 187–2006.

Fioretos, Orfeo. 2011. "Historical Institutionalism in International Relations." *International Organization* 65(1): 367–299.

Fioretos, Orfeo. 2017. *International Politics and Institutions in Time*. Oxford: Oxford University Press.

Graham, Erin. 2017. "The Institutional Design of Funding Rules at International Organizations: Explaining the Transformation in Financing the United Nations." *European Journal of International Relations* 23(2): 365–390.

Graham, Erin R. 2015. "Money and Multilateralism: How Funding Rules Constitute IO Governance." *International Theory* 7(1): 162–194.

Graham, Erin R., and Alexandria Serdaru. 2020. "Power, Control, and the Logic of Substitution in Institutional Design: The Case of International Climate Finance." *International Organization* 74(4): 671–706.

Greenstone, J. David. 1986. "Political Culture and American Political Development: Liberty, Union, and the Liberal Bipolarity." *Studies in American Political Development* 1: 1–49.

Hacker, Jacob. 2002. *The Divided Welfare State: The Battle over Public and Private Social Benefits in the United States*. New York: Cambridge University Press.

Haftel, Yoram, and Alexander Thompson. 2018. "When Do States Renegotiate Investment Agreements? The Impact of Arbitration." *The Review of International Organizations* 13(1): 25–48.

Hosli, Madeleine, and Thomas Dörfler. 2019. "Why is Change So Slow? Assessing Prospects for United Nations Security Council Reform." *Journal of Economic Policy Reform* 22(1): 35–50.

Iannantuoni, Alice, Charla Waeiss, and Matthew Winters. 2021. "Project Design Decisions of Egalitarian and Non-egalitarian International Organizations: Evidence from the Global Environment Facility and the World Bank." *Review of International Organizations* 16: 431–462.

Idris, Kamil, and Michael Bartolo. 2000. *A Better United Nations for the New Millennium: The United Nations System—How It Is Now and How It Should Be in the Future*. The Hague/London/Boston: Kluwer Law International.

Ikenberry, G. John. 2003. "Is American Multilateralism in Decline?" *Perspectives on Politics* 1(3): 533–550.

Ivanova, Maria. 2021. *The Untold Story of the World's Leading Environmental Institution: UNEP at Fifty*. Cambridge, MA: M.I.T. Press.

Jenks, Bruce, and Jennifer Topping. 2016. *Financing the United Nations Development System: Current Trends and New Directions*. Uppsala: Dag Hammarskjöld Foundation.

Kahler, Miles. 1992. "Multilateralism with Small and Large Numbers." *International Organization* 46(3): 681–708.

Kaya, Ayse. 2015. *Power and Global Economic Institutions*. New York: Cambridge University Press.

Kentikelenis, Alexander, and Erik Voeten. 2021. "Legitimacy Challenges to the Liberal World Order: Evidence from United Nations Speeches 1970–2018." *The Review of International Organizations* 16: 721–754.

Koremenos, Barbara, Charles Lipson, and Duncan Snidal. 2001. "The Rational Design of International Institutions." *International Organization* 55(4): 761–799.

Lipscy, Phillip. 2017. *Renegotiating the World Order: Institutional Change in International Relations*. Cambridge: Cambridge University Press.

Mahn, Timo. 2012. "The Financing of Development Cooperation at the United Nations: Why More Means Less." Briefing Paper 8/2012, German Development Institute.

Mahoney, John, and Kathleen Thelen, eds. 2010. *Explaining Institutional Change: Ambiguity, Agency and Power*. New York: Cambridge University Press.

Mantilla, Giovanni. 2020. *Lawmaking under Pressure: International Humanitarian Law and Internal Armed Conflict*. Ithaca, NY: Cornell University Press.

Michaelowa, Katharina, Bernhard Reinsberg, and Christina Schneider. 2017. "Multi-bi Aid in European Development Assistance: The Role of Capacity Constraints and Member State Politics." *Development Policy Review* 35(4): 513–530.

Moschella, Manuela, and Eleni Tsingou. 2013. "The Financial Crisis and the Politics of Reform: Explaining Incremental Change." In *Great Expectations, Slow Transformations: Incremental Change in Post-Crisis Regulation*. Edited by Manuela Moschella and Eleni Tsingou. Colchester, UK: ECPR Press, 1–33.

Murphy, Craig. 2006. *The United Nations Development Programme: A Better Way?* Cambridge: Cambridge University Press.

Murphy, Sean D. 2013. "The Relevance of Subsequent Agreement and Subsequent Practice for the Interpretation of Treaties." In *Treaties and Subsequent Practice*. Edited by Georg Nolte. Oxford: Oxford University Press, 82–94.

Muttukumaru, Romesh. 2016. "Toward Enhancing Core (Unrestricted) Funding to the UN Development System in the Post-2015 period." A report prepared for the United Nations Department of Economic and Social Affairs for the 2016 Quadrennial Comprehensive Policy Review, January 25.

Nolte, Georg. 2013. "Introduction." In *Treaties and Subsequent Practice*. Edited by Georg Nolte. Oxford: Oxford University Press, 1–10.

Pierson, Paul. 2003. "Big, Slow-Moving, and … Invisible: Macrosocial Processes in the Study of Comparative Politics." In *Comparative Historical Analysis in the Social Sciences*. Edited by James Mahoney and Dietrich Rueschemeyer. New York: Cambridge University Press, 177–207.

Posner, Elliot. 2009. *The Origins of Europe's New Stock Markets*. Cambridge, MA: Harvard University Press.

Pouliot, Vincent. 2011. "Multilateralism as an End in Itself." *International Studies Perspectives* 12: 18–26.

Pouliot, Vincent. 2020. "Practice Theory Meets Historical Institutionalism." *International Organization* 74(4): 742–772.

Putnam, Tonya. 2020. "Mingling and Strategic Augmentation in International Legal Obligations." *International Organization* 74(1): 31–64.

Reinsberg, Bernhard. 2017. "Trust Funds as a Lever of Influence at International Development Organizations." *Global Policy* 8(S5): 84–95.

Reinsberg, Bernhard, Katharina Michaelowa, and Stephen Knack. 2017. "Which Donors, Which Funds? Bilateral Donors' Choice of Multilateral Funds at the World Bank." *International Organization* 71(4): 767–802.

Rixen, Thomas, Lora Anne Viola, and Michael Zürn. 2016. *Historical Institutionalism & International Relations: Explaining Institutional Development in World Politics.* Oxford, UK: Oxford University Press.

Schauer, Frederick. 1991. *Playing by the Rules.* Oxford: Oxford University Press.

Schlesinger, Stephen. 1997. "Can the United Nations Reform?" *World Policy Journal* 14(3): 47–52.

Schmid, Lisa Katharina, Alexander Reitzenstein, and Nina Hall. 2021. "Blessing or Curse? The Effects of Earmarked Funding in UNICEF and UNDP." *Global Governance* 27(3): 433–459.

Scholte, Jan Aart, and Jonas Tallberg. 2018. "Theorizing the Institutional Sources of Global Governance Legitimacy." In *Legitimacy in Global Governance: Sources, Processes, and Consequences.* Edited by Jonas Tallberg, Karin Baackstrand, and Jan Aaart Scholte. Oxford: Oxford University Press.

Sridhar, Devi, and Ngaire Woods. 2013. "Trojan Multilateralism: Global Cooperation in Health." *Global Policy* 4(4): 325–335.

St. John, Taylor. 2018. *The Rise of Investor-State Arbitration: Politics, Law, and Unintended Consequences.* Oxford: Oxford University Press.

Thelen, Kathleen. 2003. "How Institutions Evolve: Insights from Comparative Historical Analysis." In *Comparative Historical Analysis in the Social Sciences.* Edited by James Mahoney and Dietrich Rueschemeyer. New York: Cambridge University Press, 208–240.

Thelen, Kathleen. 2004. *How Institutions Evolve: The Political Economy of Skills in Germany, Britain, the United States and Japan.* New York: Cambridge University Press.

Thorvaldsdottir, Svanhildur, Ronny Patz, and Klaus Goetz. 2022. "Mandate or Donors? Explaining UNHCR's Country-Level Expenditures from 1967 to 2016." *Political Studies* 70(2): 443–464.

Topping, Jennifer, and Bruce Jenks. 2021. "Financing the UN Development System: Time to Meet the Moment." Dag Hammarskjold Foundation and the UN Multi-Donor Trust Fund Office.

UN General Assembly. 2019. "Operational Activities for Development: Operational Activities for Development of the United Nations System. Funding Compact. Report of the Secretary-General. General Assembly 74th Session, A/74/73/Add.1-E/2019/4/Add.1.

UN General Assembly and Economic and Social Council (ECOSOC). 2012. "Analysis of Funding for Operational Activities for Development of the United Nations System for 2009." Geneva, Switzerland.

United Nations Multi-donor Trust Fund Office. 2016. "Financing the United Nations Development System: Current Trends and New Directions." UN MPTF Office and the Dag Hammarskjold Foundation.

UN Secretary-General. 2012. "Quadrennial Policy Review." May 31.

Voeten, Erik. 2000. "Clashes in the Assembly." *International Organization* 54(2): 185–215.

von Borzyskowski, Inken, and Felicity Vabulas. 2019. "Hello, Goodbye: When Do States Withdraw from International Organizations?" *The Review of International Organizations* 14: 335–366.

Weinlich, Silke, Max-Otto Baumann, Erik Lundsgaarde, and Peter Wolff. 2020. "Earmarking in the Multilateral Development System: Many Shades of Grey." Studies, No. 101. ISBN 978-3-96021-112-9. Deutsches Institut für Entwicklungspolitic (DIE).

Yusef, Muhammad, Juan Luis Larrabure, and Cihan Terzi. 2007. *Voluntary Contributions in United Nations System Organizations: Impact on Program Delivery and Resource Mobilization Strategies*. Geneva, Switzerland: UN Joint Inspections Unit.

2

How International Institutions Transform

How did the United Nations evolve from a system that relied primarily on mandatory funding governed by egalitarian multilateralism to one that relies primarily on earmarked voluntary contributions governed by a multitude of bilateral contracts between UN programs and individual member states? Put simply, how did we get from there to here? We can easily identify how it did not happen. First, the transformation did not occur through rule replacement. Mandatory funding rules at the UN remain on the books and no serious effort to repeal those rules has succeeded. While compliance with the mandatory system varies, it remains, having weathered all major storms to date, and is protected by a diverse and strong majority of UN member states. Second, change did not occur through replacement or reform of Charter rules that grant the General Assembly authority over the United Nations regular budget. Nor did it occur through the replacement of rules that assign the multilateral governing bodies of various programs, like UNDP or UNEP, authority over their respective budgets. The founding institutional designs that give rise to multilateral practices and produce multilateral governance remain intact.

In identifying how change did not occur, we see the constraining effect of rules. Two critical sets of rules in the UN Charter—the mandatory assessments system and egalitarian voting rules, combined with Assembly control over burden-sharing and budgeting—were drafted with the UN's original membership in mind. This included fifty-two states that were mostly Western, and mostly favorable to US leadership. Membership doubled by 1960 as decolonization progressed. Newly independent states brought demands for economic assistance and did not reliably vote with the West. It is difficult to imagine that the US and its allies—or the Soviet Union—would ever have agreed to mandatory funding rules with this expanded membership, but that mattered little. They now faced rigid constraints. The drafters of the UN Charter intentionally incorporated flexibility to amend it, but in practice the exercise is prohibitively difficult. The relevant rules could not be changed because the vast majority of member states now had a stake in the status quo. There was no way to amend rules to curtail Assembly control over the budget or negotiate a formal escape clause to mandatory commitments. Powerful states were, it seemed, stuck with their "mistakes," the product of low visibility—an inability to see 1960 clearly from 1945.

Can rule change occur in contexts in which status quo rules are entrenched and supported by the majority? And if so, how? At any time in the United Nations'

Transforming International Institutions. Erin R. Graham, Oxford University Press. © Erin R. Graham (2023).
DOI: 10.1093/oso/9780198877936.003.0002

history, it would have been politically impossible to legislate the contraction of multilateral governance. Yet the politically impossible occurred through other means. This chapter offers a theory of *how* rules are altered through an uncoordinated, subterranean process to transform fundamental organizational principles even when those fundamental principles are favored by the majority.[1] It begins with the insight from historical institutionalism that incremental change can produce transformation.[2] Put in context, lifting earmark prohibitions at UNDP in 1967, a small, even technical change, plays an important role in shrinking multilateralism at the UN in the 2000s, a big, transformational change. The idea that an incremental change can produce transformation might strike some readers as paradoxical and others as obvious. Some strands of rationalist IR scholarship draw a line between incremental or adaptive change on the one hand and transformational change on the other.[3] In this view, a change has *either* an incremental or a transformational effect and it can be identified as such when it occurs. By contrast, an HI approach sees transformational potential in incremental change. What looks incremental at Time$_1$ might evolve to greater significance at Time$_2$. Whether change proves incremental or transformative is best judged in retrospect.

I develop a framework that illuminates the subterranean, uncoordinated nature of gradual transformation. The path to transformation does not occur through incremental but steady, linear accumulation. This is not a theory of small, incremental steps intended to add up to a bigger one. Rather, incremental change transforms over time because (1) rule drafters cannot fully anticipate the future or how rules will be interpreted or deployed in that future; (2) they cannot do this in part because rules contain an inherent indeterminacy or permissiveness; and (3) creative actors can subsequently exploit this permissiveness to interpret and enact rules in ways that serve their distinct interests. The theoretical foundations of genuine uncertainty, rule permissiveness, and creative agency open space for incremental change to set transformation in motion *because the transformational potential of incremental change is not foreseen.* This allows the possibility that those who object to the downstream effects that incremental change sets in motion, that is, to transformation at T$_2$, may nevertheless support incremental change at T$_1$.

---

[1] The framework is not intended to provide a causal theory that articulates the conditions under which transformational change occurs. It is intended to illuminate how change occurs under the condition that rewriting rules, through replacement, renegotiation, or amendment processes is unattainable. For reasons articulated below it assumes this condition is widespread, that is, it is often difficult to revise international institutions through replacement, renegotiation, or amendment, particularly in ways that transform the institution's fundamental principles.

[2] For an overview, see Mahoney and Thelen 2010. This framework draws especially on insights from Tulis 1987; Hacker 2002; Pierson 2003; and Thelen 2004.

[3] E.g., Koremenos et al. 2001, 773.

I characterize the institutional design environment as one of *low visibility*, in which designers cannot anticipate a range of phenomena that affect how design features or their adaptations will affect institutional development, especially, but not exclusively, in the long run. Some features of a low visibility environment are unavoidable—the possibility of an exogenous shock that upends anticipated outcomes always looms, and the combination of permissive rules and creative actors always leaves some room for unanticipated developments. Low visibility enables *uncoordinated* change: multiple individuals can contribute to the same change trajectory over time without an awareness of their role in the larger process. It also lends itself to a *subterranean*, under-the-radar dynamic. Those whose behavior can be retroactively identified as starting a transformational process may not fathom transformation as a possibility. If they had, they may not approve of it.

I integrate international legal interpretive strategies with an HI approach by mapping those strategies onto the gradual change processes of layering and conversion theorized by historical institutionalist scholars. Evolutive treaty interpretation and modification by subsequent practice are legal pathways to a conversion process in which "rules remain formally the same but are interpreted and enacted in new ways."[4] Reading a treaty through the lens of subsequently negotiated agreements illuminates the inherent tension and "churning"[5] that layering—or the adding of new rules alongside old ones—is known to produce. These processes exemplify the uncoordinated nature of individual contributions to transformational change. The behavior of states or international organizations with regard to a treaty may be identified as subsequent practice by international courts en route to reinterpreting obligations. Actors may craft rules that have a clear and intended meaning in the context they were designed only to see them muddied with unintended effects when interpreted in light of new rules and circumstances. In both instances, the initial actors' behavior contributes to the path of change, but in neither case is it necessarily intended.

Three rule features lend themselves to low visibility: rules that are perceived as technical or procedural rather than substantive, rules that are not perceived to be constitutive of fundamental institutional principles, and rules that are proposed by those perceived as friendly to the status quo (and therefore less likely to threaten it). Rule changes that exhibit these features are less likely to draw skepticism and scrutiny or to be perceived as having transformational potential.

Transformation through incrementalism does not directly challenge status quo rules favored by the majority. The layering of voluntary funding rules alongside mandatory counterparts, and the removal of earmark prohibitions, were not undertaken to boost wealthy states' control of the UN or to undermine multilateralism; they were expedient solutions to political disagreements. Years after

---

[4] Mahoney and Thelen 2010, 17.
[5] Orren and Skowronek 2004, 113.

changes were made for distinct purposes, states redeployed rules to fulfill new ends. The UN's transformation away from egalitarian multilateralism qualifies as what Paul Pierson has called a "slow-moving" outcome.[6] So slow and discreet (and offering benefits to a diverse set of actors) that by the time many became aware and wary of the changes to governance it entailed, reliance on the financial resources it begot had already entrenched the new mode of governance in the system.

This chapter proceeds with a review and critique of IR literature on institutional change, divided into sections on why and how international rules change. Functionalist theories tell us rules will change when they are inefficient and ineffective and disliked by powerful actors. Emphasizing the constraining aspect of norms and positive feedback respectively, constructivist and path dependent arguments help to explain why institutions often fail to change in line with functionalist expectations. International legal scholars tell a related and even simpler story: changing international rules through formal negotiation or amendment processes is almost always too hard. These approaches help us to understand how change did not occur at the UN, but are less helpful in understanding the trajectory of actual change over time, that is, how change did occur. After identifying shortcomings of the predominant approaches, I draw on historical institutionalism and international legal scholarship, to develop the theoretical framework outlined above.

Change and International Institutions

How do international institutions develop over time? Theories of international cooperation and institutional design do not always direct explicit attention to institutional development, but they contain implicit theories of change. Broadly construed, these approaches fall under the labels of functionalist, realist (focused on power and distributional effects), and constructivist theories. In IR, functionalist theories remain central and dominant and thus require a sustained discussion.[7] In the 1970s, the persistence of international institutions in the presence of the United States' relative economic decline posed an empirical puzzle for those who understood hegemony as a necessary condition for the provision of international order. Keohane (1984) explained continued cooperation by training attention on the demand side of the equation. International institutions would persist because they served important purposes for states, reducing transaction costs and increasing transparency—functions in high demand under anarchy. *After Hegemony* became the foundational work for neoliberal institutionalist scholarship in IR, which conceived of international institutions as vehicles through which states could achieve joint gains.

---

[6] Pierson 2003.
[7] In proposing their "design by bricolage" approach, Kalyanpur and Newman (2017, 374) similarly note the continued "primacy" of rationalist approaches to explaining institutional outcomes in IR.

Although some realist scholars dismissed international institutions as epiphe-nomenal to state interests, others responded to the neoliberal institutionalist thesis by directing attention to distributional issues. By posing the question, *functional for whom,* realist scholars highlighted distributional consequences, arguing that the gains from cooperation were skewed toward the most powerful actors in the system.[8] The realist thesis challenged the conclusion drawn by neoliberal insti-tutionalists that international institutions raised all ships, but not its underlying functionalism. The implication of neoliberal institutionalism is that institutions should persist so long as they are functional for their member states; for realists they should persist so long as they are functional for their *powerful* member states. When international institutions no longer serve these purposes, they should be reformed to address the shortcoming or abandoned if no longer needed.

It is worth noting that Keohane (1984), and certainly Krasner, explicitly rec-ognized that while functionalist expectations for change sounded fine in theory, they might prove problematic in practice. In *After Hegemony,* Keohane acknowl-edges that "functionalist arguments (...) must be used with caution. Even if the institutions in question perform the functions ascribed to them, they may have emerged for different reasons."[9] Krasner's early writing on sovereignty is an impor-tant work in the historical institutionalist cannon. Indeed, his 1988 article begins with the assertion that while sovereignty historically served as an instrument of human progress, "It is no longer obvious that the state system is the optimal way to organize political life."[10] But while some acknowledged that rules were unlikely to adapt efficiently when they ceased to serve functional needs, the tendency was to treat the problem as if it represented the exception rather than the normal state of affairs. The starting point for Krasner (1988), "that outcomes at some given point in time cannot be understood in terms of the preferences and capabilities of actors existing at that same point in time" did not become central to IR thinking on international institutions.

Indeed, as the rationalist research program progressed, these concerns largely fell away. The contemporary functionalist thesis is embodied by the rational design (RD) project, which brings welcome attention to variation in international insti-tutional design. RD seeks to explain features of international agreements with reference to the type of cooperation problem states face. For example, flexibil-ity mechanisms are incorporated in response to situations of risk, which allows states to protect against undesirable compliance costs. In some ways, it also seeks to synthesize the neoliberal and realist strands of functionalism with conjectures that emphasize distributional problems. With regard to change, the RD research program provides a micro version of the general neoliberal institutionalist expec-tation: when individual features of institutional design become dysfunctional

---

[8] Krasner 1991; Gruber 2000.
[9] Keohane 1984, 81.
[10] Krasner 1988, 67.

or no longer serve their purpose, they should be reformed or replaced. Some works have integrated distributional and functionalist approaches to explain when change will occur.[11] But in contrast to earlier work, the concern that features of design would resist change even when they cease to be useful was, in the words of Hug and König (2007, 107), only "indirectly and rather summarily acknowledged" by rational design scholarship. Occasional reminders that the origins of international institutions should not be inferred from the function they perform[12] have not altered the working assumption that international institutions are designed to be, and for the most part continue to be, functional instruments to facilitate joint gains.

When international institutional histories are revealed in any detail, problems with functionalist expectations become clear. Take the example of quota rules at the IMF. These rules simultaneously determine how much a member state contributes to the IMF *and* the limits on how much they can borrow. Wealthy industrialized states with larger quotas also have higher borrowing limits. Poorer, developing states are required to contribute less financially but also have lower borrowing limits. This might strike the reader as strange since for the last fifty years it has been developing states that most often borrow from the IMF and demand its resources. Bird and Rowlands (2006) provide an explanation. The IMF "was initially established in the form of a credit union where most members were seen as being equally likely to require the temporary financial assistance the IMF was designed to provide."[13] "Balance of payments problems were viewed as cyclical rather than endemic,"[14] and the relationship between financial contributions and borrowing limits made sense because big wealthy economies would require larger loans. But in the post-Bretton Woods IMF, states quickly sorted into "lenders" and "borrowers." Although "this division made the quota structure increasingly untenable and unsuitable as a means of determining simultaneously contributions and access (...)"[15] the rules were not changed to unlink the two.

Both constructivist and path dependent arguments help to explain why international rules often do not experience change consistent with functionalist expectations. For constructivists, the content of formal institutions is explained by conformity to norms of appropriate behavior in international society. Rules will conform to norms even when doing so undermines effectiveness. For example, Paris argues that the association of international trusteeship with colonialism prevents the United Nations from employing temporary trusteeship arrangements even when facts on the ground demand it.[16] In Paris's argument, the UN opts

---

[11] Koremenos 2016, especially chapter 10; Zangl et al. 2016.
[12] Wendt 2001; Duffield 2003; Pierson 2004; Thompson 2010.
[13] Bird and Rowlands 2006, 157.
[14] Bird and Rowlands 2006, 157.
[15] Bird and Rowlands 2006, 157–158.
[16] Paris 2003.

for more modest options that are normatively appropriate, but less effective. With regard to change, the primary implication is that when international norms of appropriate behavior evolve, formal rules should follow. But norms can also explain the absence of change when functionalist theories expect it.

For its part, historical institutionalism is best known for explaining why rules persist in the face of functionalist expectations. The concept of path dependence, and the importance of sequencing in explaining variation in outcomes, are both central to the approach. At a basic level, the idea is that choices made early in the life of an institution have consequences that outlast the circumstances that gave rise to those choices. As one continues down the path, it becomes costlier to reverse course.[17] Pierson explains how, once in place, institutional rules "will often generate self-reinforcing dynamics."[18] Positive feedback processes provide incentives to reproduce status quo rules rather than break from them. Path dependence has been an attractive entry point into historical institutionalist scholarship for IR scholars.[19] For example, Hanrieder deploys path dependence to explain obstacles to meaningful reform at the World Health Organization. Fragmentation at the WHO is "locked in" due to the relative autonomy of its regional offices—itself a product of historical contingency.[20] An emphasis on path dependence makes sense given contemporary challenges to reform and the empirical demonstration by Gray that many IOs neither live nor die, but rather become "zombies" that continue to operate "without any progress toward their mandate."[21] Yet path dependence does not imply *no change*, rather it suggests that institutional rules will constrain how change occurs.[22] In this way, path dependence is essential to explaining how changes in UN financing rules and governance *did not occur*. It sets certain parameters of possibility, but it tells us little about how change *does* unfold over time. In what follows, I explicate the foundations of an approach to understand how such change can occur. First, however, I briefly consider a prominent alternative (and complementary) model to explain transformational change, the punctuated equilibrium model.

Theories about How International Rules Change

Punctuated equilibrium models are frequently employed by political scientists to explain or describe institutional change. In these models, institutions experience (relatively) long periods of stasis followed by periods of significant or even

[17] Pierson 2004, chapter 1.
[18] Pierson 2004, 10.
[19] E.g., see Hanrieder 2015; Goldstein and Gulotty 2017; Hanrieder and Zürn 2017; Ikenberry 2017; Weaver and Moschella 2017.
[20] Hanrieder 2015, 12–13. See also Graham 2014.
[21] Gray 2018.
[22] Graham and Serdaru 2020, 681–682.

radical change. Causes of change are typically conceived as exogenous to the institution. As Thelen points out, both rational choice and historical institutionalist approaches that employ a narrow definition of path dependence gravitate toward punctuated equilibrium models.[23] For rational choice scholars, an exogenous shock that alters the incentives for cooperation will cause reform or rule replacement. For HI scholars, the shock must be of such a size that it overrides the status quo bias toward current arrangements.

Patterns of international institutional change are often depicted as consistent with punctuated equilibrium models.[24] Colgan et al.'s interpretation of the international energy regime complex provides an example. In examining the regime's forty-year history, they argue that de novo innovations, that is, the emergence of new institutions, will occur when states that are dissatisfied with the regime possess heterogeneous interests.[25] The logic is that disagreement prevents incremental reform from gaining the support necessary for implementation within existing arrangements. Under these conditions, entrepreneurial splinter groups break off to build new institutions that better suit their interests. Young uses a similar approach in applying the concept to the development of the Antarctic Treaty System (ATS).[26] Though ecumenical in his theoretical inclinations, Young's interpretation of ATS development suggests institutional arrangements have generally changed to reflect the emergence of new functional needs. He cites a multitude of endogenous and exogenous sources to explain the discontinuous pattern of change.[27]

There is no doubt that change sometimes occurs in a punctuated fashion. It is difficult to regard the end of World War II as anything other than a critical juncture in international politics, and a moment of "punctuated" international institutional development. Events of similar importance—the fall of the Berlin Wall and breakup of the Soviet Union—and surely some of lesser importance, have caused substantial change all at once. Yet there are reasons to be skeptical that a punctuated pattern of change, which has emerged as "the most common way of thinking of institutional change in political science,"[28] is actually the most common mode of international institutional development. The first is simply that it is difficult to build and sustain broad coalitions behind major institutional change and the thresholds required to implement major changes to international rules are often high. Although the rational design literature "assumes that IOs will be renegotiated if they do not fulfill their original purposes,"[29] in practice doing so is often difficult. This is widely acknowledged by scholars of international law. Buga

---

[23] Thelen 2004, 28.
[24] E.g., Young 2010; Colgan et al. 2012; Lundgren et al. 2018.
[25] Colgan et al. 2012, 119–122.
[26] Young 2010.
[27] Young 2010, chapter 3.
[28] Thelen 2004, 35.
[29] Gray 2018, 1.

(2018) usefully describes the disparity between the demand for change and the ability to implement it:

> To stay relevant, treaty provisions must keep pace with new policies, technological developments, changing economic and social interests, the proliferation of international institutions and actors, and evolving moral conceptions. They must likewise allow for the possibility of redressing shortcomings and ineffective compromises by the drafters, as well as intended ambiguities. At the same time, States often have (highly) divergent interests, making it challenging to reach agreement on specific rules and (further) politicizing the amendment process.[30]

The failure to alter IMF quota rules despite radical change in the nature of its clients, along with standard examples of the Doha Round at the WTO and the 1982 UN Convention on the Law of the Sea, provide illustrations of how difficult it can be to make substantial change. Recent analysis of EU institutions demonstrates that in the context of the Eurozone crisis—a circumstance one might expect to produce punctuated change—enacting major change was exceedingly difficult.[31] Even in a crisis compared to the Great Depression and a post-crisis analogous to a "Bretton Woods moment," "the post-crisis regulatory reform process has proceeded quite slowly and by way of marginal adjustments."[32] Change at the United Nations is no exception. International legal scholars have written extensively about the difficulties of implementing significant change at the UN, especially when it involves the Charter.[33] Charter amendments must be approved *and ratified* by two-thirds of the UN member states *including the five permanent members of the Security Council.* The sheer difficulty of passing major institutional change—and its rarity—suggests a healthy skepticism about whether it is the dominant mode through which international institutions evolve.

Other reasons for skepticism about the dominance of change via punctuated equilibrium are related to its visibility relative to the incremental, gradual counterpart. An insight from Thelen (2004) above notes that scholars who employ a *narrow definition* of path dependence are inclined toward thinking about change in a punctuated fashion. A narrow definition, which has certain analytical advantages,[34] also "implies and encourages the analyst to draw a sharp line between 'critical juncture' moments in which institutions are originally formed (or perhaps reformed) and long periods of stasis characterized by institutional continuity."[35] Questions of concept formation immediately emerge: how stable

---

[30] Buga 2018, 3.
[31] Moschella and Tsingou 2013; Fioretos 2016; Schmidt 2016; Jabko and Sheingate 2018.
[32] Moschella and Tsingou 2013, 193. For a similar argument, see Fioretos 2016, 68.
[33] E.g., Kelsen 1951; Gross 1956; Liang 2012; Buga 2018.
[34] Mahoney 2000, 510ff.
[35] Thelen 2004, 28. Also, see Streek and Thelen 2005.

must an institution be to code as static? There is a concern that if conceptions of institutional stasis actually tolerate considerable change, and conceptions of change require major breaks with developmental paths, the eye will catch punctuation, but incremental evolution will be rendered invisible. As Moschella and Tsingou put it: "the disproportionate attention given to revolutionary change risks reducing our understanding of change itself."[36]

A second reason is distinct, but related. Independent of how stasis and change are conceived, punctuated change is more visible than its incremental counterpart and easier to identify empirically. As important, it is easier to infer its significance when it occurs. The fact that punctuated change is easier to see and easier to judge does not mean that incremental change does not occur or is insignificant to institutional development, but it does stack the deck against its discovery. For example, in their analysis of the development of the energy regime complex, Colgan et al. define institutional innovations as "significant organizational changes."[37] Three categories of change are included: the creation of new organizations or links between them, the inclusion of "major new members," and "major internal structural changes."[38] As the authors note, "The advantage of this approach is that organizational changes are relatively easy to observe and thus provide a convenient metric to measure institutional innovation in the regime complex."[39] This is surely the case, but such an identification strategy is unlikely to produce a complete account of innovation or change.

In IR, accounts of incremental change complement and sometimes challenge punctuated models. In the wake of the 2008 financial crisis, this scholarship—much but not all grounded in the historical institutionalist tradition—illuminated an empirical middle ground between punctuated change and stasis. In this work, incremental change is conceived in opposition to radical (punctuated) change and whether it proves significant is an empirical question. Fioretos characterizes changes to financial market regulation as "intense incrementalism" that cumulatively produced "a more robust regulatory regime."[40] In a distinct but related realm, Rixen characterizes incremental reforms intended to close regulatory gaps around offshore financial centers as "feeble," "at best, minor improvements over the status quo."[41] These accounts are compelling in their message that the absence of punctuated change should not be mistaken for stasis. One cannot dismiss incremental change as unimportant; its effects require empirical investigation and may be critical to understanding how international institutions develop.

[36] Moschella and Tsingou 2013, 2.
[37] Colgan et al. 2012, 122.
[38] Colgan et al. 2012, 123.
[39] Colgan et al. 2012, 123.
[40] Fioretos 2016, 68–70.
[41] Rixen 2013, 95–96.

For the most part, this work does not aim to provide a theoretical frame-work for how incremental change produces transformation.[42] The possibility of transformation is occasionally noted,[43] but there is no theory to explain why what is incremental at T_1 contributes to transformation at T_2. Further, HI concepts are more often deployed to identify forces that hold back transformation rather than those that propel it forward. For example, Baker argues that despite the "radical and rapid" evolution of macroprudential *ideas* after the 2008 crisis, macropru-dential *policy* change was "distinctly incremental" owing to existing institutions and politics.[44] Fioretos similarly deploys HI to explain how more radical regu-latory reforms were stymied: "entrenched interests often prevailed in regulatory battles."[45] Although persuasive in the argument that we not dismiss incremental reform as unimportant, this work leaves the reader with the impression that HI is primarily about how change is obstructed (even in ostensible critical junctures) rather than how it is propelled forward despite institutional constraints.

A few studies in IR focus on the relationship between incremental reforms and transformational outcomes and deploy HI to understand how institutional constraints shape opportunities for change.[46] Farrell and Newman's work on cross-national layering provides an example.[47] In their argument, transnational regulatory forums are a response to pressure from firms to resolve "rule overlap" across domestic jurisdictions. Initially, new layers of agreement produced in these forums are informal and non-binding (read: incremental), but later they "can sub-sume and replace the domestic rule," ultimately transforming the sector.[48] Another example comes from Posner's argument that over a fifteen-year period, the routine activities of EU bureaucrats caused the emergence of new European financial mar-kets modeled on the Nasdaq.[49] These works exhibit the hallmarks of pioneering HI work on gradual transformation: radical change is initially blocked, but the incre-mental reforms made instead create opportunities for disruption that facilitate subsequent transformation.[50]

These analyses provoke questions about intentionality on the part of change advocates and the perceptions of opponents who prefer the status quo. In these empirical stories, the actors who enact incremental reform desire transforma-tion. They pursue incremental reform not because their aims are incremental but because radical change (big change all at once) is opposed by those with a stake in the status quo. If the actors pursuing change are known to intend transformation,

---

[42] Exceptions are noted below.
[43] Moschella and Tsingou 2013, 4.
[44] Baker 2013a, 417–418.
[45] Fioretos 2016, 68–70.
[46] Posner 2009; Chwieroth 2014; Farrell and Newman 2015; St. John 2018.
[47] Farrell and Newman 2015.
[48] Farrell and Newman 2015, 503.
[49] Posner 2009.
[50] E.g., Streek and Thelen 2005; Mahoney and Thelen 2010.

why are their incremental reforms not perceived by opponents as a step down a slippery slope? These questions are not directly addressed at length, but two possibilities can be inferred. The first has to do with exclusion and its distributional effects. Transnational forums include some actors and not others; those inclined to oppose change may not be in a position to object.[51] Second, the actors who pursue change may not be perceived as capable of affecting transformation, or they may act surreptitiously. Posner's bureaucrats pursued "their aims in ways that cover their tracks," their activities were "seemingly mundane" and tended "to take place in the background."[52]

Building from this work, I offer an alternative framework to understand how incremental change can, over time, transform international institutions. It allows that the actors who pursue incremental change do not intend or even conceive of its potential to produce transformative outcomes. They often pursue incremental change for purposes distinct and detached from the transformative outcomes they set in motion. Like in Posner's work, the subterranean nature of the process is important. But change is subterranean not primarily because actors who pursue change conceal their efforts, but because the link between incremental reform and transformational effects has not been conceived. This points to a novel element of my framework: the uncoordinated nature of subterranean transformation. The layering and conversion processes theorized by historical institutionalists, and the legal interpretive strategies of subsequent agreement and subsequent practice articulated by international legal scholars, occur over extended periods of time. We can connect the dots to identify these as change processes in retrospect, but the individuals and groups who we identify as having participated in the process may not have conceived of that process or recognized their role within it. Their contributions are not coordinated over time. This process requires a set of theoretical assumptions about uncertainty, rules, and agents, that are distinct from those that provide the backbone of rationalist approaches in IR, and are often left unsaid by HI scholars in IR.

The Foundations of Gradual Transformation in International Institutions

"Transformational change" often escapes definition, but in the context of institutional rules, it is widely used to refer to change that involves reorganizing fundamental relationships. Comparative political economists use the term to describe the slow but steady liberalization of the advanced political economies in the second half of the twentieth century. During this period, the state ceded

---

[51] Farrell and Newman 2015, 502.
[52] Posner 2009, 15, 35.

"ever more economic transactions from public-political control and turn[ed] them over to private contracts."[53] This is a transformative outcome because it alters fundamental relationships between the state, markets, and society. The process is gradual because it unfolds incrementally over decades. In another example, Jeffrey Tulis's classic work explains the transformation of the American presidency from a federalist model in which presidents shunned public appeals, and communication was usually directed toward Congress, to a "rhetorical presidency," in which the president often spoke directly to the people to win public support.[54] The outcome was transformational because it altered the institution of the presidency as conceived by the founders, and its relationship to Congress and the public. It was gradual because while it began with the twenty-sixth president, Theodore Roosevelt, it was fully realized only by Ronald Reagan, the fortieth.

Consistent with these examples, I define *transformation* as a change in fundamental relationships and principles of governance. The UN case qualifies as transformation because changes in funding ultimately reorganized relationships between member states and United Nations entities and between the member states themselves. In its first thirty years, UN governance was dominated by *collective* decision-making by member states seated on various governing bodies. This is not to say that equal representation meant that all member states exerted equal influence in collective decisions. Rather, it is to say that to act, member states had to make a collective, that is, multilateral, decision. It also meant that the primary accountability relationship of UN entities (i.e., UN programs and funds) was to the multilateral governing body. The introduction and expansion of earmarked voluntary funding reordered these relationships. No longer was a collective decision necessary to motivate UN action. An individual member state could—on its own in consultation with a UN entity—initiate UN projects. As more member states chose to engage in earmarking, and as other types of funding stagnated, collective decision-making came to govern a minority of funds and individual donor decisions came to govern the majority. UN entities' primary accountability relationship was no longer with the multilateral body, but rather with a multitude of donor-specific contracts. Once primarily instruments of multilateralism, UN entities became contract agencies for bilateral aid agendas.

Gradual is used in the conventional sense; it refers to a process of change rather than the accomplishment of change by a single act. It also implies a slow rather than swift pace, and multiple, incremental steps rather than single, large leaps. Gradual change processes generally do not involve replacing rules outright. Two prominent processes involve layering (adding new rules alongside old ones, which alter outcomes over time), and conversion (repurposing old rules to achieve new ends). These processes share much with those used by legal scholars to

[53] Streek and Thelen 2005, 4.
[54] Tulis 1987.

describe the ways that international law evolves. Gradual change processes can be usefully deployed to describe empirical phenomena without much theoretical elaboration. When the International Court of Justice (ICJ) or European Court of Human Rights (ECtHR) explicitly relies on subsequent practice to arrive at decisions that alter the meaning of the law, we can describe the change as having occurred through subsequent practice, consistent with the general category of conversion.

But understanding how changes that are ostensibly incremental gradually transform requires unpacking theoretical assumptions. Transformational potential rests on a particular understanding of agents, rules, and the environment in which they operate. In particular, a decision-making environment characterized by genuine uncertainty (in addition to risk), rules that contain an inherent permissiveness (rather than only serving as constraints), and agents with a potential for creativity (rather than machine-like calculators or predictably biased), provide a foundation for understanding how gradual change transforms institutions over time.

Uncertainty

Katzenstein and Seybert write that "Important strands of international relations scholarship have followed the intellectual ascendency of economics. These approaches focus attention on the controllable world of risk, while largely neglecting the uncontrollable world of uncertainty."[55] The rationalist literature on international rules is one such important strand of IR scholarship. Uncertainty is defined in a probabilistic way; future states of the world are identifiable but cognitive limits and environmental complexity make it difficult to know which will occur for *certain*. In this conception, Blyth explains, "life is uncertain in the sense that rolling a dice is uncertain, and this is why it is not uncertain at all."[56] The disadvantage of defining uncertainty in a probabilistic way is that it conflates uncertainty with risk when in fact the two connote very different decision-making environments.[57] Genuine uncertainty refers to situations in which the past is not a good predictor of the future and future states of the world are not foreseeable. One cannot assign probabilities to unforeseeable events, and as a practical matter, one cannot design institutions proactively to anticipate them. By defining uncertainty in probabilistic terms, actual uncertainty is assumed away.

This is not only an abstract point. In decision-making environments characterized by genuine uncertainty, actors engaged in institutional design (or reform)

[55] Katzenstein and Seybert 2018, 86.
[56] Blyth 2006, 495.
[57] North 1990; Blyth 2006; Nelson and Katzenstein 2014; Lockwood 2015; Katzenstein and Seybert 2018.

are more likely to make "mistakes." This is because they cannot anticipate how unforeseen events will alter the consequences of their design choices. Unforeseen events come in many forms, and in both exogenous and endogenous varieties. A recurring theme in the archival record of postwar institutions is the failure to anticipate changes in membership that would occur in the decades to come. Barton et al. explain how the loose rules of the GATT functioned well for the original, mostly like-minded member states.[58] But GATT designers did not fully contemplate an increasingly diverse membership or the effects that flexible rules would have in that context. The United Nations story is similar. Writing his dissent in the *Certain Expenses* decision at the ICJ regarding whether peacekeeping costs constituted "expenses of the Organization," Judge Percy Spender wrote, "the wisest among them could never have anticipated the tremendous change which politically, militarily, and otherwise have occurred in the comparatively few years that have elapsed since 1945."[59]

Another type of unforeseen event bleeds into the categories of rule permissiveness and creative agency, but can be previewed here. Actors engaged in institutional design cannot exhaustively foresee how the rules they design will be used in the future. The unforeseen "event" might be the redeployment of a rule for a purpose distinct from or even contradictory to designers' original intent. Búzás and Graham demonstrate how, in the twenty-first century, judges at the ECtHR interpreted rules in ways states parties never contemplated when they designed them in the 1950s, and these reinterpretations altered parties' obligations under the European Convention on Human Rights.[60] Genuine uncertainty exists in part because one cannot anticipate how creative agents (in this example, ECtHR judges) will interpret and repurpose rules at a later date.

Scholars have explained that when applied to a world of uncertainty, theories that assume a world of risk perform poorly.[61] For our purposes there is another important implication specific to institutional change. Genuine uncertainty around the downstream effects of rules leaves room for rules to be adopted *because their transformational potential is unforeseen.* Actors that would be unsupportive or oppose downstream rule effects nevertheless approve rule enactment because they do not see a causal connection between the two. Indeed, it allows that some such actors may even *pursue* rule changes that contain transformational potential. Genuine uncertainty allows that actors may set in motion transformational change without intending to do so. This stems in part from rule permissiveness.

---

[58] Barton et al. 2006.
[59] Judge Spender Opinion in *Certain Expenses* Advisory Opinion, 1962.
[60] Búzás and Graham 2020.
[61] On this point, see especially Blyth 2006.

Rules

Rationalist arguments about international institutions emphasize the constraining aspect of rules. The role rules play in this regard is undoubtedly important: International institutions facilitate cooperation by making states' commitments to constrain their behavior more credible. States make public, explicit commitments to refrain from some circumscribed set of behaviors. These commitments are often buoyed by rules that make regulated behaviors more transparent, delegate dispute settlement to third parties, and outline penalties for non-compliance. Rationalist accounts allow that rules can be more or less constraining but variation is the result of intentional design. These accounts of designed flexibility are increasingly nuanced; they incorporate a wide range of design features, and recognize substitution and interaction effects among and between those features.[62] Rule makers design rigid rules, for example, with narrowly drawn escape clauses and precise language when they want tight constraints, and design flexible rules, for example, by designing broad conditions for escape and employing ambiguous language when they want room to maneuver.

On its face, nothing appears unreasonable about the rationalist account. States surely design more or less flexibility in their agreements in a strategic fashion with the goal of making them more or less constraining. The problem arises only if that which is intended is regarded as the *only* source of rule permissiveness. In addition to sometimes being the product of intentional design, permissiveness is also an ever-present and inescapable characteristic of written rules.

In a prominent example from American political development, Greenstone (1986) employs Wittgenstein's *Philosophical Investigations*, which outlines a philosophy of language emphasizing the "open texture" of human speech to provide a critique of Louis Hartz's *Liberal Tradition in America*. Greenstone explains, "For Hartz, American politics was not just pervasively, but also consensually, liberal. But the discussion of rules considered here suggests that even if Americans have one set of liberal rules, it by no means follows that these rules are entirely unambiguous."[63] In Greenstone's view, rule ambiguity is "a fact," that has the potential to produce conflict and change: "Because the rules do not always speak clearly, a conflict over their interpretation is always possible."[64] As Sheingate provides, this gives rules a "double-edged quality."[65] Rules "do more than limit alternatives or set the parameters for strategic interaction. Rules also provide actors with creative leeway. In this way, rules are at once constraining and empowering."[66]

---

[62] E.g., Koremenos 2005; Pelc 2011, 2016; Graham 2017.
[63] Greenstone 1986, 19.
[64] Greenstone 1986, 48.
[65] Sheingate 2010, 168.
[66] Sheingate 2010, 168.

Writing in a different field, international lawyer Isabelle Van Damme describes the VCLT in remarkably similar terms: The VCLT contains "principles of logic and order that both constrain and empower the interpreter."[67] At root, this empowering potential is the result of "semantic indeterminacy" in written laws; their application requires interpretation.[68] Empirically grounded accounts that chart how international laws evolve often employ the language of "open texture" to refer to rule permissiveness. A classic illustration comes from Article 27(3) of the United Nations Charter, which specifies Security Council decision-making. The provision reads: "Decisions of the Security Council on all other [non-procedural] matters shall be made by an affirmative vote of seven members [now nine members] including the concurring votes of the permanent members; (...)." As Buga (2018) explains, the word "concurrence" itself is formulated using "active language" that "does not, at first sight, leave much room for ambiguity." The archival record confirms Buga's analysis, demonstrating that the drafters of Article 27(3) intended for concurring to mean affirmative.[69] Permanent Security Council members would have to vote "yes" for a resolution to pass. Yet in just a few years, the Council reinterpreted "concurring" to mean "non-objection," rather than affirmative. This allowed resolutions to pass despite abstentions by permanent members.[70] The reinterpretation facilitated the work of the Council while simultaneously allowing permanent members a third way on politically sensitive issues. Despite drafters' attempts at clarity and rigidity, the inherent permissiveness of language offered room for consequential change via reinterpretation that was likely impossible through formal renegotiation.[71]

If rules could only be interpreted in one way and could only be employed for one purpose, then placing a given rule on a continuum between constraining and permissive as a function of intentional design would not be problematic. But this is far from the case. In the realm of international law, not only is there regular disagreement about how to interpret the obligations states incur in individual treaties, there is a lively meta-debate about how to interpret sections of the VCLT that outline how to interpret treaties.[72] What is clear, however, is that it is not only the formal amendment of treaty rules, but subsequent practice and adjacent bodies of law deemed germane, that are appropriate to include in the interpretive process. Further, having reached a certain threshold, subsequent practice can go beyond reinterpretation to modify treaty obligations.[73] This all occurs without any formal renegotiation process or rewriting of rules.

[67] Van Damme 2009, 38.
[68] Putnam 2020, 32.
[69] Stavropoulos 1967, 739ff; Búzás and Graham 2020.
[70] For a detailed account of this case, see Búzás and Graham 2020.
[71] Stavropoulos 1967, 739ff; Buga 2018, 240ff; Búzás and Graham 2020.
[72] For a review, see Waibel 2011.
[73] International Law Commission 2013; Nolte 2013; Buga 2018.

Genuine uncertainty suggests that downstream effects of rules may be different than what rule makers anticipate and rule permissiveness fuels this uncertainty. Permissiveness makes it hard to know how rules will be interpreted and used. Creativity plays a similar role. The unpredictability of agents renders forecasts of rule effects unreliable. When creative agents tap into the "empowering," permissive aspect of international rules, it can drive institutional development in significant and unanticipated ways.

Agency

Above I elaborated an assumption that genuine uncertainty is an ordinary rather than extraordinary state of affairs in world politics. The assumption recognizes that social life at T_2 is unpredictable from the vantage point of actors designing rules at T_1. This is especially true as the span of time between T_1 and T_2 grows. As postwar international rules "reach a certain age,"[74] an assumption that the actors who designed the international order in 1945 were operating in an environment of genuine uncertainty with regard to the world of 2020, and the effects of their rules in that world, would seem to reflect common sense. A growing political psychology literature in IR demonstrates that cognitive biases affect agents' cost-benefit calculations.[75] But it is important to note that genuine uncertainty is a characteristic of the environment rather than the agent. Even the perfect, idealized actor, free from biases, is prone to "mistakes," not because *she* did not predict future events but because *future events were unpredictable*. In practice, both the uncertainty of the decision-making environment and cognitive bias are likely to contribute to the unintended consequences of design choices.

These environmental limits do not lead to a second-rate view of agents, but incomplete forecasts do alter how and when agents affect institutional development. Rationalist arguments tend to be optimistic about agents' ability to anticipate future events. In this view, institutional designers are proactive. They anticipate potential futures and design rules to deal with them. In the framework proposed here, genuine uncertainty renders these expectations unreasonably high. To be sure, institutional designers will behave consistent with rationalist expectations around easy-to-anticipate challenges, but they will fail to anticipate others, and surprises will accumulate as time passes. Agents shine not in their proactive efforts to control the future, which are often bedeviled by the unforeseen, but in how they creatively cope with unanticipated events and the undesirable status quo that results. In this way agents are reactive rather than proactive. They often

[74] Nolte 2013, 6.
[75] Kertzer and Tingley 2018. On bounded rationality and international institutions, see Jupille et al. 2013. On prospect theory and historical institutionalism in international relations, see Fioretos 2011.

respond to outcomes that emerge rather than anticipate their emergence. Yet they may react in creative ways that allow them to navigate unpredictability while simultaneously contributing to it.

One fundamental aspect of this conception of creativity requires elaboration. I emphasize the potential for, and importance of, creativity in normal times and tight spots, when actors find wiggle room between a rock and a hard place. More often, creativity is associated with exceptional moments at critical junctures.[76] This is true for prominent strands of historical institutionalism that conceptualize critical junctures as "unsettled times" in which "different possibilities of development are possible" but "prior structural conditions do not necessarily determine the type and direction of subsequent institutional developments."[77] During critical junctures, structure is indeterminate and there is room for agency to play an important role in deciding the course of future events. A similar view on the temporal bounds of creativity is seen in Katzenstein and Seybert's useful conception of protean power, or the power "that results from practices of agile actors coping with uncertainty."[78] The authors make a strong case for taking genuine uncertainty seriously, and recognize that agents creatively cope rather than clairvoyantly plan, but they appear to see the exercise of protean power primarily in "fluid" periods, or critical junctures, "in response to crises that catch everyone by surprise—such as China's unexpected rise, the opening of the Berlin Wall, and the Arab Spring."[79]

Creativity undoubtedly matters when structural bounds are loosened in the wake of exogenous shocks, but I emphasize that creativity also matters during periods aptly characterized as normal, or even those in which institutions appear decidedly stuck. When standard, direct processes of change—like persuading others to vote to repeal a rule or amend it—are unavailable, creative actors can pursue change by tapping in to rule permissiveness. As the discussion of permissiveness makes clear, this does not imply an absence of constraints. On the contrary, rules constrain by blocking some paths of change and can even be said to "pull" actors toward other possibilities by virtue of the opportunities for change they offer.[80] These possibilities might be found in the clear edges of rules that allow actors to take advantage of what is not said, ambiguity that allows for new, self-serving interpretations, or tensions in meaning that result from dense, complex rule environments.[81]

[76] See Andonova 2017, 41ff on the related concept of entrepreneurship and its importance to change within international organizations.

[77] Capoccia 2016, 89.

[78] Katzenstein and Seybert 2018, 80.

[79] Katzenstein and Seybert 2018, 80–81.

[80] This conception of path dependence is consistent with Pouliot's "pulling theory of agency" developed at the nexus of practice theory and historical institutionalism (Pouliot 2020). See also Adler-Nissen and Drieschova 2019.

[81] See Búzás and Graham 2020.

Mechanisms of Transformation from International Law

HI scholars have written extensively about mechanisms of gradual change, including layering, and conversion. Conversion occurs when "rules remain formally the same but are interpreted and enacted in new ways."[82] Layering works by adding new rules, which over time can alter the effects of old ones. This section aims to accomplish two goals. The first is to introduce and illuminate how international legal interpretive strategies provide novel pathways for conversion and layering processes. The second is to highlight the "subterranean"[83] and uncoordinated nature of these processes that have not received sustained attention in IR.

Evolutive Interpretation, Subsequent Practice, and "Reading Down" in International Law

Gradual change processes of conversion and layering occur when repeal, replacement, or revision of a particular status quo rule is not possible. They become relevant in situations where institutions are somewhat *stuck*. Layering has been imported to IR to explain patterns of institutional development across a wide range of issues and organizations, including the non-proliferation regime, the Basel regulatory framework, the International Monetary Fund, and the World Health Organization.[84] The language of conversion is not employed as often, but arguments consistent with its logic can be found. For example, Hurd (2017) explains how actors have strategically stretched the "self" in the self-defense exception to the UN Charter's prohibition on war from the territorial state to the interests of the state abroad. In doing so, he argues the "self" is expanded to such an extent that the rule now serves to legitimate war, a purpose that directly contradicts its initial goal of prevention.[85]

Legal interpretive strategies employed in international law map nicely onto conversion and layering processes. Arato outlines how evolutive treaty interpretations and subsequent practice are "capable of establishing *change*, by which I mean to include all kinds of treaty development, ranging from fleshing out an ambiguous term to reinterpreting a treaty in ways not foreseen by the text, or even against the weight of its plain meaning."[86] A central problem of treaty interpretation is the passage of time; evolutive or "dynamic" interpretation regards the treaty as a "living instrument" "which can change its meaning in accordance with developments in

---

[82] Mahoney and Thelen 2010, 17.
[83] This term is used by Hacker 2004.
[84] Baker 2013b; Hanrieder 2015; Moschella 2016; Solingen and Wan 2017; Weaver and Moschella 2017.
[85] Hurd 2017.
[86] Arato 2010, 456. Emphasis original.

State and society."[87] As in a conversion process this means that the meaning of a rule is subject to change without any renegotiation or rewriting.

Two sets of actors are important in facilitating conversion through reinterpretation and subsequent practice. The first is perhaps most obvious. International courts like the ICJ and the ECtHR engage in evolutive interpretation and take into account subsequent practice in interpreting treaty obligations. Article 31 of the VCLT, which outlines General Rules of Interpretation, begins: "A treaty should be interpreted in accordance with the ordinary meaning to be given to the terms of the treaty in their context and in light of its object and purpose." The relevant *context* refers to the treaty text, including the preamble, as well as any subsequent related agreements adopted by the parties involved. Notably, taking into account the intent of the original rule makers—those who negotiated the agreement—in the act of interpretation is optional from a legal perspective. Article 32, which outlines Supplementary Rules of Interpretation notes that, "Resource *may* be had to supplementary means of interpretation, including the preparatory works of the treaty and the circumstances of its conclusion (...)."[88] According to the VCLT, then, "the original intentions of the authors of the treaty are taken into account only in a subsidiary way (...)."[89] This allows courts to interpret rules in light of changing societal norms but also in light of subsequent practice, which points to a second set of actors who are critical to conversion processes in international law.

Beyond the plain meaning of the text, the VCLT's General Rules of Interpretation (Article 31 3b), directs interpreters toward "any subsequent practice in the application of the treaty which establishes the agreement of the parties regarding its interpretation." Legal scholars interpret subsequent practice broadly; any verbal or physical action or the absence of action from one or more of the actors relevant to an agreement can constitute subsequent practice.[90] The logic is that how actors behave should provide insight into how they understand their obligations and, in turn, the meaning of the law. Most often the actors whose "subsequent practices" are significant are the states bound by international agreements, although international organizations are also noted as relevant in the VCLT. These statements, actions, and non-actions by parties to an agreement can lead to new interpretations and even modifications of international law. This can occur when international courts rely on subsequent practice in their decisions, but also when new understandings based on state practice emerge among the parties themselves even in the absence of a court ruling. The example from the modification of UN Security Council voting rules away from affirmative consent provides an instance in which

---

[87] Bernhardt 1999, 12.
[88] Emphasis added.
[89] Bernhardt 1999, 16.
[90] International Law Commission 2013, 45; Buga 2018, 24; Búzás and Graham 2020, 4.

the permanent UNSC member states indicated acceptance of the new interpretation based on subsequent practice. Later statements from the ICJ and UN Secretary-General affirmed this new interpretation by taking states' subsequent practice into account.[91]

If evolutive treaty interpretation and change through subsequent practice provide novel pathways to conversion, the legal interpretive strategy of reading one body of law through, or in light of, another[92] provides new insight into how layering processes can produce rule change in the international context. In addition to ordinary meaning and subsequent practice, the VCLT's general rules of interpretation call for consideration of "any relevant rules of international law applicable in the relations between the parties."[93] Beyond amendments or revisions of the original law, interpreters are directed to consult outside bodies of law where applicable. For instance, starting in 2011, the ECtHR interpreted the European Convention on Human Rights "in light of IHL [International Humanitarian Law]."[94] Having expanded the ECHR's extraterritorial application to armed conflicts abroad, the Court takes into account relevant IHL, including the Geneva Conventions, when interpreting ECHR obligations.[95] Scholars and policymakers predict a similar process may produce change in the meaning of trade treaty obligations— like those governing subsidies—if and when they are read in light of environmental agreements.[96] When a new law or body of law is incorporated in the interpretive exercise—either because it has recently entered into force or because a court has only just decided it is relevant, as occurred in the ECHR case, it can alter the meaning of the law.

In practice, international courts sometimes look to outside agreements or decisions that lack the force of international law. This is especially relevant in the United Nations system where the General Assembly provides an important and prolific voice for the member states but (outside its legal authority over mandatory dues and the budget), its decisions lack legal force. The ICJ often refers to General Assembly resolutions (alongside other evidence) to interpret the United Nations Charter.[97] In legal terms these resolutions may be better understood as subsequent practice since most GA resolutions do not legally obligate UN member states. But the resolutions can also be construed to represent a version of the layered rules that over time come to shape interpretation in ways similar to outside legal agreements. Resolutions from the General Assembly or other UN agencies are ultimately written texts that pass through a formal vote. Such resolutions and

---

[91] Búzás and Graham 2020, 8.
[92] Sometimes referred to as "reading down" by legal scholars, e.g., Milanovic 2011; De Koker 2015.
[93] VCLT Article 31(3c).
[94] Milanovic 2011, 299; also, Búzás and Graham 2020, 9–10.
[95] See especially *Hassan v. United Kingdom*.
[96] E.g., Dong and Walley 2008; Das et al. 2019.
[97] High profile cases include advisory opinions on *Certain Expenses* (1962) and *Namibia* (1971).

decisions passed in multilateral bodies may or may not be written with specific Charter implications in mind. In sum, a range of actors contribute international rule change through these legal interpretive strategies. Some of these actors, especially, but not exclusively early in the process, may contribute to those changes unwittingly.

The Uncoordinated Nature of Gradual Transformation

The legal processes of gradual change articulated here, evolutive interpretations, modification through subsequent practice, and reading the meaning of one rule through another, illuminate that change is dynamic, that individual contributions to change are often asynchronous and decentralized, and that those individual contributions need not be intended to cause transformation. Indeed, early in the process it is likely that their actions do not conceive of a transformative project.

Three vantage points help to illuminate these aspects of international rule change, T_1 (when an agreement is negotiated), T_2 (when an incremental act occurs), and T_3 (when transformative opportunities associated with T_2 become visible). Genuine uncertainty increases the likelihood that between T_1 and T_2 demand for change to the original agreement will emerge among some set of actors. The framework applies to situations in which, for practical reasons discussed earlier, the barriers to formal rule change are high and status quo rules produce interests with a stake in their persistence. In this context, states will have a difficult time revising rules or replacing them outright. It is important to note that in this early phase the incremental act is *not* associated with the potential to transform the institution.

The distance between intent and effect can be yawning. Rules that ultimately transformed and entrenched privatization of retirement savings in the United States provide an enlightening example of how this can work. In the example, the addition of Section 401(k) represents an incremental change to the broader US tax code.

> The legislative language that would become Section 401(k) of the tax code appears to have been merely intended to clarify the tax status of certain types of profit-sharing plans that had been under Treasury scrutiny for some time (...) Section 401(k) passed completely beneath the radar screen of public debate. Certainly no one in Congress recognized how significant it would become. (...) "The 401(k) provision," the Joint Tax Committee estimated, "will have a negligible effect upon budget receipts."[98]

---

[98] Hacker 2004, 165.

Why did this small addition to the tax code at T_2, intended to clarify certain profit-sharing plans (an issue distinct from setting the trajectory in favor or against privatization), and expected to have no effect, go on to alter the private pension landscape? Put differently, why the chasm between what the US Congress thought it was doing and what it actually did? In Jacob Hacker's meticulous telling, the answer lies in what happened at T_3, when Ted Benna, a private benefits expert, lobbied the IRS to interpret Section 401(k) to cover wages voluntarily set aside by workers. Although the extension was "not self-evident," the Reagan IRS agreed.[99]

This example illustrates that multiple actors—in this case Congress, an independent private benefits expert, and the IRS—all participate in the process of change. However, Congress did not do so knowingly. Their addition of Section 401(k) to the tax code at T_2 made transformational change possible because what they wrote was permissive; it could be used in a way they did not anticipate or intend. That potential was identified and creatively accessed by Ted Benna who forwarded a creative "not self-evident" interpretation of the rule at T_3, which was then endorsed and formalized by the IRS.

It also illustrates empirically the framework's crucial implication that incremental acts can produce transformational change precisely because the transformational potential is unforeseen by those who engage in the incremental action. In an example from international law, in *Hassan v. United Kingdom*, the ECtHR relied on *non-behavior* by states parties as subsequent practice to effectively modify Article 5 regarding detentions and security of person of the ECHR. Like in the case of Congress above, "there is no evidence that states' non-behavior—the absence of derogation—was intended to be used by the ECtHR to alter the law."[100] At the same time, like for Benna and the IRS, the ECtHR interpretation was made possible by other actors' behavior. In this case, states' decentralized, uncoordinated (non)behavior in the preceding years.

These examples highlight gradual change processes as the cumulative product of multiple actors acting. But they often act at different moments and stages in the process and for different purposes, and they need not share collective intent.[101] Put in generic terms, the initial circumstances that lead Actor X at T_2 to offer an expanded interpretation of Rule A may be different from the circumstances and concerns that lead Actor Y at T_3 to expand the interpretation of Rule A further. Actor X may not have foreseen the circumstances that would hold at T_3 and may not approve of Actor Y's response to them. Nevertheless, Actor X's initial

---

[99] Hacker 2004, 166.

[100] Búzás and Graham 2020, 10.

[101] Collective intent about the purpose of design or change may also be missing at any given moment. Schickler's (2001) theory of disjointed pluralism emphasizes that different groups often pursue the same rule for different purposes. Grynaviski (2014) theorizes how distinct understandings of particular rules and their likely effects can be essential to successfully negotiating international cooperative agreements. This diversity of purpose is even more likely in dynamic settings.

reinterpretation provides a building block for Y's expanded interpretation of Rule A. Actor X acted intentionally, but only unwittingly passed the baton to Actor Y, who pushed the process of change along further.

Visibility

The question of when transformative potential becomes "visible" in the gradual change process is an empirical one. In the examples just provided, actors at T_2 do not contemplate that their incremental actions have the potential to transform at all. Rather, they intend them to be incremental or to have nothing to do with the outcome they ultimately affect. In some instances, such transformational effects may be imagined by some small set of actors but deemed improbable and beside the point given the distinct goals of the moment. Given the uncertainty assumption of the framework, what is crucial is that the transformative outcome is not contemplated as a plausible future state of the world. To be clear, transformative potential can remain forever latent. But it is more likely to become visible some time after incremental change is implemented, especially when a subset of actors become dissatisfied with the status quo and have an interest in fundamental change. Within the UN development system, as state representatives learned how earmarked funding worked, it became apparent that if employed on a larger scale it could be used to reorient the system away from multilateral governance. Once this was clear, *and* representatives from some member states became increasingly critical of the UN bureaucracy, they could creatively repurpose earmark rules to achieve that goal. At this later moment of repurposing, not all actors understood that transformation was being pursued, but the actors involved now saw the transformative potential of their actions clearly.

The underlying assumptions of the framework make space for transformation that is initially unintended and the preceding examples make clear that sometimes those who set the process in motion do not intend to do so. On the other hand, we know that choices made in the realm of international cooperation are often not taken lightly. Choices about institutional design, how to interpret and behave in response to international rules, and whether or not to support or impede others' attempts at change are (often) arrived at carefully. Assuming a mindset of rigorous attention to decisions, it may seem unlikely that transformational potential is "missed" very often, and thus easy to discard these instances to the realms of the exceptional.

There are reasons to be skeptical of this thinking. With the benefit of history, the retrospective observer may be biased toward higher expectations about what actors can reasonably anticipate as they gaze ten, twenty, or fifty years into the future. Reorienting one's perspective to understand that some things are only "missed" in retrospect may prove useful. When a rule is initially designed or altered, the expectation that actors involved envision how the same rule will be deployed, manipulated, or interpreted by actors of a future generation who operate in a distinct global (rule) context is probably unreasonable. In addition, I outline three characteristics that can further insulate incremental acts with transformational potential from being seen, and lend themselves to subterranean change processes. The starting point is that incremental change is helped by the fact that it is small. Its very definition as incremental undercuts the likelihood of large-scale effects. But the reasons why a change is perceived as incremental at T_2 requires attention. I focus on characteristics associated with the nature of the rule change, its perceived association with fundamental principles of the broader rule system, in this case, those that underlie the international organization, and the actors who pursue incremental change.

The first characteristic stems from sociological approaches that emphasize how perceptions of bureaucracies as technical, apolitical actors undergird their authority.[102] The political agendas of domestic partisans or sovereign states provide constant cause for suspicion regarding their motivations. By contrast, perceptions of bureaucrats as apolitical actors whose decisions stem from professional expertise may insulate their actions from the same scrutiny. Posner's EU bureaucrats fit this bill. Their activities are judged "mundane" and "routine," and as such tend to escape notice.[103] Here I do not emphasize technical knowledge or expertise on the part of the actors who implement incremental change, but related perceptions of the nature of the rule change itself. When changes are understood by involved parties to be "technical" or "procedural" or "bureaucratic," rather than "substantive," transformational potential is especially difficult to envision.

A second characteristic is a function of the perceived relationship between a proposed incremental change and the fundamental principles of an organization or body of law. Fundamental principles, like multilateralism, are upheld, produced, and reproduced by a set of rules and practices. Some of these rules and practices are consciously understood to be constitutive of those principles. In these cases, actors perceive a tight relationship between particular rules and the identity of an organization or body of law. Touching these rules—even to tinker—is almost certain to draw scrutiny and concern about the potential effects of change. In the context of most international organizations, voting rights and rules are viewed as crucial elements that produce multilateral governance, and shape the relationship between member states and between member states and the international organization's bureaucracy. When representation issues arise, they are immediately treated as important questions worthy of attention and energetic response. When change is made to rules that are *not* regarded as constitutive of fundamental

---

[102] Barnett and Finnemore 2004.
[103] Posner 2009.

principles, they are likely to receive less attention and more likely subject to subterranean change processes.

Related is the relationship between the rule subject to proposed change and existing rules that *are* perceived to constitute underlying principles. If particular rules are viewed as essential to an organization's fundamental character, any attempt to undermine them will raise concerns about undermining underlying principles. By contrast, if changes are understood to be divorced from the relevant rules, or are understood to complement, strengthen, or supplement them, transformative potential is less likely to be contemplated. Another example from Hacker's work on the rise of private benefits systems in the United States helps to illuminate this point. Hacker explains that private benefits systems did not directly repeal Social Security, nor were they initially viewed as a threat to public benefits.[104] Indeed, important labor groups supported private retirement protections as a temporary *supplement* to public benefits, until the latter could be further expanded. The consequences in the long term were of course distinct: an expansion of privatization and a correspondent narrowing of public benefits.

A third characteristic involves the question of which actors propose changes and how they are perceived in relation to fundamental principles and status quo rules. If change proposals come from actors known to be critical of the organization or dissatisfied with fundamental aspects of its operation, they are more likely to be received skeptically by those who support the status quo. This is likely to be true regardless of substantive content; suspicion about motivations can draw attention independent of the proposed change itself. By contrast, proposals from actors who are supportive of the institution's fundamental principles are less likely to be received with suspicion. In Hacker's retirement example,[105] the potential negative effects of new private pension rules on public benefits were perhaps less likely to be considered because they were supported by labor groups who were advocates of the public system. Since one would anticipate that those who advocated and relied on Social Security and would benefit from a public pension system would not seek to unravel those benefits, actors were less likely to contemplate scenarios that would lead to that outcome.

Tensions Produced by Subterranean Change

The framework put forward here makes clear that a gradual, decentralized process can produce change that is as consequential for institutional development as the formal negotiation and amendment processes typically associated with major change in IR. Yet the character of change produced by these gradual processes is

---

[104] Hacker 2002.
[105] Hacker 2004, 255.

distinct in an important way. When attempts to alter the status quo are intentional, direct, and visible, and when the relevant groups formally or publicly endorse change, there is some agreement that status quo rules are inadequate and require alteration. Formal, collective revision indicates a rejection of old rules as lacking in some way, functionally, normatively, or otherwise. New rules are collectively deemed the best way to move forward.

Transformation that occurs through a decentralized, gradual process is less likely to benefit from this collective endorsement. These processes are not initiated based on widespread agreement that old rules were deficient. On the contrary, many accept initial acts of conversion or layered rules as acceptable only because they did not anticipate transformational effects. When a layer is added to an institutional foundation, it can "alter" the original layer without "obliterating" it.[106] There is no formal, collective rejection of the original institutional architecture, which often retains its proponents. The absence of a clean, intentional break produces tension and churning because rules now entail contradictory practices and support contradictory principles that are difficult to resolve. In the United Nations case, the effects on multilateralism ushered in by changes in financing rules were never "approved" by the membership, rather they "happened." Multilateralism maintains its normative value within the UN and remains a key component of the UN's institutional identity. For this reason, as transformational effects of the bilateral funding system became clear, it became a source of tension and criticism within the system.

Sources and Observable Implications of the Framework

The chapters that follow constitute a longitudinal case study of institutional change at the United Nations from its negotiation during World War II through the early 2000s. I employ process-tracing to evaluate the empirical purchase of my framework. In doing so, I produce an analytically informed narrative[107] that weaves together various threads—including funding rule design in the Charter, the emergence of peacekeeping and its effects, the introduction of voluntary funding rules to fund technical assistance, and the effects of a growing UN membership—that ultimately altered and produced UN governance as it exists today. Here I summarize the source material that informs the book and develop a set of theoretically informed observable implications with regard to "context, process, or mechanism."[108] Some of the observable implications follow from the framework's assumptions of uncertainty, rule permissiveness, and creativity, and others follow from the framework's mechanisms of change, layering and conversion, and specific

---

[106] Tulis 1987, 17.
[107] See George and Bennett 2004, chapter 10.
[108] Seawright and Collier 2004, 277.

varieties of those processes in the international legal space. Some correspond with specific stages in the process (i.e., T_1, T_2, T_3), while others characterize the process as a whole.

Source Material

The analysis of the UN's negotiation and founding (Chapter 3) draws on three primary sources: the Papers of Leo Pasvolsky held at the US National Archives in Washington, DC; the Foreign Relations of the United States (FRUS) series; and the *travaux préparatoires* from the United Nations Conference on International Organization in San Francisco, in addition to the memoirs and diaries of several of the principals in UN negotiations (e.g., Sir Alexander Cadogan of the United Kingdom, Andrei Gromyko of the USSR, and Cordell Hull of the United States).

The initial period of the UN's operation, from 1945 through the early 1960s (Chapter 4) covers two major events in the UN's financial history. To analyze the first, the introduction of voluntary funding rules for technical assistance, I draw on the Yearbook of the United Nations (the UN's official record of meetings), documents from the Dag Hammarskjold Library at the UN in New York, and the Papers of Sir David Owen, held by Columbia University in New York. Owen launched the UN's first technical assistance programs and was a key figure promoting their growth. To cover the second major event, the UN's budget crisis caused by member states' refusal to pay for two peacekeeping missions (the UN Emergency Force and the UN Operation in the Congo), I draw extensively on the Lyndon B. Johnson Presidential Library archives in Austin, Texas, the Papers of Arthur Goldberg in Washington, DC,[109] and the record of the International Court of Justice on the *Certain Expenses* case that evaluated the question of whether member states were obligated to pay for peacekeeping.

The analysis of the introduction of permissive earmark rules at the UN Development Program (Chapter 5) draws on the United Nations Juridical Yearbook, which covers the work and advice of the UN Office of Legal Affairs and a key evaluation from the UN Joint Inspection Unit, in addition to sources already mentioned. Analysis of the late 1970s and 1980s (Chapter 6) draws on the official documents from a number of UN programs, including the Governing Councils of UNDP and UNEP, US Congressional Hearings, and the papers and speeches of Jeane Kirkpatrick, the US Ambassador to the UN during much of the Reagan administration.

These archival sources are complemented where helpful and appropriate by resolutions from the General Assembly and Economic and Social Council, news coverage of the UN, scholarly works from the relevant period, and especially legal analysis on the interpretation of UN rules. Throughout the book, I evaluate

---

[109] Goldberg was US Ambassador to the United Nations during the Article 19 Crisis.

the observable implications below and begin each chapter by describing which implications are relevant to the pages that follow.

Observable Implications from Genuine Uncertainty

At the design stage (T_1), the primary observable implications of the framework flow from genuine uncertainty. When designing rules, negotiators will fail to anticipate major developments or events that in retrospect prove significant to the organization's trajectory. In contrast to a decision-making environment characterized by risk, relevant future states of the world will not be identified, and because they are not identified rules will not be designed for them. From a methodological perspective, conducting such an assessment requires that we "sit with" institutional designers in their historical moment and learn, through the archival record, diaries, and their retrospective analysis, how they expected the future to unfold.[110] If the framework holds purchase, we should observe that while designers undoubtedly identified and were concerned about future developments, some future challenges were effectively invisible. We should be able to identify precisely what they missed.

In the United Nations case, this methodological task is critical to evaluating the framework against alternative explanations that assume and derive expectations based on a world of risk. In a risk world, we would observe that designers *could* foresee the potential problems associated with egalitarian multilateralism produced by the voting and funding rules they designed, but chose those rules anyway for other reasons.

Similar observable implications flow from the framework's uncertainty assumption when incremental change is considered and implemented (i.e., at T_2). Most broadly, the initial act of incremental change—whether it involves the introduction of a layered rule or an act that contributes to reinterpretation—is not understood to implicate and affect fundamental principles or reorganize fundamental relationships within the organization. That is, the incremental act that sets gradual change in motion is not undertaken with an intention to transform the organization. The framework implies that they should be undertaken for alternative reasons (i.e., other than to transform the organization) and these reasons should be empirically identifiable. As in the initial design phase, these observable implications are critical to evaluating the framework against the rationalist alternative in which the evidence suggests that actors are either intending to pursue

---

[110] On the importance of investigating intentions rather than assuming them, see Wendt 2001; Pierson 2004.

transformation or, at the very least, have contemplated that their action may have that effect. As in the initial design phase, the archival record is used to reveal the interests, purpose, and expectations of the actors engaged in incremental change when it first occurs.

Evidence of genuine uncertainty at T_1 and T_2 can also be usefully revealed by identifying when actors make a link and connect the path of gradual change to a potential transformational effect. Although identifying precisely the moment this happens for an actor is challenging, when possible I identify actors who were among the first to suggest that the gradual change trajectory could fundamentally alter the organization as well as the point at which that view becomes widely shared.

Observable Implications from Permissive Rules

Rule permissiveness implies two observable implications. The first is that actors' understanding of what a rule means can change even when the written words of the rule have not. This path of change is obviously distinct from rewriting rules through revision, replacement, or a formal amendment process that is often the focus of IR scholarship. Patterns through which meaning changes can vary. A rule's meaning may begin as settled in the eyes of its designers, become contested over time, and then converge on a new interpretation. Alternatively, some rules are designed to accommodate contested interpretations from the start; these rules begin with unsettled meanings, but over time one interpretation may emerge as dominant and accepted. The empirical record of what individuals believed a rule to mean is of course imperfect. But in many cases, archives and diaries allow us to observe how key negotiators understood the rules they designed. Over time, the record should allow us to trace whether subsequent actors' understandings evolved. Court rulings and opinions also provide useful and explicit evidence of changes in interpretation. In the United Nations context, the advisory opinions of the ICJ offer evidence of whether change occurred in the interpretation of Charter rules, and provide a roadmap for how change in meaning occurred in the eyes of the Court.

Shifts from settled to unsettled meanings or to new settled meanings can also have observable, behavioral effects. Actors generally behave in ways that reflect their understanding of the rule. If meaning changes over time, behavior should reflect that change. For example, if the meaning of Security Council abstentions evolved such that abstentions were no longer regarded as "no" votes, there are clear behavioral implications. Member states would abstain with the expectation that resolutions will nevertheless pass (rather than expect that they are blocking the resolution). Having seen a resolution "pass," abstaining states should not object to the implementation of the resolution.

A second implication of rule permissiveness is that rules can be repurposed, or used for something other than their original, intended purpose, without formal revision. Repurposing does not imply that meaning has changed, only that the actors are applying or employing the rule in a new way. Identifying repurposing empirically first requires an analysis of the rule's initial purpose and the ways in which actors regarded and employed the rule at the start. With this established, instances of rules being used in new ways can be identified and compared against that baseline. The scale of repurposing and the response it receives from other actors is also of interest. Large-scale repurposing occurs when many actors or key actors deploy rules to the new, repurposed end.

Agents

The framework assumes that actors are capable of creativity. Further, it holds that creative acts reinforce the unpredictable nature of institutional development. Scholars of creativity recognize that identifying creativity empirically can be challenging and contested.[111] How do we know creativity when we see it? Psychologists focus on individual level attributes that are understood to be indicators of creative potential. By contrast, and in the vein of scholars of practice theory and of HI scholars studying political entrepreneurship, I focus empirically on creativity as *making*.[112] Combined with the emphasis that most definitions of creativity place on originality or novelty, creativity involves making something novel. Making something novel should not be conflated with requiring novel *component parts*. Often novelty is produced from borrowing that which exists in other contexts and applying it to a new realm, or from recombining existing ideas and institutions in new ways.[113]

Identifying creativity empirically underlines the importance of establishing a baseline for how rules are initially expected to be interpreted and used. Observing creativity goes beyond identifying rule permissiveness in the sense that evidence must demonstrate not only that actors can identify ways in which rules are permissive but that they act upon those possibilities to create something new. By contrast, actors that use or interpret rules in ways that were intended and anticipated by designers are not engaged in creative action. Note that actors who merely violate rules or offer opposition when compliance costs increase or distributional effects are undesirable are not acting creatively. Violation or opposition on its own does

---

[111] See Martin and Wilson 2017 for a review.

[112] This is consistent with the original etymology in which "to create" means to produce or to make, see Götz 1981. Also see Allan and Meckling 2021.

[113] This is consistent with bricolage approaches to institutional design and change, see: Kalyanpur and Newman 2017; Therien and Pouliot 2020.

not create anything new, and violation behavior in response to increased costs is predictable based on rationalist expectations.

The Process

The framework theorizes a process of *gradual* change that can *transform* institutions. Gradual change is defined in contrast to punctuation. In the latter, transformation occurs (and can be observed) in one fell swoop, for example actors alter a rule, which transforms the organization. A gradual change process unfolds and is observed over time. No single change accomplishes transformation, rather a series of smaller incremental actions produce transformation over a long period. If the framework has empirical purchase, we should observe gradual change occurring through uncoordinated, sequential actions. We should observe its subterranean nature: those who act early in the process do not intend to transform the institution, and do not anticipate or intend others to subsequently "pick up the baton" to expand or exploit their incremental change to create transformation.

In addition to the contrast with punctuated change, a process of uncoordinated action over time looks different than a gradual change process in which actors *begin* with transformational goals but are simply limited in what they can achieve. Evaluating this distinction empirically requires careful analysis of actors' goals and intentions during the periods in which they designed rules and worked to implement incremental change.

Throughout the book's chapters, gradual change occurs through layering and conversion processes, which ultimately interact when layered rules are converted to serve new purposes. In some but not all instances, gradual change processes occur via the legal interpretive strategies described above. The task of observation is somewhat easier here, as advisory opinions from the ICJ clearly articulate legal reasoning.

Chapter 3 centers on negotiations over the design of the UN Charter during and following World War II. It provides an account of the core rules in the UN Charter that produce egalitarian multilateralism. I address not merely what the rules say, but also their intended meaning based on the archival record, as well as memoirs and diaries of the principal negotiators. This provides an important basis for evaluating any subsequent reinterpretation in later years. Chapter 3 also provides the first opportunity to evaluate observable implications of the framework regarding the decision-making environment. If designers operate in a world of risk, they can identify potential downstream states of the world that are associated with their rule choices. We see, by contrast, that the future was opaque to UN architects in important ways and they did not foresee a world in which General Assembly control over financial matters would be problematic.

References

Adler-Nissen, Rebecca, and Alena Drieschova. 2019. "Track-Change Diplomacy: Technology, Affordances, and the Practice of International Negotiations." *International Studies Quarterly* 63(3): 531–545.

Allan, Bentley B., and Jonas O. Meckling. 2021. "Creative Learning and Policy Ideas: The Global Rise of Green Growth." *Perspectives on Politics* 1–19. https://doi.org/10.1017/S1537592721000037.

Andonova, Liliana B. 2017. *Governance Entrepreneurs: International Organizations and the Rise of Global Public-Private Partnerships.* Cambridge, UK: Cambridge University Press.

Arato, Julian. 2010. "Subsequent Practice and Evolutive Interpretation: Techniques of Treaty Interpretation Over Time and Their Diverse Consequences." *The Law & Practice of International Courts and Tribunals* 9(3): 443–494.

Baker, Andrew. 2013a. "The Gradual Transformation? The Incremental Dynamics of Macroprudential Regulation." *Regulation and Governance* 7: 417–434.

Baker, Andrew. 2013b. "When New Ideas Meet Existing Institutions: Why Macroprudential Regulatory Change Is a Gradual Process." In *Great Expectations, Slow Transformations: Incremental Change in Post-crisis Regulation.* ECPR—Studies in European Political Science. Edited by Manuela Moschella and Ellen Tsingou. Lanham, MD: Rowman & Littlefield, 35–56.

Barnett, Michael, and Martha Finnemore. 2004. *Rules for the World: International Organizations in Global Politics.* Ithaca, NY: Cornell University Press.

Barton, John H., Judith L. Goldstein, Timothy E. Josling, and Richard H. Steinberg. 2006. *The Evolution of the Trade Regime.* Princeton, NJ: Princeton University Press.

Bernhardt, Rudolph. 1999. "Evolutive Treaty Interpretation, Especially of the European Convention on Human Rights." *German Yearbook of International Law* 42: 11–25.

Bird, Graham, and Dane Rowlands. 2006. "IMF Quotas: Constructing and International Organization Using Inferior Building Blocks." *The Review of International Organizations* 1: 153–171.

Blyth, Mark. 2006. "Great Punctuations: Prediction, Randomness, and the Evolution of Comparative Political Science." *American Political Science Review* 100(4): 493–498.

Buga, Irina. 2018. *Modification of Treaties by Subsequent Practice.* Oxford, UK: Oxford University Press.

Búzás, Zoltán I., and Erin R. Graham. 2020. "Emergent Flexibility in Institutional Development: How International Rules Really Change." *International Studies Quarterly* 64(4): 821–833.

Capoccia, Giovanni. 2016. "Critical Junctures." In *Oxford Handbook of Historical Institutionalism.* Edited by Orfeo Fioretos, Tulia Falleti, and Adam Sheingate. Oxford, UK: Oxford University Press, 95–108.

Chwieroth, Jeffrey. 2014. "Controlling Capital: The International Monetary Fund and Transformative Incremental Change from within International Organizations." *New Political Economy* 19(3): 445–469.

Colgan, Jeffrey, Robert Keohane, and Thijs Van de Graaf. 2012. "Punctuated Equilibrium in the Energy Regime Complex." *Review of International Organizations* 7(2): 117–143.

Das, Kasturi, Harro van Asselt, Susanne Droege, and Michael Mechling. 2019. "Making the International Trade System Work for the Paris Agreement: Assessing the Options. *Environmental Law Reporter* 49: 10553–10580.

De Koker, Cedric. 2015. "Hassan v United Kingdom." *Utrecht Journal of International and European Law* 31(81): 90–96.

Dong, Yan, and John Walley. 2008. "Carbon, Trade Policy, and Carbon Free Trade Areas." National Bureau of Economic Research, Working Paper No. 14431, Cambridge, MA.

Duffield, John. 2003. "The Limits of 'Rational Design.'" *International Organization* 57(2): 411–430.

Farrell, Henry, and Abraham Newman. 2015. "The New Politics of Interdependence: Cross National Layering in Trans-Atlantic Regulatory Disputes." *Comparative Political Studies* 48(4): 497–526.

Fioretos, Orfeo. 2011. "Historical Institutionalism and International Relations." *International Organization* 65(2): 367–399.

Fioretos, Orfeo. 2016. "Retrofitting Financial Globalization: The Politics of Intense Incrementalism after 2008." In *Historical Institutionalism & International Relations*. Edited by Thomas Rixen, Lora Anne Viola, and Michael Zürn. Oxford, UK: Oxford University Press, 68–95.

George, Alexander, and Andrew Bennett. 2004. *Case Studies and Theory Development in the Social Sciences*. Cambridge, MA: MIT Press.

Goldstein, Judith, and Robert Gulotty. 2017. "The Limits of Institutional Reform in the United States and the Global Trade Regime." In *International Politics and Institutions in Time*. Edited by Orfeo Fioretos. Oxford, UK: Oxford University Press, 196–213.

Götz, Ignacio L. 1981. "On Defining Creativity." *The Journal of Aesthetics and Art Criticism* 39(3): 297–301.

Graham, Erin R. 2014. "International Organizations as Collective Agents: Fragmentation and the Limits of Principal Control at the World Health Organization." *European Journal of International Relations* 20(2): 366–390.

Graham, Erin R. 2017. "The Institutional Design of Funding Rules at International Organizations: Explaining the Transformation in Financing the United Nations." *European Journal of International Relations* 23(2): 365–390.

Graham, Erin R. and Alexandria Serdaru. 2020. "Power, Control, and the Logic of Substitution in Institutional Design: The Case of International Climate Finance." *International Organization* 74(4): 671–706.

Gray, Julia. 2018. "Life, Death, or Zombie? The Vitality of International Organizations." *International Studies Quarterly* 62(1): 1–13.

Greenstone, J. David. 1986. "Political Culture and American Political Development: Liberty, Union, and the Liberal Bipolarity." *Studies in American Political Development* 1: 1–49.

Gross, Leo. 1956. "Progress Towards Universality of Membership in the United Nations." *The American Journal of International Law* 50(4): 791–827.

Gruber, Lloyd. 2000. *Ruling the World: Power Politics and the Rise of Supranational Institutions*. Princeton, NJ: Princeton University Press.

Grynaviski, Eric. 2014. *Constructive Illusions: Misperceiving the Origins of International Cooperation*. Ithaca, NY: Cornell University Press.

Hacker, Jacob. 2002. *The Divided Welfare State: The Battle Over Public and Private Social Benefits in the United States*. Cambridge, UK: Cambridge University Press.

Hacker, Jacob. 2004. "Privatizing Risk without Privatizing the Welfare State: The Hidden Politics of Social Policy Retrenchment in the United States." *American Political Science Review* 98(2): 243–260.

Hanrieder, Tine. 2015. *International Organizations in Time: Fragmentation and Reform*. Oxford, UK: Oxford University Press.

Hanrieder, Tine, and Michael Zürn. 2017. "Reactive Sequences in Global Health Governance." In *International Politics and Institutions in Time*. Edited by Orfeo Fioretos. Oxford, UK: Oxford University Press, 93–116.

Hug, Simon and Thomas König. 2007. "Domestic Structures and Constitution-Building in an International Organization: Introduction." *Review of International Organizations* 2(2): 105–113.

Hurd, Ian. 2017. "The Permissive Power of the Ban on War." *European Journal of International Security* 2(1): 1–18.

Ikenberry, G. John. 2017. "The Rise, Character, and Evolution of International Order." In *International Politics and Institutions in Time*. Edited by Orfeo Fioretos. Oxford, UK: Oxford University Press, 59–75.

International Law Commission. 2013. "First Report on Subsequent Agreements and Subsequent Practice in Relation to Treaty Interpretation." UN Doc. A/CN.4/660.

Jabko, Nicolas, and Adam Sheingate. 2018. "Practices of Dynamic Order." *Perspectives on Politics* 16(2): 312–327.

Jupille, Joseph, Walter Mattli, and Duncan Snidal. 2013. *Institutional Choice and Global Commerce*. Cambridge, UK: Cambridge University Press.

Kalyanpur, Nikhil, and Abraham Newman. 2017. "Form over Function in Finance: International Institutional Design by Bricolage." *Review of International Political Economy* 24(3): 363–392.

Katzenstein, Peter J., and Lucia A. Seybert. 2018. "Protean Power and Uncertainty: Exploring the Unexpected in World Politics." International Studies Quarterly 62(1): 80–93.

Kelsen, Hans. 1951. "Recent Trends in the Law of the United Nations." *Social Research* 18(2): 135–151.

Keohane, Robert. 1984. *After Hegemony: Cooperation and Discord in the World Political Economy*. Princeton, NJ: Princeton University Press.

Kertzer, Joshua, and Dustin Tingley. 2018. "Political Psychology in International Relations: Beyond the Paradigms." *Annual Review of Political Science* 21: 319–339.

Koremenos, Barbara. 2005. "Contracting Around International Uncertainty." *American Political Science Review* 99(4): 549–565.

Koremenos, Barbara. 2016. *The Continent of International Law: Explaining Agreement Design*. Cambridge, UK: Cambridge University Press.

Koremenos, Barbara, Charles Lipson, and Duncan Snidal. 2001. "The Rational Design of International Institutions." *International Organization* 55(4): 761–799.

Krasner, Stephen. 1988. "Sovereignty: An Institutional Perspective." *Comparative Political Studies* 21(1): 66–94.

Krasner, Stephen. 1991. "Global Communications and National Power: Life on the Pareto Frontier." *World Politics* 43(3): 336–366.

Liang, Jessica. 2012. "Modifying the UN Charter through Subsequent Practice: Prospects for the Charter's Revitalisation." *Nordic Journal of International Law* 81(1): 1–20.

Lockwood, Erin. 2015. "Predicting the Unpredictable: Value-at-Risk, Performativity, and the Politics of Financial Uncertainty." *Review of International Political Economy* 22(4): 719–756.

Lundgren, Magnus, Theresa Squatrito, and Jonas Tallberg. 2018. "Stability and Change in International Policy-making: A Punctuated Equilibrium Approach." *Review of International Organizations* 13: 547–572.

Mahoney, James. 2000. "Path Dependence in Historical Sociology." *Theory and Society* 29(4): 507–548.

Mahoney, James, and Kathleen Thelen. 2010. *Explaining Institutional Change: Ambiguity, Agency and Power.* Cambridge, UK: Cambridge University Press.

Martin, Lee, and Wilson, Nick. 2017. "Defining Creativity with Discovery." *Creativity Research Journal* 29(4): 417–425.

Milanovic, Marko. 2011. *Extraterritorial Application of Human Rights Treaties: Law, Principles, and Policy.* Oxford: Oxford University Press.

Moschella, Manuela. 2016. "Negotiating Greece: Layering, Insulation, and the Design of Adjustment Programs in the Eurozone." *Review of International Political Economy* 23(5): 799–824.

Moschella, Manuela, and Eleni Tsingou. 2013. *Great Expectations, Slow Transformations.* Colchester: ECPR Press.

Nelson, Stephen, and Peter Katzenstein. 2014. "Uncertainty, Risk, and the Financial Crisis of 2008." *International Organization* 68(2): 361–392.

Nolte, Georg. 2013. *Treaties and Subsequent Practice.* Oxford: Oxford University Press.

North, Douglas. 1990. *Institutions, Institutional Change and Economic Performance.* Cambridge, UK: Cambridge University Press.

Orren, Karen, and Stephen Skowronek. 2004. *The Search for American Political Development.* Cambridge, UK: Cambridge University Press.

Paris, Roland. 2003. "Peacekeeping and the Constraints of Global Culture." *European Journal of International Relations* 9(3): 441–473.

Pelc, Krzysztof. 2011. "How States Ration Flexibility: Tariffs, Remedies, and Exchange Rates as Policy Substitutes." *World Politics* 63(4): 618–646.

Pelc, Krzysztof. 2016. *Making and Bending International Rules: The Design of Exceptions and Escape Clauses in Trade Law.* Cambridge, UK: Cambridge University Press.

Pierson, Paul. 2003. "Big, Slow-Moving, and … Invisible: Macrosocial Processes in the Study of Comparative Politics." In *Comparative Historical Analysis in the Social Sciences.* Edited by James Mahoney and Dietrich Rueschemeyer, Cambridge, UK: Cambridge University Press, 177–207.

Pierson, Paul. 2004. *Politics in Time: History, Institutions, and Social Analysis.* Princeton, NJ: Princeton University Press.

Posner, Elliot. 2009. *The Origins of Europe's New Stock Markets.* Cambridge, MA: Harvard University Press.

Pouliot, Vincent. 2020. "Practice Theory Meets Historical Institutionalism." *International Organization* 74(4): 742–772.

Putnam, Tonya. 2020. "Mingling and Strategic Augmentation of International Legal Obligations." *International Organization* 74(1): 31–64.

Rixen, Thomas. 2013. "Offshore Financial Centres, Shadow Banking and Jurisdictional Competition: Incrementalism and Feeble Re-regulation," In *Great Expectations, Slow Transformations: Incremental Change in post-Crisis Regulation.* Edited by Manuela Moschella and Eleni Tsingou. Colchester, UK; ECPR Press, 95–124.

Schickler, Eric. 2001. *Disjointed Pluralism: Institutional Innovation and the Development of the U.S. Congress.* Princeton, NJ: Princeton University Press.

Schmidt, Vivien. 2016. "Reinterpreting the Rules 'by Stealth' in Times of Crisis." *West European Politics* 39(5):1032–1052.

Seawright, Jason, and David Collier. 2004. "Glossary." In *Rethinking Social Inquiry: Diverse Tools, Shared Standards*. Edited by Henry E. Brady and D. Collier. Plymouth: Rowman and Littlefield, 273–313.

Sheingate, Adam. 2010. "Rethinking Rules: Creativity and Constraint in the U.S. House of Representatives." In *Explaining Institutional Change: Ambiguity, Agency, and Power*. Edited by James Mahoney and Kathleen Thelen. Cambridge, UK: Cambridge University Press, 168–203.

Solingen, Etel, and Wilfred Wan. 2017. "International Security: Critical Junctures, Developmental Pathways, and Institutional Change." In *International Politics and Institutions in Time*. Edited by Orfeo Fioretos. Oxford, UK: Oxford University Press, 167–195.

St. John, Taylor. 2018. *The Rise of Investor-State Arbitration: Politics, Law, and Unintended Consequences*. Oxford, UK: Oxford University Press.

Stavropoulos, Constantin. 1967. "The Practice of Voluntary Abstentions by Permanent Members of the Security Council Under Article 27, Paragraph 3, of the Charter of the United Nations." *American Journal of International Law* 61(3): 737–752.

Streek, Wolfgang, and Kathleen Thelen. 2005. *Beyond Continuity: Institutional Change in Advanced Political Economies*. Oxford, UK: Oxford University Press.

Thelen, Kathleen. 2004. *How Institutions Evolve: The Political Economy of Skills in Germany, Britain, the United States, and Japan*. Cambridge, UK: Cambridge University Press.

Therien, Jean-Philippe, and Vincent Pouliot. 2020. "Global Governance as Patchwork: The Making of Sustainable Development Goals." *Review of International Political Economy* 27(3): 612–636.

Thompson, Alexander. 2010. "Rational Design in Motion: Uncertainty and Flexibility in the Global Climate Regime." *European Journal of International Relations* 16(2): 269–296.

Tulis, Jeffrey. 1987. *The Rhetorical Presidency*. Princeton, NJ: Princeton University Press.

Van Damme, Isabelle. 2009. *Treaty Interpretation by the WTO Appellate Body*. Oxford: Oxford University Press.

Waibel, Michael. 2011. "Demystifying the Art of Interpretation." *European Journal of International Law* 22(2): 571–588.

Weaver, Catherine, and Manuela Moschella. 2017. "Bounded Reform in Global Economic Governance at the IMF and the World Bank." In *International Politics and Institutions in Time*. Edited by Orfeo Fioretos. Oxford, UK: Oxford University Press, 274–292.

Wendt, Alexander. 2001. "Driving With the Rearview Mirror: On the Rational Science of Institutional Design." *International Organization* 55(4): 1019–1049.

Young, Oran. 2010. *Institutional Dynamics: Emergent Patterns in International Environmental Governance*. Cambridge, MA: MIT Press.

Zangl, Bernhard, Frederick Hueßner, Andreas Kruck, and Xenia Lazendörfer. 2016. "Imperfect Adaptation: How the WTO and the IMF Adjust Shifting Power Distributions among Their Members." *Review of International Organizations* 11: 171–196.

3

Vision over Visibility

Designing the United Nations Charter

The basic contours of the United Nations design were settled before states arrived in San Francisco for the United Nations Conference on International Organization in April of 1945. The nature of the Security Council and General Assembly were discussed by the Allied powers in Tehran in 1943. By the end of the Dumbarton Oaks Conference in October of 1944, the United States, the Soviet Union, the United Kingdom, and China agreed that the Assembly would employ egalitarian voting rules; each state would have a single vote. The Allied powers had further agreed to make funding mandatory for all member states, to grant the General Assembly the authority to determine how much each state would pay, as well as control over all budgetary matters. At San Francisco, the Charter came to specify that member states would share "collective financial responsibility" for the "expenses of the Organization." The language of "capacity to pay," was proposed by the UK and added to the Charter to guide the Assembly in the task of allocating dues across member states. Taken together, these rules instantiated multilateral governance at the UN in 1945 and provide the foundation on which subsequent change occurs.

This chapter serves two purposes. The first is to account for the core rules that provide the foundation for the study. This involves knowing what the rules say but also what they meant and how they were intended to work by those who drafted them. For example, knowing the extent to which member states understood "the expenses of the Organization" in Article 17 of the Charter to have a clear and settled meaning is crucial to evaluating later disputes over mandatory funding and to identifying attempts at rule conversion. The second purpose is to begin to assess the book's theoretical framework, which includes expectations about design that are distinct from rationalist accounts. The most important implications for this chapter stem from the assumption of genuine uncertainty. The framework expects egalitarian multilateralism to be codified in UN rules *because powerful states did not anticipate a future state of the world in which GA control of financing would be problematic.* By contrast, in a decision-making environment characterized by risk, the expectation is that powerful states would foresee such a possibility and design rules to protect themselves against its costs. Possibilities that would have accomplished that goal include weighted rather than egalitarian voting rules, voluntary rather than mandatory funding rules, or an escape clause to opt out of mandatory

Transforming International Institutions. Erin R. Graham, Oxford University Press. © Erin R. Graham (2023).
DOI: 10.1093/oso/9780198877936.003.0003

obligations under certain conditions. Each of these design features was in use at other international organizations by 1945. Yet not only were none incorporated in the Dumbarton Oaks draft agreed upon by the Allied powers or considered at San Francisco, these possibilities were not discussed at length or in great detail by the powerful states involved.

The archival record, memoirs, and diaries of the participants reveal a design process that—in retrospect—looks remarkable for what is absent. First, the core rules that affect funding—egalitarian voting, General Assembly control of the budget, and mandatory assessments based on capacity to pay—received only limited attention from the major powers. The great powers did not anticipate that Assembly control of the budget would prove problematic down the road. Given its emergence as an area of growing concern by the mid-1950s, the failure to anticipate the issue is striking. Second, these core rules were not the result of concessions to smaller states, but rather were the product of "Big Three" negotiations that occurred before smaller powers became involved in the process. After Dumbarton Oaks and prior to San Francisco, when drafts circulated among the broader group of potential UN members, a few smaller countries raised questions about the scope of members' financial obligations. The major powers in general, and the US in particular, gave answers that affirmed their obligations and indicated these were not areas of great concern. The third remarkable feature of the design process is the outcome of egalitarian, multilateral governance. That a two-thirds vote of the world's countries—large and small, powerful and weak—governs the allocation of assessments to the United Nations and determines the content and size of its budget is no small thing. Stoessinger nicely captures its importance: For the members to "accept the principle that a state can be legally bound to pay an authoritatively determined assessment in support of a given United Nations program is to restrict the right to use the financial weapon as an instrument of control."[1]

How did this surprising outcome come to pass? I argue that genuine uncertainty prevented powerful states from understanding why this "restriction" would become problematic for them at the UN in the future. A careful review of the archival record and publications during that period allows us to identify how policymakers' expectations about future developments were off the mark in critical ways. Assumptions they held about the future led them to believe egalitarian multilateralism in financial matters would be unproblematic, and a number of these expectations turned out to be wrong.

In the course of the chapter, I consider two alternative explanations. The first possibility is that rules instantiating egalitarian multilateralism at the UN were selected due to a poor decision-making process. In the overwhelming context of World War II, perhaps design choices were made in haste, prompting mistakes that could have been avoided had a careful and thorough process been undertaken. The

---

[1] Stoessinger 1964, 27.

archival record allows us to reject this alternative rather quickly. The negotiation and design process detailed below took place over several years, involved heads of state, high-level diplomats, outside experts, legislators, and was subject to public debate. Big and small issues were debated in excruciating detail—just not those related to funding, which was a blind spot.

The second alternative is more consistent with traditional rational design accounts and stems from a decision-making environment characterized by risk. It is difficult to imagine the United States, the Soviet Union, or France agreeing to mandatory funding rules with General Assembly control over budgeting had 1960 been visible to them in 1945. Nevertheless, if risk rather than uncertainty characterized the decision-making environment, we should see, at the very least, that the adoption of core rules that produced egalitarian multilateralism was controversial, and subject to considerable debate. In fact, we see very little evidence to support the argument that powerful states foresaw potential problems with these rules and chose them reluctantly for other reasons.

In evaluating competing explanations for the design of UN Charter rules, I uncover the working assumptions held by UN negotiators in 1945 about how the world would move forward in the years ahead and how the United Nations would develop. The archival record reveals the potential problems that were on the forefront of negotiators' minds—and there were many—but it also reveals what they were not worried about. With the benefit of hindsight, one can evaluate what was "missing" from negotiators' vision of the future. I complement primary source material from multiple archives, and the diaries of the principal actors, with scholarly literature from the early postwar period in international law and international relations. At the time, there was considerable overlap between the individuals who were involved in the UN's design and those publishing in scholarly journals. Their accounts often reflect upon whether and how the trajectory of the UN's development and international events matched or departed from the expectations of UN drafters, thereby providing critical insight into the role played by uncertainty in 1945.

In what follows, I first summarize the timeline and process that led to the UN's establishment. I then present archival evidence to demonstrate who pursued which rules, whether there was any controversy or debate surrounding the wisdom of these decisions, and whether any alternative rules were considered. In particular, I demonstrate that while decision makers were forward-looking, indeed intently so, they did not anticipate that egalitarian multilateralism regarding financing would be problematic. The third section uncovers how decision makers' assumptions in 1945 were wrong in two important respects. First, they misjudged decolonization in various ways. They failed to anticipate how quickly new states would gain independence, they failed to anticipate how many new states decolonization would produce, and they could not conceive of the possibility that many new small states would be members of the United Nations. Even if they had, which they did not, they failed to appreciate that the preferences these new states would pursue within the UN would be at odds with their own. Second, and related, in 1945 the great powers did not anticipate the potential for UN costs to rise significantly because they did not anticipate that the Organization would have a substantial operational arm. They did not foresee that the UN would evolve to see peacekeeping and economic and social development programs as central to the work of the Organization. In a counterfactual world where the US, the Soviet Union, and the UK anticipated these developments, it is very likely that UN rules would be different.

Timeline and Process

Planning for a postwar world organization began as World War II raged. In the US State Department, the work started in earnest a year before the attack on Pearl Harbor. On November 22, 1940, Leo Pasvolsky, an official at State who played a prominent role in postwar planning and would later lead the US delegation in negotiations at San Francisco, proposed that a "Division of Special Research" be established to analyze and appraise both war and postwar problems.[2] With the war upending much that had been taken for granted in international life, participants in the process were aware of the ground shifting under their feet. Harley Notter,[3] a State Department official who participated in postwar planning from its inception through the UN's establishment, and who wrote the "definitive treatment"[4] on the subject, wrote of the time:

> In the political field, basic uncertainties rendered it more difficult to determine the problems that might, or were even likely to, confront the nation at the end of war. The future circumstances to be dealt with were subject to possibly radical change, since many of the attributes of international life, and even its basic character, were no longer firmly fixed. It had become necessary to think in terms of questions concerning the conditions or arrangements that would exist, or could or should be brought into existence at the end of the war: What kind of nations? What kind of international relations? What kind of transitional arrangements? What kind of permanent arrangements?[5]

Pasvolsky and others at State sought to cope with these uncertainties by organizing teams to engage in in-depth research and careful analysis of potential outcomes

---

[2] Notter 1975, 41.

[3] Notter was a Stanford-trained historian who taught at Stanford and Smith College before joining the State Department in 1937.

[4] Congressional Information Service, 1987. Post World War II Policy Planning. State Department Records of Harley A. Notter, 1939–1945, viii.

[5] Notter 1975, 55.

and policy options. It would be difficult to find a process more in accord with rationalist accounts of how decision-making should work than those described in State Department records. Officers in the political section at State "undertook to formulate an inclusive program of studies in light of alternatives with respect to possible future conditions and resulting problems and of such official expressions of policies as had already been enunciated."[6] Emphasis was placed on the importance of avoiding hasty decisions and evaluating all possible options. The attitude "insistently maintained by the Secretary of State, was that the use of precious time to mature views and plans outweighed the value of the rapid reaching of decisions, which might involve fatal gambles."[7]

In selecting the postwar planning staff, effort was made to incorporate individuals from different areas of government, from the academy, and from others with specialized expertise. They sought "to obtain a balance of experience and maturity in persons of sufficiently youthful age to make possible a fresh but well-grounded approach to problems (...)."[8] When the Subcommittee on International Organization was established in July of 1942, its initial task was to survey and learn from the past experiences of other international organizations, with an emphasis on the League of Nations. This included "an appraisal, article by article, of the Covenant of the League of Nations in terms of its strength or weakness in international action."[9]

The United States was hardly alone in its engagement with postwar questions in 1941. Indeed, by the fall of that year the US received queries from the United Kingdom and Australia about postwar reconstruction plans as well as the design of an international juridical organization.[10]

The respective domestic plans for a postwar world organization moved to the interstate negotiation phase beginning in August of 1943 with Anglo-American talks in Quebec.[11] In this phase, each state's designs for a future world organization became subject to scrutiny from one another. In October, the foreign ministers of the Soviet Union, the United Kingdom, and the United States met in Moscow to prepare the groundwork for a meeting between the heads of state. Roosevelt, Churchill, and Stalin met in Tehran from November 28 to December 1, 1943. Here, the Big Three discussed plans for a general international organization in broad terms, including issues related to universal participation and trusteeship. With a commitment to work together to design a world organization now certain, the period between December of 1943 and the start of the Dumbarton Oaks Conference in August of 1944 was characterized by intense and detailed planning. In the

---

[6] Notter, 1975, 55.
[7] Notter, 1975, 93.
[8] Notter, 1975, 153.
[9] Notter 1975, 109.
[10] Notter 1975, 57.
[11] Notter 1975, 186. Stalin was invited but was unable to attend.

US, the team worked almost entirely through drafts and revisions. Keen to avoid the League's fate in the Senate, Members of Congress were regularly and thoroughly consulted about US drafts, including prominent Republicans. Governor Dewey, the presumptive Republican nominee for President, was also included.

The Dumbarton Oaks conference itself involved nearly three months of intense negotiations and two sets of talks. The first occurred between the Soviet Union, US and UK, and the latter between the US, UK, and China. The sequential nature of the talks meant that the proposals negotiated among the Big Three were immediately subject to another round of close scrutiny. Once agreed to, the Dumbarton Oaks proposals were widely circulated and subject to public debate. Ample opportunity was provided to voice concerns or take issue with aspects of the draft. As Clyde Eagleton, a member of the US Delegation at the United Nations Conference for International Organization explains, the Dumbarton Oaks proposals "were at once published for study and criticism of the world. Thousands of letters poured into the Department of State (...) Scholars and organizations sent in or published detailed criticisms and suggestions, all of which received careful study."[12] Indeed, each of the major powers made changes to the Dumbarton Oaks proposals after the Conference. After an Inter-American Conference held in Mexico City with the US and Latin American states, the amended Dumbarton Oaks draft was again subject to intense negotiation, revision, and further specification during the San Francisco Conference, held from April 25 to June 26, 1945, which included the initial fifty-one member states. Only after four years of planning, input from hundreds of carefully selected individuals, and scrutiny from Congress and the public, did the US Senate ratify the United Nations Charter on July 28, 1945.

In what follows, I detail why and how, despite this exemplary process, the Allied powers failed to anticipate that core rules would be problematic to them down the road. To begin, I examine when and how the Big Three designed the rules regarding the General Assembly and its control of funding.

The Design of Egalitarian Multilateralism in 1945

It is difficult to overstate the openness with which the US Department of State began its planning for a postwar international organization. At the outset, two alternative models were briefly on the table: a cooperative organization (as the UN would become) and a federal organization that would put in place world government. Despite advocacy from a number of prominent individuals, the latter option was set aside due to concerns that the peoples and nations of the world were not yet ready for such a thing. Consistent with the open nature of the research and planning process, provisions changed quickly as early drafts were revised multiple

---

[12] Eagleton 1945, 935.

Table 3.1 Egalitarian Multilateralism in the UN Charter

Article 9.1	*The General Assembly shall consist of all Members of the United Nations*
Article 17.1	*The General Assembly shall consider and approve the budget of the Organization*
Article 17.2	*The expenses of the Organization shall be borne by the Members as apportioned by the General Assembly*
Article 18.1	*Each member of the General Assembly shall have one vote*
Article 18.2	*Decisions of the General Assembly on important questions shall be made by a two-thirds majority of the members present and voting. These questions shall include: (...) budgetary questions.*

times. However, through the entirety of the process, several core elements that would produce egalitarian multilateralism were unchanged. All drafts included mandatory funding for the Organization. Indeed, there is no mention of voluntary funding in either negotiated or US drafts. No draft excluded the General Assembly from a role in apportioning mandatory dues or controlling the budget. And in all but a single US draft in July of 1944, just before the Dumbarton Oaks Conference, the General Assembly was always to employ a one country, one vote rule to make decisions on *all* questions.

The core rules in the UN Charter are listed in Table 3.1. The first, Article 9.1 ensures that the General Assembly will include all UN Member States. The drafting of Article 9.1 was uncontroversial. From the earliest phases, the Big Three envisioned the Organization to include an Assembly where all member states were represented (often referred to as the General Conference in the early stages of negotiations) and a smaller executive (Security) Council. The issues left for debate were not whether all member states would sit in the Assembly, but rather about what authority it would exercise. The Soviet Union pressed for tight limits, with all important powers vested in the Council. The US and UK held somewhat more moderate views, envisioning the Assembly as a forum for discussion and recommendations to facilitate coordination on economic and social issues.[13] In addition, some in the American group saw a potential role for the Assembly in security affairs. Attempting to break a logjam in negotiations with the USSR over whether permanent members could use the veto to block Council action when they were party to the dispute in question, one of the American negotiators, Breckinridge Long, proposed that in such instances "the Council shall refer the entire matter to the General Assembly which shall reach decision by a three-quarters vote of all members (including all parties to the dispute) which decision shall be final."[14]

---

[13] E.g., Hull 1948, 1635, 1677; Israel 1966, 370–371; Pasvolsky Papers, Washington Conversations on International Organization. Informal Record of The First Plenary Session. Assembly Hall, Dumbarton Oaks. 10:30 a.m.–11:40 a.m. Conv. A. Plenary Record 1, August 22, 1944.

[14] Israel 1966, 380. Long's proposal was not adopted.

Smaller powers sought to expand the purview of the Assembly to a greater extent. Responding to the Dumbarton Oaks draft, Australia's H.V. Evatt noted that the role of the General Assembly and Economic and Social Council required more thoughtfulness, and argued that "more attention should be given by the world organization to social, economic and humanitarian problems."[15] Among the ambitious amendments Australia proposed at San Francisco, was one that sought to "give the General Assembly a wider jurisdiction over, and a fuller share in, the general work of the Organization and in disputes from becoming frozen in the Security Council (...)."[16] Many Latin American states responded similarly. At the Inter-American Conference on Problems of War and Peace in February of 1945, the US formally shared the Dumbarton Oaks proposals with Latin American States. The delegation of Mexico proposed that the Assembly should have a larger role in Security affairs, and specifically suggested that three-fourths of the General Assembly should be required to give binding force to some decisions of the Security Council.[17]

Although the Big Four (i.e., China, UK, USSR, US,)[18] resisted proposals to empower the Assembly in security affairs, they saw no problem in empowering the Assembly on budgetary issues. Articles 17(1) and 17(2), which grant the Assembly the power to approve the budget and obligate member states to bear the "expenses of the Organization," were drafted by the Big Four and were not concessions to smaller powers at San Francisco. Early in the postwar planning process in 1943, a US draft had granted the General Conference (later Assembly) the authority to apportion the expenses of the United Nations among the Members but required the (Security) Council to approve the apportionment.[19] But this provision was revised by December 1943 when the role of the Security Council in budgetary matters was eliminated, never to return. A US draft dated December 29, 1943 stated, "all administrative and budgetary arrangements should require approval of the General Assembly" with no mention of the Council.[20] This change reflected the desire to avoid a flaw in the initial design of the League of Nations, which had briefly divided budgetary authority between the Assembly and the Council,[21] before the Assembly asserted its exclusive control early on.[22]

---

[15] Hasluck 1980, 145, 155–156.
[16] Hasluck 1980, 208.
[17] Pasvolsky Papers. Inter-American Conference On Problems Of War And Peace. Report of The Spokesman of Committee II, Doctor C. Parra-Perez, Minister Of Foreign Relations of Venezuela, Concerning The World Organization For The Maintenance Of International Peace And Security. NO. 292, C2-V-19. FEB–MARCH, 1945. P. 8.
[18] The Big Four also consulted with France on matters related to the Security Council.
[19] Notter 1975, appendix 23. "The Charter of the United Nations" (Draft). August 14, 1943. See also, Singer 1961, 2.
[20] Notter 1975, 580, appendix 33. "Plan for the Establishment of an International Organization for the Maintenance of International Peace and Security." December 29, 1943.
[21] Singer 1961, 2.
[22] Goodrich et al. 1969, 149.

Granting the General Assembly legal authority over UN financing would not be so puzzling if not for the egalitarian voting rules that accompany it. The Big Four anticipated they would pay a disproportionate share of the UN's expenses, yet the Dumbarton Oaks proposal specified not only that the General Assembly would control the budget, but that each state would have a single vote. Alternatives were considered only fleetingly. A US draft on July 18, 1944, just before the Dumbarton Oaks Conference, included language that specifies weighted voting. Section C of the draft, which governs representation and voting in the Assembly, specifies that, "with respect to the budget of the organs and agencies of the Organization (...) each member state should have voting power in proportion to its contribution to the expenses of the organization."[23] Weighted voting rules had not been included in any prior American drafts and the provision applying weighted rules to budgetary questions disappeared "just as quickly as it had arisen."[24] A subsequent mention of weighted voting comes as the US delegation is preparing for the San Francisco Conference, when the State Department Representative explains, almost in passing, that weighted voting was not an option.

The sudden emergence of weighted rules, followed by a quick and somewhat unceremonious exit, requires investigation, yet the archival record leaves one wanting. The detailed record of Harley Notter, the Pasvolsky Papers, and the Foreign Relations of the US Series are silent on the issue, save for mentioning that weighted rules appeared in a single draft. The memoirs and diaries of the American, British, and Soviet principals are similarly silent. It is clear that weighted rules did not receive sustained advocacy from any state, and that egalitarian rules were adopted without substantial discussion of the issue. On its face, the absence of debate is surprising. By 1944, weighted voting arrangements of various kinds had been used in a number of international organizations.[25] In 1878, the Universal Postal Union assigned certain states extra votes through their colonies, including the Netherlands, Spain, Portugal, Denmark, and France.[26] More similar to weighted voting formulas used today, the International Institute of Agriculture (1905) and the International Office of Public Health (1907) "divided states into classes according to the amount of their financial contribution with corresponding differences in voting strength."[27] The United States had recent experience negotiating a weighted voting system as part of the Inter-American Coffee Agreement (1940), which distributed more votes to larger exporters than to smaller ones.[28]

---

[23] Notter 1975, 598. [United States] Tentative Proposals for a General International Organization. July 18, 1944.

[24] Singer 1961, 3.

[25] Weighted rules were also discussed in scholarly literature, e.g., Sohn 1944.

[26] The UPU was organized as the General Postal Union in 1878. McIntyre 1954, 486.

[27] McIntyre 1954, 486.

[28] McIntyre 1954, 487.

In light of these examples, it makes sense that the great powers would have considered weighted rules and also that they would have a sense of their usefulness. Indeed, the sudden emergence of weighted voting in the American draft of July 1944 occurred during the Bretton Woods negotiations where the US proposed a similar formula to apportion votes at the International Bank for Reconstruction and Development (IBRD) and the International Monetary Fund (IMF).[29] While the formula was adopted at those institutions, it was quickly removed at Dumbarton Oaks.[30]

The archival record demonstrates that the debates that did occur on voting rules at the Assembly took egalitarian voting for granted and centered on the smaller issue of whether to employ simple or super-majority thresholds to pass resolutions. It was settled that a simple majority be used except for special questions, including "budgetary questions," which would require a two-thirds threshold.[31] At San Francisco, the only substantive modification on budgetary issues came when several delegations, including Australia, India, the Netherlands, and Norway, made proposals that states failing to pay dues would face penalty.[32] After consultation, the Big Four supported a proposal that became Article 19 of the Charter, which states: "A Member of the United Nations which is in arrears in the payment of its financial contributions to the Organization shall have no vote in the General Assembly if the amount of its arrears equals or exceeds the amount of the contributions due from it for the preceding two full years."

That the great powers did not take issue with General Assembly authority over financing is all the more surprising given they clearly understood and anticipated that they would pay a disproportionate share of UN expenses. The details were left out of the Dumbarton Oaks proposals, but at San Francisco, negotiators granted the Assembly authority to allocate assessments across member states. Interim arrangements reflected the British proposal to rely on the scale of assessments from the Food and Agriculture Organization, in which wealthy states paid more than poorer ones.[33] Moving forward, the British proposed that the *capacity to pay* principle should guide the Assembly's allocation of assessments across member states.[34] The principle was later adopted by the Assembly and remains the

---

[29] The Bretton Woods Conference took place in New Hampshire, July 1–22, 1944.

[30] Few texts take note of the brief appearance of weighted voting rules in US postwar plans for the General Assembly. Those that do (i.e., Singer 1961, 2 and Hilderbrand 1990, 110), do not provide evidence for the origins of the provision or explain why it was removed so quickly.

[31] Pasvolsky Papers. Washington Conversations on International Organization. Informal Record of The Second Meeting of The General Organization Subcommittee, Assembly Hall, Dumbarton Oaks, 10:50 a.m.–12:10 p.m. Conv. A. General Organization Record 2, August 24, 1944; Pasvolsky Papers. Office Memorandum United States Government. Memorandum to Pasvolsky from Gerig. Subject: Draft Charter. April 5, 1945; Cadogan 1972, 8.

[32] Pasvolsky Papers. National Archives. Washington, DC. The United Nations Conference on International Organization. U.S. Delegation. Restricted. US GEN 86 (V-B-5). May 11, 1945.

[33] Singer 1961, 10–11, 18–19.

[34] Singer 1961, 14.

underlying principle for allocating assessments.[35] The UK proposals received no opposition from their fellow great powers at San Francisco.

Summary of Design

With egalitarian voting, Assembly control of the budget, and a capacity to pay principle to distribute assessments, the great powers created a system in which they would be obligated to provide the bulk of UN financial support even if they voted against the budget. Indeed, exactly this state of the world emerged within fifteen years. The following section seeks to explain why and how wealthy states in general, and the United States, the Soviet Union, and the United Kingdom in particular, failed to anticipate this possibility. In particular, I demonstrate that in 1944–45, the Big Three did not fathom the political realities they would face in 1960. With regard to the pace and consequences of decolonization and the substantive nature of UN operations, the UN's architects operated in a world of uncertainty rather than simply one of risk, which affected their design choices.

Explaining Egalitarian Multilateralism

The outcome of egalitarian multilateralism in the UN design appears puzzling in retrospect. The Soviet Union regretted UN financing rules quickly, complaining about rising costs by 1948. Within a decade's time, the United States also expressed misgivings before publicly stating its displeasure with the design in the 1960s. Further, with the benefit of hindsight, key dynamics that altered the effects of egalitarian multilateralism come to appear as natural, if not inevitable developments. For example, the Big Three knew that UN membership would grow. The trusteeship system itself was intended to facilitate the independence of many colonial territories, suggesting that a growing membership would include those that would gain their independence in the coming decades. The seeds for the UN's involvement in economic and social development—a primary source of budget growth in the twentieth century—appear clearly planted in the Charter. Its preamble states that the UN system would "employ international machinery for the promotion of economic and social advancement of all peoples."

A rationalist perspective, which assumes forward-looking designers operating in a world of risk, would expect negotiators to design rules to protect against future states of the world less favorable to their interests. In this case, a significantly expanded membership with preferences distinct from the UN's primary

---

[35] See Rule 160 of the Rules of Procedure of the General Assembly. https://www.un.org/en/ga/contributions/reference.shtml.

architects, which translated into a willingness to increase budgets and expand economic and social development work, would clearly merit different rules. Why did the Big Three fail to design for this state of the world?

The answer becomes clear only through the process of uncovering the working assumptions that negotiators held in 1945 about how the UN and the world would develop in future decades. The research reveals that the UN's architects simply could not *see* the 1960s from 1945. A number of prominent scholars and commentators noted as much during that latter turbulent decade. Lawrence Finkelstein observed, "... the United Nations today would be hardly recognizable to those (...) who played significant roles in the Conference but who did not survive to watch the Organization mature. Those leading figures who are still with us (...) must be surprised when they view it today against their images of what they thought they were creating in 1945."[36] Writing his opinion on the *Certain Expenses* decision at the International Court of Justice in 1962, Judge Spender assessed the UN's architects in much the same way: "The wisest among them could never have anticipated the tremendous changes which politically, militarily, and otherwise have occurred in the comparatively few years which have elapsed since 1945."[37]

How did the vision for the future held by UN architects differ from the future that actually unfolded? Two elements are key. First, they did not anticipate an operational role for the UN in economic and social development *or* security affairs. In both areas, they imagined a coordinating role for the UN rather than an operational one. States would carry out any action, whether required by a Security Council resolution, or encouraged by the General Assembly or Economic and Social Council. In the major powers' imagination, the costs of operational activities would be incurred by the states undertaking the action or determined by ad hoc arrangement if needed. Related, the UN's architects did not foresee peacekeeping, a term and activity that did not exist in 1945. This vision of a limited operational role had an important consequence: it produced few concerns about the potential for rising costs. As Thomas Schelling explained about the UN's combination of egalitarian voting and funding rules in 1955: "One can afford to be fair, moral, and logical about a tax system when the total tax is not going to be large; as a matter of fact, the immediately foreseeable United Nations budget was small enough to cause some countries to seek larger shares for added prestige."[38]

The second area in which the UN architects' vision of the future went astray is even more central to the UN's development. Of course, the Big Three were aware that anticolonial sentiment had grown in recent decades, and, to varying degrees, they were sometimes supportive of policies to move colonial territories toward self-government. However, they underestimated the *pace of decolonization*, and

---

[36] Finkelstein 1965, 369.
[37] Separate opinion of Judge Sir Percy Spender, *Certain Expenses Advisory Opinion.* July 20, 1962.
[38] Schelling 1955, 5.

the number of new states it would produce that would become UN members, along with *the extent to which those states would hold a distinct vision of the UN as a proponent for economic development* and a voice for their concerns. The fact that the US, and UK simply did not anticipate that there would be so many independent states, and that those states would join the United Nations, meant that they did not foresee a time when their majority status in the General Assembly would be threatened. Since a 120-state United Nations was beyond their imagination, they did not anticipate that such a membership might use the mandatory funding system, which they had designed, to promote and expand operational activities for economic and social development against their wishes.

Envisioning a Limited Operational Role in Economic and Social Development

With regard to economic and social development, the UN's primary architects shared a modest vision for the Organization. From the start, the Soviet Union held the position that the UN should be a security organization and that its mandate should be interpreted strictly.[39] The view stemmed in part from a complaint that the League of Nations had focused too much on peripheral matters rather than those central to maintaining the peace. The US and UK were more sanguine about the inclusion of language highlighting economic and social development as aspirational concerns.[40] Yet it is equally clear that the US saw a promotional, coordinating role for the UN rather than an operational one. Early in the postwar planning process, at the Hot Springs Conference, the Big Three had settled on the idea that the "Organization would not take action but rather that the nations would take the action" with regard to economic and social development.[41] This view is consistently reflected in discussions on economic and social development by the US delegation leading up to the San Francisco conference. When Senator Arthur Vandenberg, always wary of international overreach, noted that he saw an important distinction between "what are international and what are domestic matters," on economic and social development, the State Department (Mr. Taft) emphasized in response, "that the Organization would merely promote the adoption of measures by the nations and that *it would not of course undertake to do the job*

[39] Foreign Relations of The United States, Diplomatic Papers 1944, General, Volume I. Lot 60–D 224, Box 56: D.O./Conv.A/JSC Mins. 1–12 *Informal Minutes of Meeting No. 5 of the Joint Steering Committee Held at 11 a.m., August 25, at Dumbarton Oaks*, Washington, August 25, 1944, 11 a.m. See also: Hull 1948, 1677; Israel 1966, 370.
[40] Hull, 1948, 1677; Israel 1966, 370–371.
[41] Foreign Relations of The United States, DP 1945, General: The United Nations Volume 1. RSC Lot 60–D 224, Box 96: U.S. Cr. Min. 12 "Minutes of the Twelfth Meeting of the United States Delegation," Held at Washington, Wednesday, April 18, 1945, 9:10 a.m. Washington, April 18, 1945, 9:10 a.m.

itself."[42] This vision is further reflected in proposed language by the US delegation to "encourage separate and cooperative action" among member states in the field of economic and social development, clarifying that the states rather than the UN would undertake activity to spur development.[43] Finkelstein summarizes the Big Three's thinking as follows:

> the Great Powers were by and large fairly conservative about the role the Orga-nization might have with respect to economic and social matters (...) These considerations, coupled with memories of what a fractious Senate had done in 1919–1920, led the U.S. to resist any notions (...) that the Organization should have powers going beyond the hortatory. It was with some satisfaction that the chairman of the United States delegation was able to report to the President that "the Economic and Social Council was not to have any coercive powers ... Its tools and procedures are those of study, discussion, report, and recommenda-tion." *There was no hint* that the new economic and social machinery would have any operating responsibilities.[44]

The common wisdom that the UN's economic and social development activi-ties would not be costly extended to the US Senate. During Hearings on the UN Charter in the summer of 1945, Secretary of State Stettinius and Leo Pasvolsky both testified with lengthy statements that included reference to the Economic and Social Council and the powers of the General Assembly to "initiate stud-ies and make recommendations" across a range of areas, including "promoting cooperation in the economic, social, cultural, educational and health fields."[45] Senators did not raise questions or concerns about costs generally or about obli-gations under Article 17 specifically. That this apparent lack of concern extended to Senators with a history of concern for the US incurring too many obligations abroad is notable. For instance, the US worked with other countries during the war to establish the UN Relief and Rehabilitation Administration (UNRRA). About their proposal for UNRRA, former Secretary of State Dean Acheson wrote, they "expected about as much comment [from Congress] as a Red Cross drive evokes, and could not have been more wrong."[46] Led by Senator Vandenberg, resistance

---

[42] Foreign Relations of the United States: Diplomatic Papers, 1945, General. The United Nations. Volume 1 RSC Lot 60-D 224, Box 96: U.S. Cr. Min. 8 "Minutes of the Eighth Meeting of the United States Delegation," held at Washington, Wednesday, April 11, 1945, 11 a.m. Washington. Emphasis added.

[43] Foreign Relations of The United States, DP 1945, General: The United Nations Volume 1. RSC Lot 60–D 224, Box 96: U.S. Cr. Min. 12 "Minutes of the Twelfth Meeting of the United States Delegation," Held at Washington, Wednesday, April 18, 1945, 9:10 a.m. Washington, April 18, 1945, 9:10 a.m.

[44] Finkelstein 1965, 375. Emphasis added.

[45] Charter of the United Nations, Hearings before the Committee on Foreign Relations. United States Senate. Seventy-Ninth Congress. First Session on the Charter of the United Nations for the Main-tenance of International Peace and Security, Submitted by the President of the United States on July 2, 1945. Part 1 [Unrevised] July 9, 1945.

[46] Acheson 1969, 71.

to the potential financial obligations implied by the UNRRA proposal was strong. "An ecstatic phrase in the draft, by which 'each member government pledged its full support to the Administration [of UNRRA], within the limits of available resources and subject to the requirements of its constitutional procedure,' aroused the anti-New Dealer in Vandenberg to rotund hyperbole."[47] Vandenberg voiced concern that the draft "pledged our total resources to whatever illimitable scheme for relief and rehabilitation all around the world our New Deal crystal gazers might desire to pursue ..."[48] Draft language was changed in response to concerns voiced by the Republican Senators. The episode displays that, had these same Senators thought it possible that Article 17 would leave them on the hook to support development activities approved by a majority of states they disagreed with—they would have raised the issue.

Envisioning Enforcement Operations

The vision of states, and not the "UN," as the relevant actors that would implement policy extended to security operations. It is well known that the term "peacekeeping" does not appear in the UN Charter and only emerged later through the entrepreneurship of individuals and the practices of the Security Council.[49] However, the consequential implications of the UN's architects not having conceived of peacekeeping have not been fully appreciated. The design of mandatory funding rules is easier to understand in light of Big Three conversations at the time, which reveal that they expected joint costs born under the mandatory assessments system—even with regard to security—to be administrative rather than operational. In their vision, enforcement action would be undertaken by the militaries of the Big Three themselves, and they would bear these costs outside the auspices of any UN rules.[50]

The second series of Dumbarton Oaks negotiations (between the US, UK, and China) reveal US thinking when China's representative, Dr. Victor Hoo, inquires about whether the costs of enforcement action will be included in the regular budget. Meeting minutes read that Dr. Hoo "asked whether consideration had been given to the question of participation of member states in sharing the expenses involved in enforcement action. He asked whether these expenses would be out in the regular budget and assumed by the member states on the basis of some

---

[47] Acheson 1969, 71.

[48] Acheson 1969, 71–72.

[49] See Simpson 1999, 80–81.

[50] In addition to primary evidence below, this view is confirmed by Rubinstein (1964, 121), who states that many countries' opposition to mandatory assessments for the UNEF and ONUC operations was based on the proposition that "the Charter contemplated that peace and security actions should be carried out primarily by the five permanent members of the Security Council, who would furnish their troops without cost to other UN members (...)."

quota, following the practice with respect to the regular budget."[51] Leo Pasvolsky responded with a clear distinction between administrative and enforcement costs, indicating the US had thought through the issue. He notes, "forces furnished by member states for enforcement would be maintained by the member states themselves," while expenditures "resulting from enforcement action would presumably be part of the general budget." For example, he notes, "the work of the Military Staff Committee [a committee in the secretariat] would presumably be financed by the Organization as a whole."[52] Here the working understanding on the scope of Article 17 becomes clear: enforcement actions would be endorsed by the Security Council, but carried out by member states and those member states would bear the costs (or work out cost-sharing on an ad hoc basis). But any other expenses stemming from enforcement action—planning or administrative support—would be paid from the regular budget through the mandatory assessments system.

The diary entries of Edward Stettinius, who at the time served as Undersecretary of State, echo the understanding Pasvolsky relays at Dumbarton Oaks and demonstrates that the Soviet Ambassador is on the same page. In conversations with Ambassador Gromyko of the USSR, Stettinius sought to clarify Soviet thinking on enforcement operations, especially with regard to language on an "international air force" that had come up in Soviet drafts. Stettinius recalled the following exchange with Gromyko regarding the air force in his diary:

> "Mr. Ambassador, you don't mean a new uniform with a special insignia on the plane under command of some officer of the [security] council" and he replied "Not at all." I then went on and said in effect "I understand you mean joint operations with a plane of the RAF and a plane of the Red Army and a plane of the USAF all operating together under same Allied command." The Ambassador agreed and added that the Soviets think of troops and naval vessels in the same way.[53]

The earliest UN peacekeeping missions reflected this state-based understanding. Security Council commissions that provided the forerunners to modern day peacekeeping to check Greek complaints of border violations by its neighbors, and for truce-supervision activities in Palestine, relied primarily on member state representatives rather than UN staff. "These first field missions, following League precedent, were composed of representatives of Member States and serviced

[51] Pasvolsky Papers. National Archives. Washington, DC. Washington Conversations on International Organization. Informal record of the second meeting of the joint formulation group. Assembly Hall, Dumbarton Oaks, 10:40 a.m.–12:45 p.m. CONV. B. Joint Formulation Group Record 2, October 6, 1944. Status: Secret. P. 19.

[52] Pasvolsky Papers. National Archives. Washington, DC. Washington Conversations on International Organization. Informal record of the second meeting of the joint formulation group. Assembly Hall, Dumbarton Oaks, 10:40 a.m.–12:45 p.m. CONV. B. Joint Formulation Group Record 2, October 6, 1944. Status: Secret. P. 19.

[53] Foreign Relations of The United States, Diplomatic Papers 1944, General, Volume 1. Lot 60-D224, Box 59; Stettinius 1975, 749–750.

only on a limited basis by Secretariat personnel."[54] The initial financing pattern reflected the Big Three's vision: "Initially, each government delegation on a mission was responsible for its own expenses, with the few United Nations personnel being paid from the Organization's budget. Supplies and equipment—especially for transportation and communications—were, in the conditions of early postwar Indonesia and Greece, necessarily provided by the participating governments. The salaries of military officers seconded to the missions were usually continued by their governments, with some per diem payments by the United Nations."[55] This division of labor meant that the mandatory assessments system and the principle of collective financial responsibility was respected, but "it applied to only a relatively small part of the costs."[56]

By contrast, the mandate that established the UN Emergency Force (UNEF), in response to the Suez Crisis, was an international force of 6,000 men that operated under the United Nations flag and the control of the UN Secretary-General. Russell characterizes the "truly international armed force" as a *revolutionary development* that was not consistent with the initial understanding of how the mandatory system would govern security operations.[57]

Envisioning UN Membership and Decolonization

Article 9.1 of the Charter states that "The General Assembly shall consist of all Members of the United Nations." This might appear to be among the Charter's most innocuous provisions. But at the time, whether the initial membership would include only the "United Nations," the Allied powers during the war, or a somewhat larger group of "associated nations," remained an open question.[58] Given the authoritative role assigned to the General Assembly, both to apportion assessments and approve budgets, it stands to reason that the great powers would care about who might hold those seats in the future. The evidence indicates that they did care. One of the most controversial episodes during Big Three negotiations involved the so-called "X-matter," in which the USSR demanded sixteen votes in the Assembly—one for each of its constituent republics. The "bombshell"[59] request, dropped by Soviet Ambassador Gromyko at Dumbarton Oaks, "left Stettinius and Cadogan breathless, but they lost no time in telling him that his proposal

---

[54] Russell 1966, 71.
[55] Russell 1966, 72.
[56] Russell 1966, 72.
[57] Russell 1966, 73. Emphasis added.
[58] Foreign Relations of The United States, Diplomatic Papers 1944, General Volume 1. Lot 60-D224, Box 56: D.O./P.R.16. Memorandum by the Under Secretary of State (Stettinius) to the Secretary of State. September 8, 1944.
[59] Stettinius 1975, 111.

would raise great difficulties."[60] The desire for more Assembly votes by the USSR, and the strong opposition from the US and UK, indicate that both sides were concerned about relative control in the General Assembly. The matter was settled through a compromise negotiated between Roosevelt and Stalin in which the Soviet Union received three votes, including one for the Ukrainian Soviet Socialist Republic and one for Byelorussian Soviet Socialist Republic.[61] The concern on both sides was in response to a "known unknown"—the question of whether cooperation between the Soviet Union and the West would continue after the war. Both sides were hedging their bets.

By contrast, none of the great powers raised issues about the potential for *other* states to gain majority control in the Assembly. There is no evidence that anyone imagined the actual UN membership of 1960, in which developing states—many of which had been "non-self-governing territories" in 1945—outnumbered the US and its Western European allies. I argue that this failure of imagination was the result of a decision-making environment characterized by genuine uncertainty about the future of imperialism, decolonization, and by extension, UN membership. As Rupert Emerson reflected in a special issue of *International Organization* in 1965: "the crystal ball available to even the best informed in 1945 did not disclose that the UN was shortly to fall into the hands of the ex-dependent peoples ..."[62] Below I pinpoint how the UN architects' vision of the future went wrong in anticipating the pace of decolonization and its effects, including the number of independent states it would produce, and the likelihood that those states would hold distinct preferences about the UN's development.

Gazing into the Future at War's End

The embedded nature of colonialism prior to World War II can hardly be overstated. In his classic text on the United Nations and Dependent Peoples, Emil Sady writes that "European authority—both official and personal—however much hated and resisted, seemed invincible in the colonies as the Second World War began."[63] At that time, approximately one-third of the world's population—some seven hundred million people—and about one-third of global land area was under some form of colonial rule.[64] Great Britain, the Netherlands, France, Belgium, Portugal, Italy, and Spain were the primary imperial powers, and they had not indicated that dependent territories would transition to independence. On

---

[60] Hull 1948, 1680; see also Cadogan 1972, 671.
[61] Vandenberg 1952, 159.
[62] Emerson 1965, 486.
[63] Sady 1956, 7.
[64] Sady 1956, 3.

the contrary, several had recently rejected the notion that citizens in dependent territories could obtain equal status with the so-called "metropolitan"[65] power:

> The idea that the British Commonwealth could include member states in which nonwestern peoples were dominant, although perhaps implied in British policy, had not been established. And the Netherlands, as late as 1938, had rejected a request of Indonesian nationalists for dominion status. The idea of associated states in a French Union had also not been conceived. (...) It was true of course that the principle of self-determination for all peoples had been proclaimed, but except for the Philippines [to which the US had promised independence], it had not yet been applied by the metropoles on their own initiative in any of the classical colonial situations.[66]

This historical perspective informed the views and expectations of the great powers on questions pertaining to non-self-governing territories, and especially the perspective of the United Kingdom. At Yalta (the Crimea Conference) in February of 1945, the Big Three discussed basic trusteeship arrangements to replace the League of Nations mandate system. The main agreement was that any trusteeship system would apply to three types of territories: those already under the League mandates system, territories that would be detached from Axis powers at the War's end, and any other territories that might be *voluntarily* placed under trusteeship.[67] The first indication of the great powers' expectation that they would maintain control over colonial possessions is found in this two-track system. Colonial powers would determine which territories were subject to international oversight (via the trusteeship system) and which were not.

Domestic disagreements between the Navy and State Department in the United States over US trusteeship proposals prevented those issues from being discussed at Dumbarton Oaks.[68] The Big Three intended to meet to discuss these questions prior to San Francisco, and to include France, but the meeting never occurred, and so they met to agree on terms only at the start of the San Francisco Conference.[69] Discussions from two sections of the UN Charter—Chapter XI, which pertains to non-self-governing territories, and Chapter XII, which pertains to the trusteeship system—are useful in discerning states' vision of the future on colonial questions and UN membership.

Chapter XI of the UN Charter, the Declaration regarding Non-Self-Governing Territories, begins with Article 73. Its obligations are directed toward "Members of

---

[65] "Metropolitan" is a term used to refer to the territory and citizens of the imperial power, e.g., the United Kingdom would be a metropolitan power, India would not.
[66] Sady 1956, 5.
[67] Sady 1956, 20.
[68] Gilchrist 1945, 982; Sady 1956, 20.
[69] Gilchrist, 1945, 983; Sady 1956, 20.

the United Nations which have or assume responsibilities for the administration of territories whose peoples have not yet attained a full measure of self-government (...)."[70] The language of "self-government," not independence, is repeated in Article 73(b) which commits those administering territories to "develop self-government, to take due account of the political aspirations of the peoples, and to assist them in the progressive development of their free political institutions, according to the particular circumstances of each territory and its peoples and their varying stages of advancement."[71]

Some delegations at San Francisco supported the inclusion of "independence" as a goal alongside self-government. This was strongly opposed by the United Kingdom. Eugene Chase, the Secretary of Committee II/4 on Trusteeship stated that "It [Article 73b] does *not* say 'self-government or independence' (...) for the simple reason that colonial powers led by the United Kingdom refused to approve the Declaration if it mentioned 'independence' as a possible objective."[72] Huntington Gilchrist of the UK, and the Executive Officer of Committee II summarized it somewhat differently: "Independence" was not mentioned as a goal, for the single reason that no colonial power except the United States looks upon it as a normal and natural outcome of colonial status."[73]

Unlike "independence," "self-government" fit within the lexicon of colonialism, especially in the British Empire, where colonies exercised varying degrees of "self-government" while remaining under colonial administration. In the US view, self-government could include independence, but, more consistent with the major colonial powers, "could also take the form of local autonomy within a larger association of some kind."[74] Given this understanding, it is unsurprising that the United Kingdom did not see new UN arrangements as problematic or requiring policy change. Rather, the British viewed it as a reflection of their own status quo colonial policy, with the expectation that other colonial powers would need to meet the British standard.[75]

Other colonial powers planned to reform relationships with their territories, but did not envision independence. The French moved toward a union or federal model linking its territories to metropolitan France and persisted in this vision beyond 1945. The *loi cadre* (reform act) of 1956, was "an active attempt to renegotiate imperial policy and perpetuate French influence overseas."[76] Based on archival material from France's Overseas Ministry, historian Andrew W.M. Smith notes that during the *loi cadre* planning period, "colonial officials were convinced

---

[70] UN Charter, Chapter XI, Article 73.
[71] UN Charter, Chapter XI, Article 73(b).
[72] Chase 1950, 318.
[73] Gilchrist 1945, 983.
[74] Sayre 1948, 281.
[75] Gilchrist 1945, 988.
[76] Smith 2014, 92.

of their role, as shown by confident economic and social plans projected into a colonial future."[77] Consistent with the UK's reading of "self-government," France devolved some administrative authority to colonial states while "the overarching regulatory framework remained rigged in France's favor."[78] During the war, Dutch groups worked clandestinely on plans for major colonial reforms. But even these stopped short of granting independence or full autonomy to Indonesia or other colonial possessions.[79] Rather, they envisioned a Dutch Commonwealth, in which Indonesia would be a "sort of dominion" or "a state with self-government."[80] After Indonesia gained independence in 1949, the Dutch continued working to maintain their presence in the East Indies in West New Guinea.[81] Other colonial powers, like Belgium and Portugal, were less inclined to reform.[82] In sum, the metropolitan powers envisioned a future in which they would reform relations with their territories, but they did not envision the end of empire.

To the extent that the great powers anticipated that some non-self-governing territories *would* become independent, the working expectation was that it would take a long time. This is seen in discussions and statements made around the Trusteeship System, outlined in Chapter XII of the Charter. Chapter XII, Article 76(b) specifies both "self-government" and "independence" as appropriate goals for trust territories administered by the United Nations. Initially, just ten territories were placed under UN trusteeship.[83] None of the initial trusteeship agreements specified plans for "self-government or independence."[84] Gilchrist predicted in 1945 that "In many cases, no doubt, the [dependent] status will necessarily be long-continued."[85] Two years later, the US representative at the Security Council expressed a similar sentiment when prompted to add the language of "independence" to its trusteeship agreement for the Pacific Islands. The US altered the agreement but recorded its opposition, "not to the principle of independence (...) but to the thought that it could possibly be achieved within any foreseeable future in this case."[86]

The argument proposed here—that UN architects did not envision the possibility of so many member states—is consistent with recent historical contributions that emphasize that decolonization only appeared inevitable in retrospect.[87] A

---

[77] Smith 2014, 93. See also Smith 2017, 90.

[78] Smith 2014, 92.

[79] Foray 2013.

[80] Foray 2013, 268.

[81] On Dutch plans to retain West New Guinea after Indonesian independence, see Kuitenbrouwer 2016, 309–310.

[82] Emerson 1965, 487, 489.

[83] Gilchrist 1945, 988 notes that with "the present state of nationalist feeling, it seems unlikely that any colonial power will voluntarily put a colony of its own under the system."

[84] Sayre 1948, 280.

[85] Gilchrist 1945, 992.

[86] Sayre 1948, 280. This UN DOC is listed as: S/P.V./116 March 7, 1947; Sayre 1948, 47.

[87] Shepard 2006; Darwin 2009, 610; Cooper 2014.

recent edited volume on British and French colonialism in Africa notes that only in the late 1950s did "most observers recognize that significant change loomed on the horizon (...) And yet, even at this stage, few could confidently predict how long or what shape this transformation would take."[88]

Finally, if the imperial powers could have anticipated that so many of their colonial territories would move toward independence in fifteen years' time, they could hardly be expected to predict how many states would result from the process. In some instances, states emerged from the expected geographic units. For instance, Nigeria gained independence from the UK in 1960 as a single state with a population that exceeded the entirety of French West Africa.[89] However, in other cases the number of independent states that emerged far exceeded the number of territorial units reported by the colonial powers in 1945. For example, France reported just two units in West Africa to the United Nations under Article 73. If UN architects had foreseen independence for these territories, they likely would have expected two independent states to emerge from these units. This did not prove to be the case. In part due to the French *loi cadre* policy of the 1950s, which contributed to the "Balkanization" of West Africa, twelve independent states emerged from the two reported units. In addition to the twelve, Togo, Cameroun, and Madagascar were added. As Emerson summarized in 1965 "the smaller number of heirs of the French colonial empire in sub-Saharan Africa emerged as 15 states (...)."[90]

Off the Page and into the World

The UN's architects and the Charter they designed were soon to confront a series of unanticipated developments. As colonial states gained independence and joined the United Nations, as the enforcement action envisioned by the Charter failed to materialize, as ever more robust versions of peacekeeping emerged, as demand for greater economic assistance grew, UN Charter rules governing funding were neither replaced, revised, nor amended. But the meaning of Article 17 and what constituted expenses of the Organization nevertheless changed, and a voluntary funding system nevertheless grew. Chapter 4 considers the initial incremental changes that came in response to these unanticipated developments, including the introduction of voluntary funding rules for economic and social development, and the expansion, retraction, and weakening of the great powers' commitment to the mandatory assessments system.

---

[88] Smith and Jeppesen 2017, 4–5.
[89] Emerson 1965, 494.
[90] Emerson 1965, 494.

References

Acheson, Dean. 1969. *Present at the Creation: My Years in the State Department*. New York, NY: W.W. Norton & Company.

Cadogan, Sir Alexander O.M. 1972. *The Diaries of Sir Alexander Cadogan, O.M., 1938–1945*. Edited by David Dilks. New York, NY: G.P. Putnam & Sons.

Chase, Eugene P. 1950. *The United Nations in Action*. New York: McGraw-Hill Book Company.

Cooper, Frederick. 2014. *Citizenship between Empire and Nation: Remaking France and French Africa 1945–1960*. Princeton, NJ: Princeton University Press.

Darwin, John. 2009. *The Empire Project: The Rise and Fall of the British World-System, 1830–1970*. Cambridge, UK: Cambridge University Press.

Eagleton, Clyde. 1945. "I. The Charter Adopted at San Francisco." *American Political Science Review* 39(5): 934–942.

Emerson, Rupert. 1965. "Colonialism, Political Development, and the UN." *International Organization* 19(3): 484–503.

Finkelstein, Lawrence S. 1965. "The United Nations: Then and Now." *International Organization* 19(3): 367–393.

Foray, Jennifer L. 2013. "A Unified Empire of Equal Parts: The Dutch Commonwealth Schemes of the 1920s–40s. *The Journal of Imperial and Commonwealth Studies* 41(2): 259–284.

Gilchrist, Huntington. 1945. "V. Colonial Questions at the San Francisco Conference." *The American Political Science Review* 39(5): 982–992.

Goodrich, Leland M., Edvard Isak Hambro, and Anne Patricia Simons. 1969. *Charter of the United Nations. Commentary and Documents*. Third and Revised Edition. New York, NY: Columbia University Press.

Hasluck, Paul. 1980. *Diplomatic Witness: Australian Foreign Affairs, 1941–1947*. Melbourne, Australia: University of Melbourne Press.

Hilderbrand, Robert C. 1990. *Dumbarton Oaks*. Chapel Hill, NC: University of North Carolina Press.

Hull, Cordell. 1948. *The Memoirs of Cordell Hull: Volume 2*. London, UK: Hodder & Stoughton.

Israel, Fred, ed. 1966. *The War Diary of Breckinridge Long: Selections from 1939–1944*. Lincoln, NE: University of Nebraska Press.

Kuitenbrouwer, Vincent. 2016. "Beyond the 'Trauma of Decolonisation': Dutch Cultural Diplomacy during the West New Guinea Question." *The Journal of Imperial and Commonwealth History* 44(2): 306–327.

McIntyre, Elizabeth. 1954. "Weighted Voting in International Organizations." *International Organization* 8(4): 484–497.

Notter, Harley. 1975. *Postwar Foreign Policy Preparation, 1939–1945*. Westport, CT: Greenwood Press. (Originally published by the U.S. Department of State in 1949).

Rubinstein, Alvin Z. 1964. *Soviets in International Organizations: Changing Policy toward Developing Countries, 1953–1963*. Princeton, NJ: Princeton University Press.

Russell, Ruth B. 1966. "United Nations Financing and the Law of the Charter." *Columbia Journal of Transnational Law* 5(1): 68–95.

Sady, Emil. 1956. *The United Nations and Dependent Peoples*. Washington, DC: Brookings Institution.

Sayre, Francis B. 1948. "Legal Problems Arising from the United Nations Trusteeship System." *The American Journal of International Law* 42(2): 263–298.

Schelling, Thomas C. 1955. "International Cost-Sharing Arrangements." *Essays in International Finance*. No. 24, September. International Finance Section. Department of Economics and Sociology. Princeton, NJ: Princeton University Press.

Shepard, Todd. 2006. *The Invention of Decolonization: The Algerian War and the Remaking of France*. Second Edition. Ithaca, NY: Cornell University Press.

Simpson, Erika. 1999. "The Principles of Liberal Internationalism According to Lester Pearson." *Journal of Canadian Studies* 34(1): 75–92.

Singer, J. David. 1961. *Financing International Organization: The United Nations Budget Process*. Leiden: Martinus Nijhoff.

Smith, Andrew W.M. 2014. "Of Colonial Futures and an Administrative Alamo: Investment, Reform and the *Loi Cadre* (1956) in French West Africa." *French History* 28(1): 92–113.

Smith, Andrew W.M. 2017. "Future Imperfect: Colonial Futures, Contingencies and the End of French Empire." In *Britain, France and the Decolonization of Africa*. Edited by Andrew W.M. Smith and Chris Jeppesen. London, UK: UCL Press, 87–110.

Smith, Andrew W.M., and Chris Jeppesen. 2017. "Introduction: Development, Contingency and Entanglement: Decolonization and the Conditional." In *Britain, France and the Decolonization of Africa*. Edited by Andrew W.M. Smith and Chris Jeppesen. London, UK: UCL Press.

Sohn, Louis. 1944. "Weighting of Votes in an International Assembly." *American Political Science Review* 38(6): 1192–1203.

Stettinius, Edward R. 1975. *The Diaries of Edward R. Stettinius, Jr., 1943–1946*. New York, NY: New Viewpoints.

Stoessinger, John. 1964. *Financing the United Nations System*. Washington, DC: Brookings Institution.

Vandenberg, Arthur. 1952. *The Private Papers of Senator Vandenberg*. Boston, MA: Houghton Mifflin Co.

4

Voluntary Funding and Financial Crisis

Between 1946 and 1962, the United Nations experienced two important developments in its evolution away from multilateral governance. Voluntary funding rules
were introduced when the Expanded Program of Technical Assistance (EPTA) was
established in 1949. EPTA was layered alongside the existing Technical Assistance
(TA) program that was covered by the regular budget and governed by the mandatory assessments system. EPTA's funding soon eclipsed the allocation TA received
in the regular budget. The second development involved contestation over the
scope of the UN's mandatory assessments system with regard to peacekeeping and
marked the United Nations' first budget crisis. Resolving the crisis produced contradictory effects, at once cementing the scope of the mandatory system beyond
what its designers had envisioned, while unintentionally weakening the system by
providing a rationale to withhold dues.

Taken together, these two episodes set the UN on its contemporary trajectory.
Substantively, its evolution away from the Organization that the Big Three envisioned was already visible. The UN intended by its designers would have focused
on avoiding world war and coordinating state behavior. The actual UN moved
toward an emphasis on economic development and a robust peacekeeping component. That it had also begun its path away from egalitarian multilateralism was
less visible. Voluntary funding rules at EPTA and later at the Special Fund did
not empower donors to restrict their contributions. On the contrary, they prohibited such behavior. If anything, voluntary rules were understood to protect the
mandatory system and save it from probable non-compliance should significant
economic and development activities be added to its purview. But the rules nevertheless served as an important first step in that direction, and later incremental
"tinkering" pushed the process further along.

The introduction of voluntary rules, contestation over Article 17 and the resulting budget crisis, illustrate distinct observable implications of the theoretical
framework. Voluntary funding rules exhibit a number of characteristics outlined
in Chapter 2 that are associated with *unforeseen* transformational potential and
illustrate implications that follow from genuine uncertainty and creative agency.
The framework expects that at the outset of the process, incremental changes are
not made with the intent to transform. Specific to this case, it means that the actors
proposing voluntary rules should not introduce those rules with the aim of undermining multilateralism, whether articulated broadly (i.e., we need to sidestep

Transforming International Institutions. Erin R. Graham, Oxford University Press. © Erin R. Graham (2023).
DOI: 10.1093/oso/9780198877936.003.0004

control of multilateral bodies), or narrowly (donors need to control resource distribution). Rather, the incremental change should be undertaken for reasons and purposes that are distinct from transformation. A further related expectation is that successful incremental change proposals are likely to come from those who are supporters of the UN's principles and governance, rather than from actors who are skeptical or opposed to the UN's version of multilateralism.

Creative agency implies a second set of expectations that emphasize agents' ability to tap into rule permissiveness when dissatisfied with the status quo. We see lawyers tap into Article 17's permissiveness to reinterpret UN Charter obligations and diplomats layer rules alongside the mandatory system to expand the UN technical assistance program. The framework also holds implications for the complicated episode through which member states, and ultimately the ICJ, jostled over the scope of the UN Charter's Article 17. Article 17 states that "The expenses of the Organization shall be borne by the Members as apportioned by the General Assembly." This case demonstrates that actors engaged in the process—and the USSR and United States in particular—did not fully appreciate or anticipate the downstream effects of the rules they designed. But this case is most useful in illustrating implications around rule permissiveness and creative agency in affecting change. The framework expects that formal rules change through reinterpretation because of rule permissiveness and outlines subsequent practice as one process through which conversion occurs. Specific to the case, the expectation is that Article 17 would change through reinterpretation rather than formal revision or amendment. If the contours of the framework hold, we should see creative actors use the inherent permissiveness of Article 17 to forward reinterpretations that are distinct from the ways that designers understood the rule to modify its meaning. Further, we may see international legal interpretive strategies at work in the conversion process.

The case demonstrates each of these expectations. The dispute revolved around the use of the mandatory assessments system for the United Nations Emergency Force (UNEF) and the UN Operation in the Congo (ONUC) and the refusal of two key members, the Soviet Union and France, to pay their dues. The US side was adamant that Article 17 should apply, while the Soviet Union, France, and several others, were adamant it should not. I evaluate the (re)interpretations forwarded by various actors in the dispute against designers' intent and understanding of the same rule's meaning in 1945. The unintentional permissiveness of Article 17 allowed the US to reinterpret the rule to cover peacekeeping missions of a kind not contemplated by the Charter. The evidence indicates that UN designers, including the US, intended robust military action to be funded through ad hoc agreement of the Security Council's permanent members. When the ICJ upheld the US reinterpretation, relying largely on subsequent practice, the scope of Article 17 was effectively modified without any Charter revision. But the results from this were far from straightforward. In another cunning move, the US would reinterpret the nature of French and Soviet opposition to the ICJ decision to justify its own withholding of mandatory dues through the so-called Goldberg Reservation.

The chapter begins chronologically, with the original technical assistance program followed by the introduction of voluntary rules, first for EPTA and later for the UN Special Fund, in 1959. I then step away from the economic development institutions and dive into the Article 17 case, which requires a discussion of the UNEF and ONUC missions that produced the crisis. The case tacks back and forth in time to evaluate the legal case made regarding Article 17's interpretation by both sides in 1960 against UN architects' understanding of the rule in 1945. In telling both stories, I highlight the theory's observable implications described above. The chapter concludes with a summary and status report on the UN's gradual transformation at the resolution of the financial crisis in 1965.

Demands for Economic Assistance and Rising Concerns about Costs

In Article 17, paragraph 2, the UN Charter provides that "The expenses of the Organization shall be borne by the Members as apportioned by the General Assembly." Chapter 3 demonstrates that when the great powers designed the UN Charter, they expressed little concern over the Assembly's authority over budgeting or apportioning assessments. But this lack of concern was premised on a limited vision of the Organization's future work. Operational roles in economic and social development were absent from their vision, as were robust peacekeeping missions. At the San Francisco Conference, negotiators further specified that assessments would be allocated based on *capacity to pay*. The precise details, including who would pay what portion, were left for the first meeting of the Assembly. A group of UN member states was assigned to the newly formed Contributions Committee and was tasked with making a recommendation to the Assembly regarding a scale of assessments. The Committee's discussions immediately demonstrated how keen most member states were to avoid significant monetary commitments to the new United Nations.

Given the devastation experienced by the European continent during the war, the US went into these negotiations expecting a high rate of assessment. Perhaps as high as 25 percent, they thought.[1] But the Americans quickly realized they had committed an error. The Contributions Committee's first recommendation doubled the US expectation, recommending a US rate of 49.94 percent. The second highest share, assigned to the United Kingdom, was recommended at 10.5 percent,

---

[1] Foreign Relations of the United States, 1946. General; The United Nations, Volume I. IO Files. Document 251. *Memorandum by the Deputy Director of the Office of Special Political Affairs (Ross) to the Director of the Office (Hiss)* August 29, 1946.

and the Soviet Union followed at 7 percent. On the initial discussion and recommendations, Paul Appleby, the American representative to the Contributions
Committee, reported back to the State Department:

> When we started negotiations, we thought that the idea of a ceiling would be
> acceptable to the Committee. We felt they would want no one nation to be pre-
> dominant in the organization. We found that not to be the case. (...) everyone
> seemed to think that the more the United States paid the better.[2]

The US concern was less about absolute costs, and more about the willingness of
Congress to accept such a high rate relative to other members. In framing their
arguments to the Contributions Committee, the US group, which included Senators Vandenberg and Connally, emphasized that no Organization of sovereign
equals should be so reliant on a single member. This point was sharpened by
Eleanor Roosevelt, who encouraged Senator Vandenberg to emphasize "that any
group making such a large contribution to the budget as 50 per cent would be open
to pressure by its constituency to exercise pressure on the Organization. It should
be made clear that the United States interest was not only a monetary one but
a concern that the Organization must be free."[3] Most states found US arguments
only mildly persuasive,[4] with the US being especially surprised by the United Kingdom's refusal to support its position. A compromise was ultimately adopted that
placed a 33⅓ percent ceiling on assessment rates *in principle*, with the understanding that the US rate would exceed the ceiling for the foreseeable future. The initial
US rate was set at 39.89 percent.[5]

These early negotiations demonstrate that few states were eager to invest heavily
in the new Organization. With the scale in place, the "expenses of the Organization" now implied clear costs for each member state, and its meaning became
subject to contestation. A first point of controversy involved the inclusion of what
was initially termed "expert assistance," which later morphed into the broader
category of "technical assistance." This work represented a gray area between coordination and operational activities. Standard expert assistance involved loaning

---

[2] Foreign Relations of the United States, 1946, General; The United Nations, Volume I. IO files.
Document 252. US/A/C.5/7. *Memorandum by Mr. Paul H. Appleby to the Director of the Office of Special
Political Affairs (Hiss)*. secret. [Washington] October 15, 1946. *UN Contributions.*

[3] Foreign Relations of the United States 1946, General; The United Nations, Volume I IO Files:
US/A/M (Chr.)/13 *Minutes of the Thirteenth Meeting of the United States Delegation, New York, Hotel
Pennsylvania, November 1, 1946, 9:00 a.m.* New York, November 1, 1946, 9:00 a.m. top secret *United
States Attitude Toward Contribution Ceiling.*

[4] The US was particularly taken aback by the UK's refusal to lend support to the US cause. See
Foreign Relations of The United States 1946, General; The United Nations, Volume I. IO Files:
US/A/C.5/7. *Memorandum by Mr. Paul H. Appleby to the Director of the Office of Special Political
Affairs (Hiss)* Secret. [Washington ?] October 15, 1946. *UN Contributions.* Foreign Relations of The
United States, 1946, General; The United Nations, Volume I. 501.BB Summaries/11–1446: Telegram.
Senator Austin to the Secretary of State. New York, November 14, 1946–12:30 a.m.

[5] UN Yearbook 1946–47, 219. https://www.un.org/en/yearbook

expertise (from the UN Secretariat) to provide training to member state nationals at the recipient state's request. Expert assistance seemed to go beyond the conception of coordinating state action conceived by the Big Three during UN negotiations, but it also stopped short of any significant investment or project implementation function associated with contemporary operational activity. The UN had inherited some advisory social welfare functions when they were transferred from the UN Relief and Rehabilitation Administration (UNRRA) that had operated during the war.[6] At UNRRA, the practice involved member states making requests to the Secretariat for advice and expertise across a wide range of issues, many of which had precedent at the League of Nations. The breadth of expertise offered was impressive, ranging from statistical fields and public administration, to devising domestic human rights legislation, to enacting domestic measures to combat drug addiction.[7]

During the 1946–47 period, the UN's expert assistance program continued along the lines of UNRRA. But consistent with UN architects' limited vision of the UN in economic development, and a narrow interpretation of what might constitute "expenses of the Organization," recipients paid for any expert assistance rendered.[8] That recipient states continued to pay for any services was essential, according to the Soviet Union; in their interpretation, the costs of expert and technical assistance were clearly not expenses of the Organization as intended by Article 17. The USSR held that "the United Nations was not a bank nor a relief agency,"[9] and adamantly insisted that a recipient-pays policy accompany all UN technical assistance.[10] Soviet delegates consistently opposed *any* general UN policy or formal institutionalization of technical assistance and preferred that all requests be dealt with on an ad hoc basis.[11] The Soviet position was consistent with their earlier stance at Dumbarton Oaks where they made clear their opposition to the Organization's involvement in economic and social activities. As Rubinstein writes, "This restrictive interpretation of the Charter's provisions characterized the prevailing Soviet attitude toward attempts to expand the economic competence of the United Nations."[12] Technical assistance constituted an "operational program," and as such it constituted a violation of the Charter and should not be subject to mandatory assessment.[13] "Expenses" were argued to constitute the UN's "administrative" costs, and nothing more.

---

[6] UN Yearbook, 1947–48, 657; Jacobson 1963, 117–121.

[7] UN Yearbook 1947–48, 657.

[8] UN Yearbook 1947–48. Part I: United Nations. Section 4: The Economic and Social Council. Chapter H: Other economic and social questions, p. 658. If a technical assistance assignment did not take Secretariat staff away from their other duties and was quickly resolved, payment was not required.

[9] Jacobson 1963, 230.

[10] Jacobson 1963, 119, 228–229.

[11] UN Yearbook 1947–48, 658.

[12] Rubinstein 1964, 21–22.

[13] Rubinstein 1964, 22. See also Jacobson 1963, 229.

The UN's early developing state members had reason to interpret Article 17 differently. States like Burma, Chile, Egypt, and Peru lobbied for the inclusion of technical assistance on the UN agenda in 1946, arguing that recipient-pay requirements were prohibitive for too many states.[14] The US joined developing states to oppose the recipient-pays policy, and at the Economic and Social Council (ECOSOC), both the Economic Committee and full Council rejected a Soviet amendment that would require technical services rendered by the UN to be paid for by governments requesting assistance.[15] Then, directly contradicting the Soviet Union's narrow interpretation of Article 17, the General Assembly passed Resolution 200(III) (1946), proposed by the developing states just mentioned. The resolution established the United Nations Program of Technical Assistance (TA) in the Field of Economic Development with an initial allocation of $288,000.[16] The new TA program was treated as an "expense of the Organization," funded through the mandatory assessments system and part of the regular UN budget.[17] The more expansive view of "expenses of the Organization" had won the day in 1946.

The original TA program's inclusion under mandatory funding rules demonstrates an alternative path that technical assistance and the increasingly robust economic development efforts that followed might have taken at the UN. But even in 1946, before significant membership growth, some showed signs of trepidation about including this modest program in the regular budget. The vocal opposition of the Soviet Union was often accompanied by softer expressions of concern about rising assessments from European powers. France and Belgium complained about the increasing costs of technical assistance during ECOSOC debates as early as 1948.[18] Denmark and Australia, two states with not insignificant dues, questioned whether it was wise (or legal) to make technical assistance a permanent feature of the regular budget.[19] On the other hand, the United States, playing very much against type from the contemporary perspective but consistent with its role at the time, was less concerned about costs and content to support policies opposed by the Soviet Union. Active support by the United States for a broad reading of Article 17 and specifically for the inclusion of TA in the regular budget is seen in its decision to support developing states' recommendation at ECOSOC to "ensure that the regular budget of the United Nations *shall continue* to provide the funds necessary to carry on technical assistance for economic development of under-developed countries authorized by resolution 200(III)."[20]

---

[14] UN Yearbook 1947–48, 658; Jacobson 1963, 227.
[15] UN Yearbook, 1947–48, 518; Jacobson 1963, chapter 8, especially 227ff.
[16] Jacobson 1963, 229.
[17] Jacobson 1963, 120, 229.
[18] Gibson 1967, 188–189; UN Yearbook 1948–49, 880.
[19] UN Yearbook 1948–49, 439.
[20] UN Yearbook, 1948–49, 439.

Despite the US position, the emerging problem was clear: there would be rising demand for economic development work and key member states were reluctant to see their dues rise to meet demand. This placed the United Nations at an early crossroads. The UN could remain focused primarily on security and otherwise limited to coordinating state policy, as the Soviet Union preferred. At that time and for those purposes, the mandatory system outlined in the Charter appeared adequate. Alternatively, the UN could continue to expand its work program to include economic and social development, that was preferred by its developing country membership and supported by the United States. This latter path would bring the two sides into tension and require institutional innovation in the form of voluntary rules to keep the peace.

Layering Voluntary Rules: EPTA and the Special Fund

In the context of rising demand from developing states, wavering interest among European powers, and at the dawn of American hegemony, President Truman delivered his inaugural address in 1949. The so-called "Four Points Speech" advocated increased US support for technical assistance efforts that echoed the small-scale UN TA program. Truman stated, "we must embark on a bold new program for making the benefits of our scientific advances and industrial progress available for the improvement and growth of underdeveloped areas." More specifically, he proposed:

> The material resources which we can afford to use for the assistance of other peoples are limited. But our imponderable resources in technical knowledge are constantly growing and are inexhaustible. (...) We *invite* other countries to pool their technological resources in this undertaking. Their contributions will be warmly welcomed. This should be a cooperative enterprise in which all nations work together through the United Nations and its specialized agencies wherever practicable. It must be a worldwide effort for the achievement of peace, plenty, and freedom.[21]

Following Truman's speech in March of 1949, ECOSOC adopted a resolution proposed by the United States calling for "a comprehensive plan for an expanded cooperative programme of technical assistance for economic development through the United Nations and its specialized agencies."[22] The resolution was welcomed by nearly all delegations, though with some disappointment coming from developing states that advocated for major capital investments.[23]

---

[21] President Harry S. Truman, Inaugural Address, January 20, 1949. Emphasis added.
[22] UN Yearbook 1949–50, 441.
[23] Jacobson 1963, 232.

The Soviet Union remained steadfast in its opposition to technical assistance and offered its standard proposal that recipient states pay for assistance rendered. Their suggestion was "summarily rejected" by the other members.[24] As EPTA negotiations continued, the Soviet Union opposed the necessary trappings of a voluntary funding system—they opposed the creation of a separate fund to collect contributions and they opposed proposals to organize a pledging conference.[25] But this time the Soviet Union was isolated in their opposition. The innovation of voluntary rules appeased Western European states wary of rising assessments. Since EPTA costs would fall outside the "expenses of the Organization" subject to mandatory assessments, their opposition fell away. Indeed, sensing the unpopularity of its position, even the USSR voted affirmatively to establish EPTA in 1949.[26] Consistent with Truman's inaugural address when the General Assembly formally established EPTA on November 16, 1949, UN members were not required to participate, but rather were *invited* to contribute.[27]

The path through which voluntary funding rules entered the realm of UN technical assistance is consistent with the theoretical framework and the observable implications outlined at the outset of the chapter. Incremental rules were not made with intent to undermine UN multilateralism or transform it. The new voluntary rules governing EPTA did not replace mandatory rules governing the regular TA program, rather they were layered; conceived as a supplement that would facilitate technical assistance's expansion. As critics of the regular TA program would often note, there was no functional or substantive difference between the two programs. Indeed, one could reasonably make the case at the time that voluntary funding rules "saved" technical assistance from becoming a mere footnote in the UN's history. Further, voluntary rules were not introduced by opponents of the UN's fundamental principles and governance. In 1948–49 only the Soviet Union and its satellite states could be said to hold such a position. Voluntary rule proposals came instead primarily from the US, at the time the great power most willing to provide funding and largely content with UN governance. In short, the introduction of voluntary rules does not reveal evidence they were designed to enhance donor control over resource distribution or were part of donor schemes to undercut multilateralism. Rather, they were a method to expand technical assistance work with support from a broad swath of the membership. These same dynamics are on view when UN development assistance expanded nine years later with the establishment of the UN Special Fund.

---

[24] Jacobson 1963, 233.
[25] Jacobson 1963, 233.
[26] Jacobson 1963, 235.
[27] UN Yearbook 1949–50, 452.

The Special Fund

By 1958, UN politics were shifting, but the challenge of 1949 remained: recipient demand for development assistance was growing, now more than before, and wealthier member states found the prospect of rising dues unpalatable. The Special Fund was established to support "pre-investment," which, among other activities, involved survey and evaluation work, necessary prerequisites for larger capital investment projects. This was a compromise between developing states that lobbied for a capital development fund within the UN system, and the United States and its Western European allies that opposed a new fund on that scale. Developing states' numbers in the General Assembly were growing, strengthening their position. Another important political shift had occurred: the Soviet Union now voiced rhetorical support for developing states' cause. After Stalin's death in 1952, the USSR softened its criticism of UN development work, moving toward a policy of rhetorical support for the emerging Global South, accompanied by token financial contributions to EPTA. This was politically astute; Soviet opposition had been deeply unpopular and the shift in policy put the US in a defensive position in response to demands for more resources.

This dynamic characterized the long-running politics around a potential UN capital development fund, known in proposals as the Special UN Fund for Economic Development (SUNFED). Developing states envisioned SUNFED as an institution that would combine the resources of the World Bank and the egalitarian governance of the United Nations. In another contrast to the International Bank for Reconstruction and Development (IBRD), in most of its proposed iterations, SUNFED would provide mostly grants or loans with terms much more generous than the IBRD offered. As a consequence, this meant that unlike the IBRD, SUNFED would be unlikely to generate its own revenue and would require significant financial commitments from wealthy states. The US explicitly and directly opposed SUNFED on the grounds that it could not provide the resources necessary for the initiative to be successful. Most Western European states joined the US, emphasizing that the World Bank already existed to fulfill this purpose. The US position held great sway, since it supplied more than 40 percent of voluntary funding to UN programs at the time. The European states supplied most of the balance.

Characteristically, the Soviet Union provided full-throated support for SUNFED and sharply criticized Western states for their opposition but was less forthcoming about financial commitments. In contrast to developing states, the USSR insisted SUNFED rely on voluntary contributions rather than mandatory assessments, and refused to specify the level of voluntary commitment, if any, they would make. For the purposes of understanding UN funding rules and governance, the consistency in an otherwise shifting Soviet position is worth emphasizing. The transition from Stalin to Khrushchev brought a significant and prudent update to Soviet policy at the UN. But the position on what constituted a legitimate expense of the Organization remained the same. From a UN financing perspective, the main difference between 1949 and 1958 was that the American position was beginning to trend toward the Soviet position. Western wariness about mandatory rules grew with the UN membership.

To soften the blow of its unwillingness to support SUNFED, the US offered the Special Fund to focus on pre-investment work (rather than capital development projects).[28] With no alternative funding mechanism for SUNFED, developing states agreed to move forward with the US proposal. EPTA's voluntary funding rules served as the template. With enthusiastic support from US Ambassador to the United Nations Henry Cabot Lodge Jr., who lobbied on the program's behalf, the US made a commitment to supply $1 for every $2 contributed by other countries.[29] The US commitment was intended to mobilize contributions from other states, but it is worth noting that other member states rarely contributed enough to deliver the full potential of the US match. This provides another indication of the limited enthusiasm among European states to provide development assistance through the United Nations during its first twenty years.

As the forerunners that would later merge to become the UN Development Program (UNDP), EPTA and the Special Fund established a precedent that UN operational programs were not "expenses of the Organization" as conceived under Article 17.[30] The intent of the United States and its supporters in 1949 was not to establish a pattern of support for the Soviet Union's narrow interpretation of Article 17, but EPTA's voluntary funding rules unwittingly did so, helping along the UN's subterranean transformation. The Special Fund established a pattern of using voluntary rules to fund economic development. Like in the EPTA case, wealthy states' concerns about mandatory rules were about costs, not control over resources delivered. Voluntary rules were selected because they overcame wealthy states' concerns while simultaneously expanding programs that developing states were demanding. Neither fund aimed, or was designed, to undermine and transform the UN's multilateralism. The next section provides evidence for this claim from the operational years of both funds by demonstrating how bilateral interests were opposed and resisted.

---

[28] Developing states' push for SUNFED also contributed to the establishment of the International Development Agency (IDA) at the World Bank in 1961. See Benjamin 2015, 41–42.

[29] Dag Hammarskjöld Library, New York. United Nations. General Assembly. Twenty-sixth Session. Second Committee. Agenda item 44(a). A/C.2/L.1149. October 14, 1971. Statement by Mr. Paul G. Hoffman, Administrator of the United Nations Development Programme, at the 1385th Meeting on October 14, 1971. No Time Like the Future.

[30] This distinction was later muddied by the ICJ's *Certain Expenses* in 1962, which implied that not all expenses of the Organization were paid by mandatory assessments.

The Multilateral Protections in the UN's Initial Voluntary Rules

EPTA and the Special Fund did not weaken any of the General Assembly's formal budgetary or financial powers. Rather, they laid the foundation for an alternative, voluntary system outside the General Assembly's direct control. The GA retained an advisory function, but EPTA and the Special Fund were governed by their own multilateral, executive councils. These Councils relied on voluntary funding rules and so they lacked the authority the General Assembly enjoyed, to mobilize resources in the regular budget. Some rightly note that this weakening of multilateral authority severely limits the ability of the UN to achieve its mission in the economic and humanitarian fields.[31] But in other ways these funding rules were explicitly designed to maintain and mimic the Assembly's egalitarian multilateralism (rather than to undermine or transform it). First, voting rights and representation remained favorable to developing states. Each state was assigned one vote, just as in the General Assembly, ECOSOC, and at the UN's Specialized Agencies. Indeed, outside the UNSC, strong norms of political and sovereign equality made any departure from one-country-one-vote prohibitively difficult.[32] Governing body composition required "balanced representation," which in practice meant that developing states had a small numbers advantage over net-donors.

Second, EPTA and Special Fund rules banned contributors from using earmarks. The ECOSOC resolution on EPTA states "that contributions shall be made without limitation as to use by a specific agency or in a specific country or for a specific project."[33] EPTA funds were distributed across UN Specialized Agencies (as well as to the UN Secretariat) and so the reference to "a specific agency" was meant to prevent member states from favoring some agencies over others. The reference to specific countries or specific projects was included to draw a sharp distinction between multilateral and bilateral aid. In principle, *technical* assistance was to be removed from *politics*. Assistance was rendered only by request from a recipient state (not at the initiative of the UN or a donor). Technical assistance would "not be a means of foreign economic and political interference in the internal affairs of the country concerned and not be accompanied by any considerations of a political nature."[34] The funding rules of EPTA and the Special Fund were designed to guard against bilateral motivations entering the realm of multilateral technical assistance.

The prohibition on earmarks was explicit in its wording and clear in its purpose. But despite the rule's designed rigidity, its inherent permissiveness provided some

---

[31] E.g., see Archibald 2004.
[32] Grigorescu 2015; Graham and Serdaru 2020.
[33] ECOSOC 1949. Resolution 222(IX). pp. 7–8. August 14–15, 1949. ECOSOC resolution adopted by the General Assembly establishing EPTA in Resolution 304 (IV) November 16, 1949. See also: UN Yearbook 1948–49, 444.
[34] UN Yearbook 1948–49, 448.

opportunity for motivated governments to sneak in bilateral interests. This high-lights rule permissiveness, but my primary aim is to demonstrate the widespread opposition in response to these efforts to politicize UN assistance. The disapproval and opposition in response to attempts to run bilateral policy through the UN or to have UN programming reflect powerful bilateral donor interests was strong. This disapproval provides further evidence that the initial voluntary rules were not intended to allow such behavior.

The first and most creative evasion of the prohibition on donors restricting con-tributions came when the Soviet Union shifted its policy toward the UN and began making contributions to EPTA in 1953. After three years of criticizing EPTA as a tool of western imperialism, the USSR surprised UN members on November 12 by announcing a pledge of 4 million rubles (approximately $1 million). But the announcement was accompanied by a condition prohibited by EPTA rules. The Soviet delegation "stipulated that ruble funds could be spent only on projects sponsored by organizations in which the USSR held membership."[35] This restric-tion was quite limiting since at the time the USSR lacked membership at the World Health Organization (WHO), the UN Educational, Scientific and Cultural Organization (UNESCO), the Food and Agriculture Organization (FAO), and the International Labor Organization (ILO). The problem was dealt with swiftly when the Director-General of the Technical Assistance Administration (TAA) discussed the problem with the USSR and they agreed to remove the condition in 1954.[36] But a more creative challenge posed by the Soviet Union's new contributions was just emerging.

The Soviet Union contributed to EPTA in non-convertible rubles. In practice, this meant contributions came back to the USSR since they could only be used for Soviet equipment, to hire Soviet experts and technicians on technical assis-tance missions, or to provide fellowships to study in the Soviet Union.[37] Initially, few states were eager to accept Soviet assistance, and the USSR frequently com-plained of its contributions not being utilized. As demand for EPTA assistance increased, India became the largest recipient of Soviet contributions "because of that country's readiness to accept Soviet specialists and equipment for large projects."[38]

In multilateral aid the donor is supposed to "disappear" when funds are pooled, but the use of Soviet currency ensured contributions were easily traced to the recipient and the Soviet Union was able to take full credit for the EPTA projects they funded. The evidence indicates this was not an unintended consequence of Soviet policy, but rather its intended purpose. As Rubenstein writes:

[35] Rubinstein 1964, 4.
[36] Rubinstein 1964, 37.
[37] Rubinstein 1964, 38–39.
[38] Rubinstein 1964, 40–41.

Statements from Soviet officials at TAC meetings showed that Moscow preferred to render its aid in EPTA on an essentially bilateral basis. Once plans for the Bombay project had been approved by the UN, Moscow sought to win over the Committee to the desirability of conducting all further negotiations between the Soviet and Indian Governments bilaterally. The Soviet delegate noted "that the Committee was unnecessarily complicating the problem."[39]

Although the Soviet delegate argued this practice did not undermine the multilateral principles of EPTA, the American representative, Walter Kotschnig, disagreed. He argued that a "major undertaking 'manned solely by experts from a single donor country'" undermined the multilateral basis of EPTA operations.[40] To underline his point, Kotschnig emphasized that since the US supplied half of all EPTA funds, if the US were to take the Soviet position, then "50 per cent rather than 16 per cent of all experts used in UN technical assistance programs would have to be of US nationality, 50 per cent of fellowship holders would have to be trained in the US, and 50 per cent of the supplies would have to be secured in that country."[41]

Since rubles could only be used to purchase Soviet equipment, the USSR could effectively veto any EPTA requests for Soviet machinery to be used on approved projects. At different times, they "refused to supply rolling stock, certain kinds of agricultural machinery, medical equipment, and jeeps, on the grounds that they were in short supply in the Soviet Union."[42] In conventional multilateral aid, approved projects benefit from pooled funds from all donors, but the USSR ruble policy provided an ability to pick and choose which approved projects to support.

UN officials, along with top donors like Sweden and the United States, were critical of Soviet policy.[43] Using more explicit terms than US officials at the time, Sweden's representative explicitly criticized communist countries' restricted currency policies at the Special Fund "and exhorted them to liberalize and increase their contributions to SF with [a] view [to] help meet [the] increased target level, which [the] governing council favors."[44] Close UN observers were aware of the use of restricted currencies and concerned with its implications for multilateralism. As early as 1956, just three years after the Soviet Union first contributed

[39] Rubinstein 1964, 42.
[40] Rubinstein 1964, 42–43.
[41] Rubinstein 1964, 42–43.
[42] Rubinstein 1964, 64.
[43] Rubinstein 1964, 43; LBJ Archives, Austin, TX. Incoming Telegram. Department of State. Unclassified. From: USUN New York. To: SECSTATE WASHDC 4849. Subject "Special Fund-Review of Financial Policy." June 3, 1965.
[44] LBJ Archives, Austin, TX. Incoming Telegram. Department of State. Unclassified. From: USUN New York. To: SECSTATE WASHDC 4849. Subject "Special Fund-Review of Financial Policy." June 3, 1965.

to EPTA, UN Secretary-General Dag Hammarskjöld[45] faced questions about the effect of non-convertible rubles on the program's multilateral character during a press conference:

> QUESTION: "And is it not likely that if you do get things put through the United Nations which are bilateral because of currency problems, you might transfer certain political problems to the economic field as it is being operated through the United Nations?"
>
> THE SECRETARY GENERAL: *"Yes, if you do not look out. But that is a problem, a complication, of which we are very well aware in the United Nations, and I think you can take it for granted that we are working consistently in the direction away from such bilateral elements introduced, so to say, through the back door.* Partly they are difficult to avoid, because we live in a world of rather inconvertible currencies, and dollars are a very scarce commodity, and so are Swiss francs and other international currencies, but we are working in that direction, and consistently."[46]

Hammarskjöld's language that bilateral elements were introduced "through the back door," points to an *unintended* permissiveness in the UN's voluntary funding rules. Despite an explicit prohibition on restricting contributions, inconvertible currency contributions allowed for de facto restrictions. This was not anticipated by Western states who designed the rules (and contributed in dollars) or even by the Soviet Union who had opposed technical assistance outright and had not participated in design except to oppose all funding arrangements. Since Soviet contributions to EPTA and the Special Fund were always modest, the problem of "nationalizing" contributions, as it was referred to then, was treated as an annoying but manageable one. It was regarded as an exception to the fundamentally multilateral nature of early UN development funds.

The Soviet Union was creative in its use of inconvertible currencies to engage in otherwise prohibited behavior. Initially, the United States expressed little need for a similar tool, but as the Cold War developed and communist countries requested EPTA and Special Fund projects, the domestic politics of multilateral assistance became more difficult.[47] A number of members of Congress were bothered by the idea that the US was contributing funds to UN agencies that were ultimately used

---

[45] Dag Hammarskjöld was a Swedish economist and the second United Nations Secretary-General. He served from 1953 until his death in a helicopter crash in 1961, when traveling to negotiate a cease fire as part of the UN Operation in the Congo (ONUC).

[46] Papers of David Owen. Columbia University. New York, NY. Press Conference. Transcript of The Secretary-General's Press Conference Held at UN Headquarters on Thursday, June 7, 1956. Note No. 1318 Note to Correspondents. Emphasis added.

[47] LBJ Archives, Austin TX. Incoming Telegram. Department of State. Confidential. From: USUN NEWYORK (Plimpton) To: SECSTATE WASHDC. "CUBA-EPTA" Feb 4, 1965, 6:20 p.m.

for projects in Cuba. By the mid-1960s, State Department officials feared long-term US financial support to the Special Fund was vulnerable due to growing opposition in Congress. A 1966 telegram from the State Department articulates the problem and provides direction to the USUN Mission in New York. The basic strategy involved preventing projects for Cuba from being brought to the Special Fund Governing Council for a vote:

> Recommendations to January 1966 Governing Council for two Special Fund projects for Cuba described in reftels would bring about severe crisis in U.S. and Special Fund relations. In discussions [of] this topic with senior SF, UNESCO, and FAO staffs, missions should emphasize U.S. opposition to Cuban projects making reference to Castro regime's continued attempts at subversion [of] neighbors. Would not be in best interest [of the] future of SF to force confrontation [in the] Governing Council on this issue. On one hand blocking third might for first time dfeat [defeat] Managing Director's project recommendations while on other hand approval of projects would jeopardize continued U.S. support of [the] SF.[48]

Of course, the US contributed in dollars, so did not have the ability to restrict "through the backdoor" as the Soviet Union did. As an alternative, the US tried to exercise informal influence through managing directors at both EPTA and the Special Fund. The strategy was not to oppose projects outright, but rather to encourage delays or to reject project proposals for technical reasons before they reached the full Council for a vote.[49] Most officials at State and other executive agencies were generally favorable to the UN and their concerns were primarily about protecting funding from Congressional cuts.

The US was sometimes successful in delaying projects, but its powers were somewhat less than what informal governance arguments might lead us to expect. Paul Hoffman—the American managing director of the Special Fund—allowed Cuban projects to come to the Special Fund governing council for approval despite US requests. He was "unhappy with [the] USG approach to SF projects for Cuba."[50] US telegrams demonstrate that "he [Hoffman] alleges [the] US was first to breach [the] understanding politics would not be raised in [the] Special fund."[51] The US faced similar limits at UNICEF when trying to reduce funding allocated

---

[48] LBJ Archives, Austin, TX. Outgoing Telegram. Department of State. Action: USUN New York; Amembassy PARIS NESCO 4697; Amembassy ROME FODAG 2119. Special Fund Projects for Cuba. March 10, 1965. 7:24 p.m.

[49] LBJ Archives, Austin, TX. Incoming Telegram. Department of State. Confidential. From: New York. Action: SECSTATE 3039. Subject: Cuba-EPTA. Reference: USUN's A-983. February 2, 1965.

[50] LBJ Archives, Austin, TX. Incoming Telegram. Department of State. Confidential From: USUN NEWYORK. TO: SECSTATE WASHDC 924. Subject: Special Fund Cuba Projects. September 24, 1965.

[51] LBJ Archives, Austin, TX. Incoming Telegram. Department of State. Confidential From: USUN NEWYORK. TO: SECSTATE WASHDC 924. Subject: Special Fund Cuba Projects. September 24, 1965.

for 69 Land Rovers included in a malaria eradication project for Cuba. Briefing McGeorge Bundy on the situation, the US representative, Sayre, explained:

"Our traditional position is not to oppose health projects for Cuba. Moreover, the presence of malaria in Cuba constitutes a health problem for us. But we did try to get the 69 vehicles knocked out of the program. UNICEF would not agree, but did cut the number to 52, i.e. the number required to replace worn-out vehicles." The telegram then alludes to concerns about how Congress will interpret the project and the "the embarrassing position of having our contribution to UNICEF used to buy vehicles for Cuba."[52]

While US attempts to persuade managing directors or friendly member states to sideline Cuban projects were only partially successful, they nevertheless raised the specter of violating multilateral principles. Indeed, it was multilateral principles— which included the idea that bilateral interests should not affect governing body decisions—that were used to push back against US attempts. Regarding one Special Fund project proposed by Cuba with UNESCO assistance, the US was told: "UNESCO found [the] project technically correct and, at Cuba's request, assisted in writing up [the] project proposal sent to SF. According to Adiseshia, [the] project [is] technically good, and therefore UNESCO strongly supported it."[53] The message delivered to the US was that projects appropriate to the SF mission and deemed "technically correct" would be supported regardless of the recipient country. The message is echoed in Hoffman's "unhappiness" with the US "raising politics" in the Fund. During this period, the UN leadership consistently pushed against bilateral political interests from the UN's top donor.

The process of introducing voluntary rules to the UN illustrates the framework's observable implications. EPTA and the Special Fund were established not to replace the regular TA program, but to supplement and expand its work. The new programs were proposed and endorsed by supporters of multilateral governance and economic assistance, rather than by its opponents. Developing countries and the United States had relatively short-term time horizons and sought to solve an immediate political problem: they wanted to expand UN work into the realm of technical assistance, but another important group, which included the Soviet Union and key states like France, opposed the expansion. The states who proposed voluntary rules were not those who wanted to avoid financial obligations, rather they were the ones who favored the expansion and were willing to incur

[52] LBJ Archives, Austin, TX. Memorandum for Mr. Bundy. From: Robert Sayre. Confidential. June 9, 1964.
[53] LBJ Archives, Austin, TX. Incoming Telegram. Department of State. Confidential. From: AMEMBASSY PARIS. To: RUEHCR/SECSTATE WASHDC. REF (A) DEPTEL 3880 ACTION USUN 1872 Rome 1718; (n) USUNTEL 372 ACTION DEPT 2303. ROME 37. February 17, 1965. Declassified 11/9/76.

them. Nor were the US and its Western allies concerned with controlling how their contributions were spent by the UN in 1949. Indeed, no one voiced this concern. The establishment of EPTA with voluntary rules creatively solved this problem. It expanded UN technical assistance work without drawing opposition from those who opposed increased expenses. Upon EPTA's unanimous passage in the General Assembly, the representative of Poland "pointed out, an almost unprecedented degree of unanimity in the United Nations had been achieved. That proved, he felt, that despite existing differences of opinion, it was possible to reach agreement, given enough good will."[54] That such unanimity was made possible by EPTA's voluntary funding rules escaped mention.

Consistent with the framework's implications, the evidence demonstrates that voluntary rules were not designed to undermine multilateralism. On the contrary, the rules were initially designed to protect the multilateral character of UN decision-making, and in the mid-1960s, EPTA and the Special Fund had held to those principles and practices. But while the original TA program financed by the mandatory dues was maintained, the new programs layered alongside it grew steadily. Soon, mandatory contributions to technical assistance were dwarfed by voluntary counterparts provided through EPTA and the SF, slowly normalizing the UN's reliance on voluntary funds.

The fate of economic development during this period is intertwined with another UN storyline. The crisis involved disagreement over the legality and legitimacy of peacekeeping operations and the subsequent refusal by the Soviet Union, France, and other smaller member states to pay UN dues for those missions. Among its long-term effects was to cause the US Congress to scrutinize its payments to the UN more closely and with greater skepticism. This complex story serves two purposes here. First, it further demonstrates the permissive nature of Article 17's "expenses of the Organization," and contributes to continued contestation around its meaning. Second, and most important, is that the episode created a precedent that states subsequently used as a rationale to withhold UN dues. This weakened the mandatory system while the parallel voluntary system ascended.

I begin with background on UNEF and ONUC. The summary of events highlights the legitimate legal issues the missions raised as well as their revolutionary nature in light of Charter expectations.

The Article 19 Crisis and Exceptions to the Mandatory System

The United Nations Emergency Force (UNEF), in response to the Suez Crisis of 1956, was established in controversial fashion. The United Kingdom and France blocked any Security Council action on the matter, and in response the United

---

[54] UN Yearbook 1948–49, 452.

States invoked the legally controversial "Uniting for Peace" procedure, which called for the General Assembly to weigh in on security affairs if the Security Council was paralyzed. UNEF was significant not only for its controversial start but for the robust nature of its mission. Other UN missions preceded it, but as Ruth Russell writes, UNEF was "The first United Nations peacekeeping military force."[55] "Composed of some 6,000 men, UNEF was organized in national contingents voluntarily provided by ten countries. It operated under the United Nations flag, the command of a general drawn from nearby UNTSO, and the control of the Secretary-General, while remaining politically under the Assembly's direction."[56] It "was a revolutionary development."[57]

Nearly four years later, in July of 1960, the Security Council approved the United Nations Operation in the Congo (ONUC). Although initially established by the UNSC, ONUC, too, faced controversy from the start. Congo gained independence from Belgium on June 30, 1960 with two rival leaders, Joseph Kasavubu, and Patrice Lumumba, becoming President and Prime Minister, respectively. Less than two weeks later, on July 12, Moïse Tshombe declared the southern province of Katanga an independent state. Belgium strengthened its local military presence when this occurred, and with attacks on local Belgians increasing, "found the necessary pretext for its 'humanitarian' intervention."[58] In effect, Belgium quickly found a reason *not* to leave the Congo. In response, Kasavubu and Lumumba issued an ultimatum to the United Nations Secretary-General on July 14, stating that if Belgian troops did not leave the country within forty-eight hours, they would request assistance from Soviet troops.[59]

With the guidance of Secretary-General Dag Hammarskjöld, the Security Council responded. But the initial resolution authorizing ONUC did not reconcile two divergent visions of the mission. For the USSR, the first operative paragraph of Resolution 143, 1960 that called for the peaceful withdrawal of Belgium troops was paramount. For the rest of the permanent five (P5), withdrawal was contingent on the next operative paragraph, which called on ONUC to assist the Government in providing law and order.[60] In this view, Belgium would withdraw only after law and order were restored. East–West tensions were built into the mission from the start.

In August, an additional southern province, South Kasai, declared independence under the leadership of Albert Kalonji. As internal conflict deepened, the UN mission faced difficult questions on how to proceed. ONUC was initiated in response to external (Belgian) interference. The formal Belgian intervention

[55] Russell 1966, 73.
[56] Russell 1966, 73–74.
[57] Russell 1966, 73.
[58] Aksu 2003, 101.
[59] Aksu 2003, 101.
[60] Aksu 2003, 102–103.

ended in September, but the Central Government now faced secessionist movements, and in Katanga, an informal Belgian presence continued. Hammarskjöld's position was that the UN should be involved only in upholding Congo's independence against external threats (Belgium) and should not take a position in internal matters (i.e., the secessionist movements). The USSR, and of course the Central Government in Congo, took the position that ONUC should assist the Central Government in restoring order vis-à-vis secessionists. Dissatisfied with the UN's neutral position on internal parties, the Soviet Union began providing direct military assistance to the Central Government in mid-August.[61] The situation deteriorated further in September, when President Kasavubu (favored by the West) dismissed Prime Minister Lumumba (favored by the Soviet Union) followed by a coup d'état by Joseph Mabuto. Kasavubu cooperated with the new regime, Lumumba was removed, and the Soviet Mission in Leopoldville was closed.

At this stage, even tenuous agreement on ambiguous text was elusive at the UNSC. With the UNSC paralyzed by disagreement, the matter was referred (controversially) to the General Assembly, as in the UNEF case. The GA passed a resolution authorizing the Secretary-General to continue "to assist the Central Government of the Congo in the restoration and maintenance of law and order throughout the territory of the Republic of the Congo and to safeguard its unity, territorial integrity, and political independence in the interests of international peace and security."[62] The Soviet Union voted against the resolution and France abstained. When the regular session of the General Assembly began, the member states voted on who would be seated to represent the Congo. Kasavubu, favored by the Americans and the UK, won out. As Aksu writes, "In effect, the Mobutu regime had been legitimated by the UN."[63] As time went on, the situation in the Congo did not simplify, and France and the Soviet Union continued to abstain from votes. Going far beyond even the "revolutionary" UNEF, the Congo mission involved "an unprecedented range of military and civilian responsibilities."[64] Harland Cleveland, the US Under Secretary of State for International Organization Affairs, noted in a State Department policy memo at the time that with ONUC, "the UN moved into an area of operational magnitude which placed major new strains on the organization."[65] At its height, the mission included 19,828 peacekeeping troops, by far the largest of any UN mission to date.

[61] Aksu 2003, 108.
[62] Aksu 2003, 111.
[63] Aksu 2003, 112.
[64] West 1961, 603.
[65] Foreign Relations of the United States, 1961–63. Volume XXV, Organization of Foreign Policy; Information Policy; United Nations; Scientific Matters. Doc. 206. Memorandum from the Assistant Secretary of State for International Organizations Affairs (Cleveland) to the Director of the Arms Control and Disarmament Agency (Foster). Washington, May 24, 1962. National Archives and Records Administration, RG 59, IO Files.

It also cost over 400 million dollars.[66] Taken together, the annual budgets of UNEF and ONUC cost twice the regular budget of the United Nations. Prior to UNEF, General Assembly practice treated peacekeeping expenses as regular expenses. That meant that peacekeeping costs were "expenses of the Organization" under Article 17 that "shall be borne by the member states as apportioned by the Assembly." But consistent with Russell's analysis, many saw UNEF, and ONUC even more so, to be different from earlier missions not only in degree but in kind. The costs involved in previous missions (e.g., UNTSO) were modest and included a small number of unarmed observers rather than thousands of armed troops. To some eyes, UNEF and ONUC looked more like "enforcement actions" than regular activities. And though the Charter did not speak clearly on how enforcement actions would be funded, they clearly fell outside Article 17. At the Dumbarton Oaks Conference in 1944, the prevailing view among the USSR, US, and UK was that they (with the other members of the permanent five) would be primarily responsible for enforcement action.[67] At the San Francisco Conference in 1945, discussion emerged around other member states' obligations with regard to enforcement. Chapter VII, Article 43 reflects this discussion: member states are obligated "to make available to the Security Council, on its call and in accordance with a special agreement or agreements, armed forces, assistance, and facilities including rights of passage, necessary for the purpose of maintaining international peace and security."[68]

But if UNEF and ONUC were not the expenses anticipated by the drafters of Article 17, neither were they exactly the enforcement actions envisioned by the drafters of Article 43. UNEF and ONUC were not the joint military missions discussed at Dumbarton Oaks or San Francisco, they were international missions under the UN flag. Further, the system of special agreements outlined and anticipated by Article 43 to support those missions had never been approved.[69] In short, it was hard to say how the UN was supposed to pay for missions like UNEF and ONUC because the Charter did not anticipate those missions. Despite this lacuna, the General Assembly had assumed its normal role as a financial authority. It passed and continued to pass budgets to support UNEF and ONUC. It allocated dues to support the missions, first on the normal scale of assessments, and later on an amended scale that provided rebates for developing states.

The Soviet Union and France, along with many states with smaller assessments, refused to pay dues stemming from UNEF and ONUC. Poor states argued the payments were simply too costly, but others contested the legitimacy and legality of the missions. The financial crisis produced was acute. By 1965, cash reserves

[66] Fleming 2015, 257.
[67] See Chapter 3.
[68] United Nations Charter. Chapter VII, Article 43.
[69] Hogg 1962, 1234.

at the UN in New York fell below $100,000. To keep the lights on, the Secretary-General borrowed $1 million from the UN Special Fund and alerted the US that more borrowing would occur if states in arrears did not pay their dues.[70]

The United States and most other Western European powers remained steadfast in their position that the costs of ONUC and UNEF were subject to mandatory assessment. Between 1960 and 1965 the United States and the UN Secretary-General pursued many strategies to encourage more member states, including the Soviet Union and France, to pay their assigned dues. Much of the late-game strategy hinged on what they hoped would be a favorable advisory opinion from the International Court of Justice (ICJ) on whether the costs of UNEF and ONUC constituted "expenses of the Organization" under Article 17, paragraph 2 of the Charter. Such an opinion, the Americans thought, would persuade some states to pay up. If member states persisted in withholding, they also hoped that a favorable opinion would persuade the General Assembly to invoke Article 19 of the Charter to suspend the vote of any member state whose arrears exceeded two full years' dues.

Article 17's Permissiveness

On the question of whether the expenses of ONUC and UNEF constitute "expenses of the Organization," the discussion of Articles 17 and 43 indicates that Charter rules are permissive leaving them subject to multiple and divergent, plausible interpretations. The ICJ case received written statements from twenty states, nine of which participated in oral arguments. Those seeking an affirmative answer on the question of whether UNEF and ONUC were "expenses of the Organization" argued that the justices need only look to the plain meaning of the text of Article 17. This argument is exemplified in the first part of Abram Chayes' oral statement to the Court on behalf of the United States:

> The argument for an affirmative answer is straightforward: There is only one article in the Charter dealing with financial obligations of Members, Article 17, paragraph 2. It provides: "The expenses of the Organization shall be borne by the Members as apportioned by the General Assembly." It vests the Organization the power, by resolution of the General Assembly apportioning and assessing expenses, to require Member states to pay charges lawfully incurred. This is the meaning, and the whole meaning of Article 17. It is the plain meaning of the text; it coincides with the intention of the framers of the Charter evidenced in the

---

[70] LBJ Archives. Austin, TX. Incoming Telegram. Department of State. Limited Official Use. From: USUN NEWYORK. TO: SECSTATE WASHDC. Subject: UN Borrowing from Special Fund. April 16, 1965. 7:00 p.m.

preparatory work; it is reinforced by the unbroken practice of the Organization under the Charter (...).[71]

On the plain meaning of the text, it was hard to argue with Chayes and others who made similar arguments. Article 17 is the only place the Charter explicitly deals with funding. The Preparatory Works from San Francisco also show that the only revision to the Dumbarton Oaks Proposals version of Article 17 was intended to clarify that states indeed had a legal obligation to pay the Organization's expenses.[72] It was also true that General Assembly practice was consistent with the US reading of Article 17; despite opposition, a majority of member states had passed resolutions to allocate assessments to fund UNEF and ONUC. On the other hand, the claim that the plain meaning "coincides with the intention of the framers of the Charter" is vulnerable to dispute. If one regards ONUC and UNEF as enforcement actions—hardly an implausible claim given their robust military nature—it is clear that UN architects did *not* intend their costs to fall under Article 17.

At the San Francisco Conference, substantive work was divided up into Commissions and each Commission's work was divided across various committees. Commission III dealt with the Security Council, and Commission III, Committee 3 handled enforcement arrangements. This division of labor was functionally helpful, but issues sometimes implicated more than one UN body, for example, the Security Council and the General Assembly. In these instances, cross-commission cooperation was necessary and so consultations between committees and commissions became common practice. Tellingly, during Committee 3's discussions of the costs of enforcement action, there was never a suggestion that the Committee reach out to consult with Commission II, which dealt with the General Assembly and its financial authority.[73] Instead, Committee 3 discussion made clear that the costs of enforcement action were to be covered by Special Agreements between the Security Council and individual member states (these would ultimately be outlined in Article 43 of the Charter). The US, Soviet Union, and other major powers expected to carry out most enforcement action themselves,[74] but other

[71] Oral Statement of Mr. Abram Chayes, Representing the Government of the United States of America at the Public Hearing of May 21, 1962, Afternoon. *Certain Expenses* ICJ.

[72] UNCIO. Restricted. Doc. 1094. II/1/40 June 19, 1945. Commission II. General Assembly Committee 1. Structure and Procedures. Summary Report of Fifteenth Meeting of Committee II/1. Veterans Building, Room 303. June 18, 1945. 8:30 p.m. The oral statement of Mr. Evensen (Norway) during the *Certain Expenses* case emphasized this point.

[73] See documents in United Nations Conference on International Organization. Commission III Security Council. Committee 3, Enforcement Actions.

[74] E.g., Dulles downplayed the importance of special agreements to deal with enforcement action in meetings held during the San Francisco conference: "Mr. Dulles pointed out that in any event the main burden of enforcement action would presumably rest on the major powers." Foreign Relations of The United States: Diplomatic Papers, 1945, General: The United Nations, Volume I. RSC Lot 60–D 224, Box 96: US Cr. Min. 39 *Minutes of the Thirty-Ninth Meeting of the United States Delegation, Held at San Francisco, Friday, May 18, 1945, 6 p.m.*

member state representatives were concerned that Article 43 agreements would create obligations that involved excessive costs. Concerned at the prospect of having to pay some share of enforcement action, South Africa offered an amendment seconded by Iran (and later rejected), that would specify that "aggressor nations should pay the costs of enforcement action taken against them."[75] Later, during a US delegation meeting, John Hickerson explained that the South Africans "took this amendment very seriously." To this, Senator Vandenberg "said he had assumed that it was generally understood that all costs [of enforcement action] were to be charged to us."[76]

Interventions from the Canadian delegate at San Francisco are perhaps most helpful in clarifying that the costs of enforcement were not understood to fall under Article 17.[77] Twice bringing Committee 3's attention back to the question of costs, the Canadian delegate stated that:

he was of the opinion that the language of paragraphs 10 and 11 taken together would permit arrangements to be made for sharing the costs of enforcement action among the members if this proved to be desirable. Otherwise, an inequitable financial burden might be placed on certain members who were acting on behalf of the Organization. If this interpretation was not opposed by one of the sponsoring governments he would be satisfied to have it placed on record without further discussion.[78]

This was hardly a precise statement on how enforcement action would actually be paid for, but it does make clear that Article 17 was not viewed to be relevant.

This is exactly the argument made by legal counsel for the Soviet Union, Mr. G.I. Tunkin, to the ICJ in 1964. He noted that "the province of Article 17 of the Charter must be drawn not from the analysis of this single Article, but from the analysis of the relevant provisions of the Charter as a whole. The reason for this is that a general rule does not exclude the possibility of a particular rule or rules relating to specific situations." Tunkin labeled the special agreements outlined in Article 43 as

---

[75] United Nations Conference on International Organization (UNCIO). Restricted. Doc. 649. III/3/34. May 28, 1945. Committee III. Security Council. Enforcement Arrangements. Summary Report of Fifteenth Meeting of Committee III/3.

[76] Foreign Relations of The United States: Diplomatic Papers, 1945, General: The United Nations, Volume I RSC Lot 60–D 224, Box 96: US Cr. Min. 46. Minutes of the Forty-Sixth Meeting of the United States Delegation. Held at San Francisco, Friday, May 18, 1945, 6 p.m.

[77] See: (1) UNCIO Restricted. Doc. 782 (English) III/3/41 June 4, 1945. Commission III Security Council. Committee 3. Enforcement Arrangements. Summary Report of Eighteenth Meeting of Committee III/3. Veteran's Building, Room 223, June 4, 1945, 10:35 a.m.; (2) UNCIO. Restricted. Doc 878 (English) III/3/45 June 9, 1945. Commission III Security Council. Committee 3. Enforcement Arrangements Summary Meeting of Nineteenth Meeting of Committee III/3, Veteran's Building, Room 303, June 8, 1945, 8:45 p.m.

[78] UNCIO. Restricted. Doc 878 (English) III/3/45 June 9, 1945. Commission III Security Council. Committee 3. Enforcement Arrangements Summary Meeting of Nineteenth Meeting of Committee III/3, Veteran's Building, Room 303, June 8, 1945, 8:45 p.m.

a *lex specialis* "which relates to expenditures for certain actions for the purpose of maintaining international peace and security."[79] He added, "If actions of the UN Emergency Force and the UN Operations in the Congo were undertaken and carried out in compliance with the provisions of the Charter, they would undoubtedly fall within the category of actions contemplated in Article 43 of the Charter."[80]

If UNEF and ONUC constituted enforcement actions, they faced another more fundamental legal problem. Unlike the somewhat broader category of "international peace and security" issues in which the General Assembly had a recognized, if secondary, role to play, enforcement actions were the sole purview of the UN Security Council. France and the Soviet Union held that the missions were illegal because their establishment (in the UNEF case) or continuance (in the ONUC case) had relied on the Assembly resolutions rather than those of the Council. Those member states held they could not be charged for illegal missions. This point warrants emphasis. At least on legal grounds, the Soviet Union and France were not challenging the integrity of the mandatory system writ large (i.e., they were not suggesting member states could withhold dues whenever they wanted for whatever reason they saw fit). Rather, they made the argument that the process used to authorize these missions was illegal. They further implied that in a legal process through the Security Council these would be enforcement actions, and enforcement actions fell outside of Article 17.

The ICJ was asked by the Assembly to rule only on the narrow question of whether the costs of UNEF and ONUC already authorized by the Assembly constituted expenses of the Organization under Article 17 paragraph 2 of the Charter, rather than the broader question of mission legality. Sidestepping such an important issue left the ICJ's *Certain Expenses* opinion vulnerable to contestation from detractors. On the narrow question, the ICJ found affirmatively that the costs of UNEF and ONUC were in fact expenses of the Organization. To arrive at this conclusion, the Court applied "the principle of subsequent practice," in which "settled practice" "is good presumptive evidence (and may in certain cases be virtually conclusive) of what the correct legal interpretation is (...)."[81] The Court relied especially on General Assembly practice. In response to the USSR's argument that only administrative expenses be treated as "expenses of the Organization," the majority noted that it was the "settled practice" of the Assembly to include non-administrative expenses in the regular budget.[82] The opinion further states, "The Court does not perceive any basis for challenging [that] settled practice."[83]

The member states had not precisely defined "expenses" as the Organization evolved away from the scope its architects envisioned, and agreeing on such text

---

[79] Oral statement of Mr. Tunkin (USSR). ICJ. *Certain Expenses*, 404.
[80] Oral Statement of Mr. Tunkin (USSR). ICJ. *Certain Expenses*.
[81] *Certain Expenses Advisory Opinion*, Separate Opinion of Judge Sir Gerald Fitzmaurice.
[82] *Certain Expenses Advisory Opinion, Majority*, p. 162.
[83] *Certain Expenses Advisory Opinion, Majority*, p. 162.

in writing would likely have been prohibitively difficult. Yet the ICJ identified GA funding resolutions as subsequent practice, and based on this, the Court interpreted "expenses of the Organization" broadly. The majority then rejected the argument that UNEF and ONUC were enforcement actions and so found Article 43 inapplicable, rejecting another of the Soviet Union's key claims.[84]

Two aspects of the decision illustrate how rules can be modified without a formal amendment process. First, the majority opinion affirmed and legitimated the Assembly's practice of allocating mandatory dues for robust military peacekeeping missions under the UN flag. The Prepared Works of the UN Charter indicate that such missions were not anticipated by UN architects, and in a counterfactual world where they had been, the evidence indicates that they would not have allocated the Assembly that power. On the contrary, it is likely it would have been confined to the Security Council. The majority in *Certain Expenses* advised that even when expenses included:

> expenditures for the maintenance of peace and security, which are not otherwise provided for, it is the General Assembly which has the authority to apportion the latter amounts among the Members. The provisions of the Charter which distribute functions and powers to the Security Council and to the General Assembly give no support to the view that such distribution excludes from the powers of the Assembly the power to provide for the financing of measures designed to maintain peace and security.[85]

In this way, the ICJ actually confirmed and expanded the mandatory system to include peacekeeping. The story of United Nations financing is primarily about a gradual shift away from multilateral control, but in the *Certain Expenses* case, the ICJ actually expanded the reach of the mandatory assessments system and its egalitarian multilateralism beyond what the designers intended. The ICJ did not equate all expenses of the Organization with the mandatory dues, carefully noting that expenses could be paid for through the normal scale of assessments, through some alternative scale, or, citing EPTA and the Special Fund as examples, through voluntary contributions.[86] But for the cases of immediate relevance, ONUC and UNEF, the important finding in the opinion was that the Assembly had the authority to do what it had done. Those resolutions had passed the Assembly, and as such states were now obligated to pay. This was a critical development that made modern peacekeeping with mandatory dues possible. But the decisions were not an unalloyed good for the mandatory system.

---

[84] *Certain Expenses Advisory Opinion, Majority*, p. 166. Two dissenting opinions indicated that they found ONUC and UNEF to be enforcement actions.

[85] *Certain Expenses Advisory Opinion, Majority*, p. 164.

[86] *Certain Expenses Advisory Opinion, Majority*, p. 160.

Member States' Response to the ICJ Opinion

The ICJ's advisory opinion was accepted with the adoption of a resolution in the General Assembly, but it did little to facilitate the collection of arrears from member states. From the perspective of the Soviet Union and France, which by 1965 owed $62 million and $17.7 million respectively, ONUC and UNEF remained illegal missions. The failure of the Assembly to request an ICJ opinion on the question of the missions' legality provided the rationale to reject its opinion on the narrow question. When payments for UNEF and ONUC were not forthcoming, the United States lobbied to invoke Article 19, which would suspend the vote of a member state when its arrears exceeded two years' worth of payments, a situation that would now apply to the Soviet Union. But the majority in the Assembly did not support the American plan. Some feared the Soviet Union would leave the United Nations if the Assembly voted to suspend their right to vote.[87] Others were concerned their own state might someday fall into significant arrears, and were worried by the precedent. The upshot was that the Soviet Union would not pay, and the Assembly would not levy any consequence.

From an American perspective, the Soviet Union's refusal to pay was problematic for reasons that went beyond the UN's precarious financial position. US funding for the UN was increasingly imperiled by the perception in Congress and among the US public that other countries, and especially the Soviet Union, did not pay their fair share. The view was becoming more widespread; that the Soviets were refusing to pay even their small share (relative to the US) only strengthened it.[88] The UN's use of contributions to the Special Fund to cope with inadequate funds in the regular budget increased Congressional reluctance. The contention of the Congress, which was not entirely without merit, was that US contributions to economic development programs were being reallocated to pay the Soviet Union's dues for UNEF and ONUC.

As in the first Contributions Committee meeting, it was not the amount of money per se that was problematic for US diplomats, it was the political problem that emerged when Congress perceived itself—rightly or wrongly—to be on the wrong side of inequitable international burden-sharing arrangements. To end the Article 19 crisis required the US to back down from its "no dues, no vote" position taken publicly by Dean Rusk, Harland Cleveland, and Adlai Stevenson during the Kennedy administration.[89] This delicate and thankless task was left

---

[87] "The United Nations: Conciliator Challenged." *Newsweek*, August 23, 1965. Papers of Arthur Goldberg. National Archives. Washington, DC. "Clearing the Slate at the U.N." *Business Week*, August 21, 1965; Department of State 1967, 108.

[88] Those holding this view failed to appreciate that the UN was being employed in ways the Soviet Union opposed for ends the US largely supported and often advocated. "Clearing the Slate at the U.N." *Business Week*, August 21, 1965.

[89] "The United Nations: The Conciliator Challenged." *Newsweek*, August 23, 1965. Goldberg Papers. National Archives. Washington, DC.

to Arthur Goldberg who left his lifetime appointment at the Supreme Court to become Lyndon Johnson's Ambassador to the United Nations in 1965.

More than even at the outset of the financial crisis in 1960, the UN membership was fully transformed by 1965, and the effects of that transformation were finally understood by Western states. This new General Assembly with 117 members could not be managed or controlled by the US and its Western allies. While backing down from its position was politically difficult, there was recognition that the Soviet precedent of withholding, and the insistence that peacekeeping be handled by the Security Council, was perhaps not contrary to US interests. A memorandum to McGeorge Bundy in October of 1964 noted that "occasions may arise in which we do not agree with the General Assembly and will not carry out its directives, and certainly we should expect this to be true of other states as well."[90] Of the US and like-minded delegations, *Newsweek* reported that: "... as they considered the new Afro-Asian majority in the Assembly, many Western statesmen began to see some virtue in the Soviet contention that the power to levy assessments for peace-keeping must be confined to the Security Council—where the big powers have veto."[91] Senator Frank Church of Idaho, who served as a member of the US Delegation to the 21st General Assembly and authored the Senate Report titled "The United Nations at 21," highlighted the same problem, focusing on what were then labeled "microstates." He noted the recent admission of the Maldives that had "a population of less than 100,000" that "can cast the same vote as the U.S." Church laid out the numbers to his fellow Senators as follows:

> Now, waiting in the wings, are said to be some 40 other tiny areas that are future targets for decolonization, and that may apply to become members of the United Nations. Already, the African bloc of nations in the U.N. comes to 36, with the former British protectorates of Bechuanaland and Basutoland, scheduled to be admitted when they get their independence in October. When the 36 African countries can manage to get the support of Asian members, they can muster 53 votes in the U.N. Assembly—a powerful bloc.[92]

Given the nature of the Assembly, Church reasoned that if the US found itself in the position the Soviet Union had (an increasingly plausible scenario), it would behave similarly.

---

[90] Memorandum, R.C. Bowman, to McGeorge Bundy, Spec. Asst. to the Pres. for Nat. Security Affairs. October 22, 1964. 2p. CONFIDENTIAL. Declassified Jan. 23, 1978. Johnson Library, NSF, Countries, United Nations, Memos—Miscellaneous, 11/63/11/64. Declassified Documents Online, Document ID Number: 1978070100149. http://www.history-lab.org.

[91] "The United Nations: The Conciliator Challenged." *Newsweek*, August 23, 1965. Papers of Arthur Goldberg. National Archives, Washington, DC.

[92] "United Nations at Twenty-One." Report to the Committee on Foreign Relations, United States Senate. By Senator Frank Church, Idaho. 90th Congress, 1st Session. February 1967.

Had we Americans put the shoe on the other foot, and assumed [a] possible U.N. peacekeeping venture in the future with which we found ourselves in strong disagreement—say, for example, a U.N. intervention to keep the peace in the Caribbean from which Castro were to somehow benefit—can anyone imagine an American President agreeing to pay our share of the expense, or Congress ever appropriating the money?[93]

Goldberg's creative means of backing down from the crisis involved articulating what became known as the "Goldberg Reservation." After asserting that the US would have preferred to see the General Assembly fulfill its duty to invoke Article 19 and hold Governments accountable for their obligations under the Charter, Goldberg stated:

> ... we [the US] must make it crystal clear that if any member can insist on making an exception to the principle of collective financial responsibility with respect to certain activities of the Organization, the United States reserves the same option to make exceptions if, in our view, strong and compelling reasons exist for doing so. There can be no double standard among the members of the Organization.[94]

At the time, the Goldberg Reservation was understood primarily as a face-saving device. News reports noted that while "the U.S. reserves the same option as other members to reject U.N. assessments (...) in fact the [Johnson] Administration has no intention of doing so."[95] But in the wake of an ostensibly clear defeat, the US had found a quasi-legal rationale to withhold dues from the UN, in a context in which it was increasingly clear it might wish to do so. The Goldberg Reservation was informed by other states' practice of withholding dues for UN activities they disagreed with and the General Assembly's practice (non-behavior) of not invoking Article 19 despite Soviet arrears. But few emphasize that Goldberg's statement, whether intended or not, went beyond the legal arguments made by France and the Soviet Union. Those states emphasized that mandatory assessments could not be charged for ONUC and UNEF because those missions relied on illegal resolutions. The same emphasis on keeping all aspects of peacekeeping under the sole purview of the Security Council is similarly reflected in Senator Church's statement above. The Goldberg Reservation was broader, expanding beyond the argument articulated by the Soviet Union and France. It did not state that the US could withhold if a peacekeeping mission was established by the General Assembly or if it determined that processes required by the Charter were violated. It did not distinguish

---

[93] "United Nations at Twenty-One." Report to the Committee on Foreign Relations, United States Senate. By Senator Frank Church, Idaho. 90th Congress, 1st Session. February 1967. 23–24.
[94] Goldberg, Arthur. 1965. "Statement by Ambassador Goldberg, US Representative to the United Nations, as Delivered in the Special Committee on Peacekeeping Operations," August 16, 1965. International Legal Materials, 1000-03.
[95] "Clearing the Slate at the U.N." Business Week, August 21, 1965.

between peacekeeping and the regular UN budget. Rather, it said the US could withhold mandatory dues "if, in our view, strong and compelling reasons exist for doing so." This represented a threat to the integrity of the mandatory funding system writ large. Fifteen years later, during Ronald Reagan's presidency, it would be used to justify systematic withholding from the regular budget.

Taking Stock of Gradual Change in 1965

As the United Nations muddled through the turbulent 1960s, three developments in UN operations that were unforeseen in 1945 had firmly taken hold. Decolonization had transformed the General Assembly. When Ambassador Goldberg made his statement on Article 19, Singapore had just gained independence and would soon become the 117th member of the United Nations. Enforcement action as envisioned at Dumbarton Oaks had never materialized, but the practice of international peacekeeping had. Operational programs in economic and social development were well-established and growing.

For wealthy states who paid for the bulk of UN expenses, decolonization had significant implications for peacekeeping and economic and social development. General Assembly control of the regular budget, and now, according to ICJ opinion and General Assembly practice, the peacekeeping budgets, was regarded somewhat warily. The Article 19 crisis was dominated by an East–West, Cold War narrative, but the precedent of withholding by the USSR and France and the subsequent statement from Ambassador Goldberg were important to the new North–South dynamic at the UN. With these actions and statements, the great powers signaled that their commitment to the mandatory funding system had limits. On the social and economic development front, the shift from the mandatory system to voluntary contributions had been made. The original "regular" TA program persisted in the regular budget, but its size was overwhelmed by voluntary programs that expanded its work. Here, too, the positions of East and West were more aligned than in the UN's early years. The US was now disinclined to support new mandatory obligations and no doubt thankful the Soviet Union had limited regular budget activities to the extent it had in the early years.

The implications for the UN's multilateral character appeared mixed. Multilateral bodies continued to govern both mandatory dues and voluntary contributions. But the ability of those multilateral bodies to compel financial support was weakening on two fronts. States had withheld dues without punishment, and the United States had asserted its right to do so in the wake of others' withholding. This undoubtedly weakened the strength of General Assembly decisions on financial matters. The multilateral bodies of the Special Fund, EPTA, and other similar funds passed budgets, determined program priorities, and even set aspirational financial goals for states to meet. But voluntary funding rules meant multilateral decisions could not compel financial support.

Late in the period considered here, between 1960 and 1966, wealthy states' frustrations about funding evolved from criticism that focused on costs, toward more political concerns about how money was spent.[96] For France and the USSR, this applied to peacekeeping with dues allocated by the Assembly. For the United States, this applied to voluntary contributions being used by the Special Fund, UNICEF, and other UN programs for projects in Cuba. Especially in the latter case, an incremental change to voluntary funding rules to allow donor earmarks would be quite attractive. Yet it was not the US, nor the Soviet Union or France, who proposed permissive earmark rules. As Chapter 5 will demonstrate, that job was instead done by some of the UN's most ardent supporters.

References

Aksu, Eşref. 2003. *The United Nations, Intra-state Peacekeeping and Normative Change.* Manchester, United Kingdom: Manchester University Press.
Archibald, James E. 2004. "Pledges of Voluntary Contributions to the United Nations by Member States: Establishing and Enforcing Legal Obligations." George Washington International Law Review 36(2): 317–376.
Benjamin, Bret. 2015. "Bookend to Bandung: The New International Economic Order and the Antinomies of the Bandung Era." *Humanity: An International Journal of Human Rights, Humanitarianism, and Development* 6(1): 33–46.
Department of State. 1967. "United States Participation in the United Nations: Report by the President to the Congress for the Year 1965." United States, Division of Publications.
Fleming, Keith. 2015. "A Ringside View of Contemporary History in the Making" (1950–1961). *The World is Our Parish: John King Gordon, 1900–1989: An Intellectual Biography.* Toronto, Canada: University of Toronto Press.
Gibson, J. Douglas. 1967. "The Financial Problem of the United Nations." *International Journal* 22(2): 182–194.
Graham, Erin R. 2017. "The Institutional Design of Funding Rules at International Organizations: Explaining the Transformation in Financing the United Nations." *European Journal of International Relations* 23(2): 365–390.
Graham, Erin R., and Alexandria Serdaru. 2020. "Power, Control, and the Logic of Substitution in Institutional Design: The Case of International Climate Finance." *International Organization* 74(4): 671–706.
Grigorescu, Alexandru. 2015. *Democratic Intergovernmental Organizations? Normative Pressures and Decision-making Rules.* New York, NY: Cambridge University Press.
Hogg, James Fergusson. 1962. "Peace-Keeping Costs and Charter Obligations—Implications of the International Court of Justice Decision on Certain Expenses of the United Nations." *Columbia Law Review* 62(7): 1230–1263.

[96] Graham 2017.

Jacobson, Harold K. 1963. *The USSR and the UN's Economic and Social Activity.* Notre Dame, IN: University of Notre Dame Press.

Rubinstein, Alvin Z. 1964. *Soviets in International Organizations: Changing Policy toward Developing Countries, 1953–1963.* Princeton, NJ: Princeton University Press.

Russell, Ruth B. 1966. "United Nations Financing and the Law of the Charter." *Columbia Journal of Transnational Law* 5: 68–95.

West, Robert L. 1961. "The United Nations and the Congo Financial Crisis: Lessons of the First Year. *International Organization* 15(4): 603–617.

5

Creative Cracks in Multilateralism

After an extended negotiation, the Expanded Program of Technical Assistance (EPTA) and the Special Fund merged in 1966 to become the flagship development assistance program at the UN: the United Nations Development Program (UNDP). The financial rules of EPTA and the Special Fund were reproduced in the initial UNDP design. But in fairly short order, in 1967, the new UNDP Governing Council adopted a policy that effectively lifted the prohibition on donor earmarks that had been in place at its predecessor institutions.[1] Without fanfare or even much notice, the Governing Council dislodged its exclusive authority over resource distribution. The near-term effects of the change were negligible; earmarks were used sparingly and so the Governing Council continued to control the vast majority of contributions coming through UNDP. But the institutional design now allowed for the Governing Council to lose that control. Some 25 years later, that process started in earnest when more states began to earmark contributions and the proportion of funds that many contributor countries earmarked increased. By the early 2000s, the UNDP Governing Council exercised control over only about 30 percent of financial contributions received by UNDP. Egalitarian multilateralism continued to characterize voting, but those votes no longer controlled resources, which were instead governed by a multitude of contracts negotiated between donors and the UN.

This chapter illustrates implications that follow from the framework's assumptions regarding uncertainty, rule permissiveness, and creative agency. With regard to uncertainty, the Netherlands and the UN Office of Legal Affairs, the two actors with the most responsibility for actively introducing earmarked contributions to UNDP, did not intend to transform UN governance. They had distinct, shorter-term aims in mind. The Government of the Netherlands' proximate aim was to ease UNDP negotiations troubled by Cold War tensions. The intent of the Office of Legal Affairs was to solve a technical, legal problem on a request from the UNDP Executive Director. Three features of rule change noted in Chapter 2 rendered the transformational potential of permissive earmark rules difficult to foresee. First, among member states, funding rules continued to be understood as marginal to the production or practice of multilateral governance. By contrast, representation and voting rules were understood to be part and parcel of, and indeed essential

---

[1] United Nations Development Program 1967; Graham 2017.

Transforming International Institutions. Erin R. Graham, Oxford University Press. © Erin R. Graham (2023).
DOI: 10.1093/oso/9780198877936.003.0005

to, the production of egalitarian multilateralism. Both recipient and donor states fought for council seats to ensure their influence in joint decisions. But just as in the original design of the UN Charter, few states took interest in the nuance or complexity of different funding arrangements. Despite criticism of Soviet ruble policy on the grounds it undermined multilateralism, there is little evidence that states identified trust funds as posing a similar challenge to the UN's fundamental principles.

This blind spot was undoubtedly affected by a second permissive condition, that the actors who introduced permissive earmark rules were perceived as benign. Indeed, supporters of permissive earmarks came not from the Soviet Union or the United States—whose proposals likely would have been received with suspicion—but rather from among the UN's most ardent financial supporters, Sweden, Denmark, the Netherlands, and Norway. There was little reason to think these states intended to transform UN governance (the evidence indicates they did not), or, given their relatively small size, that they were capable of transforming UN governance.[2] A third permissive condition is also present: these changes were intended to allow supplementary funding for specific purposes rather than to replace unrestricted or unearmarked voluntary contributions. They were expected to remain small relative to other resources. These factors are useful in understanding why layering permissive earmark rules was not especially contentious or concerning at the time.

The case also usefully demonstrates how creative actors access rule permissiveness to create something new. Faced with the predicament of how to make the Netherlands' contribution compliant with UNDP rules, the UN Office of Legal Affairs repurposed a financial rule that existed elsewhere on the UN books. It allowed the Secretary-General to create trust funds for special purposes. The rule was redeployed to accept contributions to be distributed by the UNDP Executive Director. The creative repurposing was consolidated into UNDP rules in an ostensibly unremarkable resolution in 1967.

All of these characteristics point to the subterranean nature of transformational change in institutions. This chapter identifies the source of early inquiries about earmarking and the intentions and interests of those involved. It then traces the process that led to the adoption of permissive earmark rules at UNDP in 1967, followed by a summary of similar changes made across UN programs in the 1960s into the 1970s. The chapter concludes by taking stock of the state of gradual change as 1980 approaches and the transformational potential of permissive earmark rules is coming into view.

---

[2] Overseas Development Institute 1968, 31–43.

Early Inquiries about Earmarks

David Owen of the United Kingdom served as the chairman of the United Nations Technical Assistance Board (TAB), a body that included the heads of the UN Specialized Agencies that received money to implement projects approved by EPTA. In 1954, he reported to UN Secretary-General Dag Hammarskjöld about private discussions that occurred at a recent meeting of the Nordic Council. His memo centered on Denmark's nascent proposal to encourage the UN to allow donors to earmark their contributions to EPTA. He reported:

> the Danish Government intended to put forward some far-reaching leading suggestions at the forthcoming meeting of European National Committees in Rome next week (23rd and 24th September). In brief, the suggestion was that Governments should, under carefully stated conditions, be permitted to make contributions to the Special Account ear-marked for special purposes.[3]

Owen went on to convey to Hammarskjöld that he "was sympathetic to this line of development, provided that we can safeguard the existence of a freely useable multilateral account." But, he noted, "The matter is so obviously one of great delicacy that I have had no difficulty in persuading the Danish Government not to raise this publicly in Rome, but to discuss it with me in a private meeting to which the other two Scandinavian delegations, and perhaps one or two others known to be interested might be invited."[4]

In the mid-1950s, the controversy and complaints surrounding the Soviet practice of providing contributions in non-convertible rubles, hence exercising a *de facto* earmark, explains why the Danish proposal qualified as "one of great delicacy." As Chapter 4 showed, the USSR was criticized for intentionally breaching EPTA's multilateral character by providing its support in non-convertible currency. The Soviet Union violated the spirit of EPTA's multilateralism, but not the letter of the law, since convertible currencies were encouraged rather than required.[5] Rubles could be used only to pay Soviet experts or to purchase Soviet equipment, which allowed the USSR to control which projects and countries

---

[3] Papers of David Owen. Columbia University. New York, NY. Technical Assistance Board. United Nations, New York. Memorandum. To: The Secretary-General, United Nations. From: David Owen, Executive Chairman, Technical Assistance Board. September 15, 1954. Notes on some recent developments on the technical assistance front.

[4] Papers of David Owen. Columbia University. New York, NY. Technical Assistance Board. United Nations, New York. Memorandum. To: The Secretary-General, United Nations. From: David Owen, Executive Chairman, Technical Assistance Board. September 15, 1954. Notes on some recent developments on the technical assistance front. Underline original.

[5] On law evasion, see Búzás 2017.

received their funds without technically specifying any restriction on contributions. The Danish Government was proposing that funding rules be altered to legalize a related behavior under "carefully specified conditions."

The Danish proposal was not accommodated at the time. EPTA rules were not altered to allow earmarks, and as Chapter 4 demonstrates, neither were they incorporated in the Special Fund's design when it was established in 1958. As negotiations started on the EPTA and Special Fund merger in the mid-1960s, the issue would eventually resurface. But in a fashion reminiscent of the great powers' inattention to funding rules in the design of the Charter, funding rules remained a marginal topic in UNDP design negotiations. For developed and developing states alike, the primary points of contention revolved around representation rights. In a system where multilateral decision-making was both primary and assumed, representation was the means to influence.

The strength of one-country-one-vote within the UN system is such that the contested design question was not about whether voting rules might be weighted, but simply about how many seats the council would include. Member states now clearly fell into the category of net-donor or net-recipient, and debate emerged over whether strict "parity" was required in allocating seats between the two groups, or whether "balanced representation," which was more flexible, would do.[6] The Americans wanted a small council of no more than 27 members. While some key donors like the United Kingdom agreed,[7] others, including the Netherlands and Belgium indicated they would insist on parity if the council included fewer than 31 seats. US memos convey the position of the Dutch representative (Lubbers) and in doing so the importance attached to representation among some donor states: "Particularly in light of Scandinavian ambitions, council according to him must be of size and composition which would permit both Dutch and Belgian participation. He could contemplate governing council of 32 with 15 donors and 17 beneficiaries."[8]

Belgium's argument in favor of strict parity went a step further by insisting that representation rights would likely affect donors' willingness to provide funds. Directing his comments to the developing countries at an ECOSOC meeting, the Belgian delegate, M.J. Woulbroun noted, "the membership formula of nineteen developing countries and seventeen developed countries that had been put forward by the developing country group might satisfy their *amour propre* but would

[6] LBJ Archives, Austin, TX. Incoming Telegram. Department of State. Limited Official Use. From: USUN New York. To: RUEHCR/SECSTATE WASH DC 1086. Subject: GA Consideration of SF-EPTA Merger. October 4, 1965.

[7] LBJ Archives, Austin, TX. Incoming Telegram. Department of State. Limited Official Use. From USUN New York. To: RUEHCR/SECSTATE WASH DC 1086. Subject: GA Consideration of SF-EPTA Merger. October 4, 1965; Economic and Social Council 1966.

[8] LBJ Archives, Austin, TX. Incoming Telegram. Department of State. Limited Official Use. From: USUN New York. To: RUEHCR/SECSTATE WASH DC 1086. Subject: GA Consideration of SF-EPTA Merger. October 4, 1965.

hardly benefit them if the rate of increase of funds available for the new Program were decreased."[9]

Strict *parity* was politically contentious; developing states favored "balanced representation," which would favor net-recipients.[10] A larger, 32 seat council was also more acceptable to developing states who, like the donors, had intra-group concerns about how to distribute seats. In a memo to the State Department, Ambassador Goldberg conveyed that Latin American and Asian member states were frustrated with African voting "domination" among developing countries and wanted to ensure they had adequate seats relative to the African group.[11] For their part, the Soviet Union lobbied for a guaranteed number of socialist states on the new council.[12] The language in the resolution adopted by the General Assembly called for "equitable and balanced representation" between the contributor and beneficiary countries, but also provided guidance for handling intra-group dynamics. On the side of economically advanced states the resolution called for giving "due regard for their level of contribution to the UN Development Program." For developing states, it called for the need for "suitable regional representation."[13]

The negotiating action centered on representation and council size, while funding rule design received far less attention. One reason is that in a system in which resources are allocated by multilateral decision—as they had always been at the UN—a seat at the table is necessary to influence resource allocation. Another reason is that the United States had made its substantial funding pledge to the new Program contingent on the understanding that EPTA and Special Fund rules would remain intact at UNDP. The US made clear during negotiations that if rules were changed, the US pledge might be reconsidered.[14] When amendments unfavorable to US preferences arose in discussion, the US delegate, James Roosevelt, reminded others "that the funds pledged by his government to the Special Fund and EPTA were dependent on the maintenance of current policies and procedures of the two programs."[15] The US knew its seat on the governing council was assured whatever the size, and so left that issue to others with stronger preferences. On other matters, the contingency of the US pledge was an effective tool to facilitate negotiation and to bias negotiations toward the status quo.

---

[9] Economic and Social Council 1966, 329.

[10] In practice, a small number of net-recipients, especially India, were also important donors. The donor states liked including such states because they tended to be more concerned with the efficient use of funds.

[11] LBJ Archives, Austin TX. Incoming Telegram. Department of State. Limited Official Use. From: USUN New York. To: SECSTATE WASHDC 1320. GA-EPTA-Special Fund Merger. October 14, 1965.

[12] Economic and Social Council 1966, 328–329.

[13] General Assembly Resolution A/RES/2029 (XX) 1965. Consolidation of the Special Fund and the Expanded Programme of Technical Assistance in a United Nations Development Programme. https://undocs.org/en/A/RES/2029(XX).

[14] Economic and Social Council 1966, 330.

[15] Economic and Social Council 1966, 330.

The status quo at EPTA and the Special Fund prohibited donors from placing any restrictions on contributions, and the US continued to object to Soviet contribution policies. At the same time, the Nordic Council and the Special Fund Administrator had quietly discussed the Danish proposal to allow earmarks a few years before. During UNDP negotiations, the US learned of a similar proposal from Sweden. Ambassador Arthur Goldberg reported:

At a luncheon with Bolin and Larsson (Sweden), MISOFFS learned that while Swedes would apparently favor separate fund for industrial development purposes, they would be willing to accept an earmarking within UNDP. Swedes also feel that developed countries should take some initiative during current GA session. They will consult us on content of initiative during next few days.[16]

The language of "an earmarking" indicates a design similar to contemporary trust funds that allow donors to select among multiple funding windows, for example, expert assistance, or industrial development. The proposal provides evidence that among the Nordic states there was a sustained interest in more permissive earmark policies, but the mention of *industrial development* is noteworthy for another reason.

Like the creation of the Special Fund, the establishment of UNDP was viewed by many developing states as a decidedly second-best institution. While supporting the merger negotiations, they continued to lobby for a major capital development fund at the United Nations to invest in industrial development. Specifically, money would be used to invest in heavy industries viewed by many as the lifeblood of industrialization, like mining, steel, electric, and chemical industries.[17] The developing world envisioned an institution with the financial resources of the World Bank, offering highly concessional loans or grants, like the International Development Agency (IDA) that had been established in 1960, but with UN governance—specifically with voting and representation rights more favorable to recipients. From the developing states' perspective, IBRD interest rates were too high, IDA (and IBRD) weighted voting rules biased decisions in favor of donors, and the Bank was infused with the liberal economic ideology of the West.

But the practice, and even the language, of "industrial development" was politicized at the UN by the Cold War. Industrial development meant state-led development, a practice that conflicted with the US liberal economic vision. The idea that state-led investment in heavy industry should be prioritized was associated with the Soviet Union and the emerging New International Economic Order

---

[16] LBJ Archives, Austin, TX. Incoming Telegram. Department of State. Limited Official Use. From: USUN New York. To: SECSTATE WASH DC 1420. Subject: Industrial Development. October 19, 1965. 7:36 p.m.

[17] This reflected domestic development priorities in the USSR as well, see Kaser 1966.

(NIEO).[18] Before the USSR's partial embrace of UN development programs in 1953, their critique of technical assistance was based in part on the fact that UN programs did *not* invest in heavy industry and as such, in their view, would not promote industrialization.[19] When the USSR changed course to make modest contributions after Stalin's death, they persisted in the argument that programs should be directed toward capital investments. Within the Special Fund, the USSR and Yugoslavia were "constant proponents of pilot projects."[20] These projects sat "on the borderline of actual 'investment'" rather than pre-investment activities.[21]

But it was the US rather than the Soviet Union that supplied the lion's share of UN funding, and the US view was that public funds should be used for "pre-investment" to create conditions to attract and catalyze private investment in developing states.[22] The timeline of the UNDP merger overlapped with debate and negotiation over the UN Capital Development Fund and UN Industrial Development Organization (UNIDO), and the period in which the first UN Conference on Trade and Development (UNCTAD) was held. During his opening speech to that conference, and after acknowledging that too little private investment flowed to too many developing countries, US Under Secretary of State George Ball indicated the US position on UN aid with the following question:

> Would it not be useful to examine carefully the experience of countries that have been attracting a flow of private foreign investment? Would it not also be useful to study the new techniques, new attitudes, and new procedures that have arisen in this field in response to the conditions of this century?[23]

Ball's questions indicated the broad contours of the American view: developing states should work to provide the conditions that would attract private investment; multilateral UN assistance should be used to help them do so. He further summarized the US view on how aid could be usefully applied:

> First, as a supplemental source of long-term capital for certain projects that will not produce immediate returns but which are a necessary base for other projects and a stimulant to the development process as a whole;

---

[18] Kaser 1966, especially 64, 71. On the role of these ideas in the NIEO, see Murphy 1983.
[19] Rubinstein 1964.
[20] Manzer 1964, 781.
[21] Manzer 1964, 781.
[22] Manno 1966, 45; Economic and Social Council. International Organization. 1962. 16(4): 835–844. (33rd session of ECOSOC), 347; "Common problems of Industrial and Developing Countries" Statement by Under Secretary Ball. Made before the United Nations Conference on Trade and Development at Geneva, Switzerland on March 25 (press release 133), 638–639.
[23] "Common problems of Industrial and Developing Countries" Statement by Under Secretary Ball. Made before the United Nations Conference on Trade and Development at Geneva, Switzerland on March 25 (press release 133), 638–639.

Second, as a source of capital to finance imports of materials and equipment that could otherwise become serious production bottlenecks in a situation of foreign exchange stringency;

Third, as a source of seed capital that can stimulate the mobilization and effective use of capital from internal sources.

We believe, in short, that foreign aid, will play an essential role if it exercises the catalytic effect it is designed to produce.[24]

In sum, international aid was to be supplemental, or to mobilize and catalyze additional funds whether public or private. This position was part and parcel of US liberal economic ideology, but it also reflected the US position as the largest provider of UN assistance. Major capital investments were expensive and donors were wary of new capital development funds, in part for that reason. The "large potential donors," including France and the United Kingdom, opposed a General Assembly resolution in 1963 to transform the Special Fund into a Capital Development Fund,[25] and Canada, Denmark, France, the Netherlands, United Kingdom, and the US had previously refused to participate in drafting a statute to establish the institution separately.[26] The USSR continued to advocate for a capital development fund and for similar additions, but as the delegate of the United Kingdom not-so-subtly put it: "Among the developed countries the most vocal in their support of such a fund were not conspicuous supporters of any other multilateral financial institutions."[27] The Soviet Union lobbied for the UN to expand its voluntary aid programs but never chose to foot the bill.

Both ideology and lopsided cost-sharing made industrial development an obstacle to negotiations. During the EPTA–Special Fund merger negotiations the Soviet Union submitted amendments to the proposal, stating that the consolidation of EPTA and the Special Fund "represented a step toward the establishment of the UN capital development fund," that UNDP would "emphasize the preeminent importance of industrial development," and that the "new Governing Council" would "consider ways of apportioning UNDP funds for investment activities."[28] The US responded simply that it would not provide funds if the amendments were adopted.[29]

In the midst of politicized debate over industrial policy, small but important donors, including Sweden and the Netherlands, held more moderate positions.

---

[24] Common problems of Industrial and Developing Countries" Statement by Under Secretary Ball. Made before the United Nations Conference on Trade and Development at Geneva, Switzerland on March 25 (press release 133), 639.
[25] Manno 1966, 46.
[26] Manno 1966, 46.
[27] Economic and Social Council 1966, 334.
[28] Economic and Social Council 1966, 330.
[29] Economic and Social Council, 1966, 328.

Like the US, they were concerned about the "absorptive capacity" of many developing states and voiced concerns that projects must be sound and conditions ripe for aid to be successful.[30] But they were not opposed to state-led industrial development in principle. Sweden's growing bilateral aid program was on the cusp of a major shift from public service investment to industrial development.[31] As their early proposal regarding industrial development demonstrates,[32] Sweden was open to creating a separate fund or a window within the Special Fund to support direct investment rather than pre-investment activity.

Sweden's position, shared by the Netherlands, opposed the establishment of new capital development mechanisms at the UN (like the US), but responded to developing states' demands and the Soviet position by supporting additional operational activities in the category of "special industrial services" under the new UNDP administrator.[33] This middle ground position was staked out by Sweden, the Netherlands, the UK, and Finland in a four-power draft resolution during negotiations, as an alternative to a draft from developing states, calling for the immediate establishment of a new bureaucracy to carry out industrial development.[34]

With merger negotiations ongoing, the Netherlands put its money behind the middle ground position, announcing in November of 1965 a contribution of 3 million guilders to UNDP that would be "earmarked for special industrial services." But EPTA and Special Fund rules clearly prohibited earmarks and UNDP negotiations anticipated no change in funding rules, leaving the status of the contribution unclear. The new UNDP Administrator sent the issue to the United Nations Office of Legal Affairs in December of 1965.[35] In issuing its request to Legal Affairs, UNDP noted that "in view of the conditions attached to it, the Netherlands' offer could not be accepted as a contribution to 'the resources' of either the Special Fund or the Expanded Programme of Technical Assistance."[36] UNDP's Director of the Division of Financial Management inquired whether the UNDP Administrator might "overcome the difficulty" by establishing a trust fund to disburse the resources on the terms specified by the Netherlands.[37] But based on its reading of EPTA and Special Fund rules, Legal Affairs found that the UNDP Administrator "would not seem to be vested with the formal authority to establish a trust fund." Based on this reading, they advised "it would not be legally possible to accept the

---

[30] Economic and Social Council 1966, 344, 355.

[31] Beckman 1979, 134ff.

[32] LBJ Archives, Austin, TX. Incoming Telegram. Department of State. Limited Official Use. From: USUN New York. To: SECSTATE WASH DC 1420. Subject: Industrial Development. October 19, 1965. 7:36 p.m.

[33] UN Yearbook 1965, 340. https://www.un.org/en/yearbook

[34] See UN Yearbook 1965, 339–340; Graham 2017, 383.

[35] UN Juridical Yearbook 1966, 234.

[36] UN Juridical Yearbook 1966, Chapter VI.A.12. Additional Pledge by the Netherlands, 234. https://legal.un.org/unjuridicalyearbook/

[37] UN Juridical Yearbook 1966, 234.

Netherlands contribution as a contribution to the UNDP to be credited to a trust fund set up by the [UNDP] administrator."[38]

But Legal Affairs advice did not end there. Instead, they looked beyond EPTA, The Special Fund, and the new UNDP's rules, to a set of financial regulations that provided the UN Secretary-General with the ability to accept "voluntary contributions, whether or not in cash (...) provided that the purposes for which the contributions are made are consistent with the policies, aims, and activities of the Organization ..."[39] The Secretary-General in the past had used this authority to accept money from non-state actors, like philanthropic agencies or non-governmental organizations.[40] These sums were typically in the tens of thousands of dollars and were usually provided to support seminars and meetings. For example, "The Population Council, Inc." served as the single donor for two trust funds operated by the Secretary-General. The first supported a population seminar for southern European countries in Athens, the second covered expenses for a seminar on census data in Santiago, Chile. Occasionally, but rarely, the dollar figures exceeded the tens of thousands as in the case of the Ford Foundation providing $335,648 for the United Nations Library in 1960.[41] These and similar examples were governed by financial regulation 7.3, which stated that such voluntary contributions accepted by the Secretary-General would be "treated as trust funds or special accounts."[42]

Based on resolutions passed by the Economic and Social Council, emphasizing the importance of increased funding for industrial development, the Office of Legal Affairs reasoned that "special industrial services" clearly met the threshold to be "consistent with the policies, aims, and activities of the Organization." They concluded that:

> It follows from the forgoing provisions that it would be permissible for the Secretary-General to accept voluntary contributions from the Netherlands and other governments for purposes of industrial development; that such contributions could be credited to a trust fund; and that the Secretary-General, being the "appropriate authority" under Financial Rule 6.7, could define the purpose and limits of the trust fund in accordance with the terms specified by the donors, provided, of course, that such terms are consistent with the policies, aims, and activities of the Organization.[43]

Legal Affairs concluded by suggesting UNDP pursue this course of action, essentially advising that an otherwise illegal UNDP trust fund for special industrial

---

[38] UN Juridical Yearbook 1966, 235.
[39] UN Juridical Yearbook 1966, 235. Cites Financial Regulation of the United Nations 7.2.
[40] Macy 1972.
[41] Macy 1972, Annex A, 1.
[42] UN Juridical Yearbook 1966, 235.
[43] UN Juridical Yearbook 1966, 235.

services would be legal if the money was formally accepted by the UN Secretary-General.[44] The money could then be used for exactly the same purpose. The Legal Affairs suggestion was followed and the trust fund for Special Industrial Services was established in 1966.[45]

Consistent with the status quo bias that favored EPTA and Special Fund rules carrying over to the new UNDP, no provision for earmarked contributions was made in the resolutions establishing UNDP in 1965. Less than two years later, in January of 1967, however, the UNDP Governing Council formally incorporated the opinion from Legal Affairs in its financial rules, in the blandly titled resolution 67/6, "Harmonization of administrative and financial procedures."[46] Section c of the resolution would permit the UNDP Administrator to accept donations "from non-governmental sources for purposes consistent with UNDP." Consistent with its rules for state donors, section c indicates that "no limitation may be imposed by the donor on the use of donations." Reading resolution 67/6 through section c shows a Governing Council protecting its control over resource distribution, even as they expand their resource base to include non-state contributions. But then comes section d, which authorized the Administrator to accept trust funds for purposes not inconsistent with the basic aims and purposes of UNDP, subject to the prior approval of the Governing Council in each case."[47]

At first glance, one might think that here, too, the Governing Council protected its control. From one perspective it had. By ensuring trust funds were subject to Council approval, it maintained an ability to veto new trust funds if they were found to be "inconsistent with the basic aims and purposes of UNDP." But from other perspectives it ceded control. Donors could initiate trust funds and determine their purpose. The substantive areas of work that trust funds would support, and the recipients who received the resources, would then also be determined by the donor. The new financial rule offered donors an opportunity to channel aid through UNDP without the Council weighing in on how their money should be used—except to say "yes" or "no." This cannot be said to ensure that donors would allocate resources to bilateral aid priorities through UNDP, but it certainly gave them the opportunity to do so.

Explaining Low Visibility

In addition to the bland, technical language, in which this ostensibly incremental change was ushered in at UNDP, three conditions facilitated the rule's adoption with little fanfare. First, the new funding rule solved a problem for UNDP. It

[44] UN Juridical Yearbook 1966, 236.
[45] UN Yearbook 1966, 297.
[46] United Nations Development Program 1967.
[47] United Nations Development Program 1967.

allowed the Program to expand its activity in ways that were politically unpalatable to the United States. Absent resolution 67/6, funding industrial development required its inclusion in UNDP's budget, agreed to by the Governing Council. But funding for industrial development was politically difficult and risked alienating the United States. Resolution 67/6 allowed other donors to provide support for industrial development or for other more contentious investments, without requiring the US or any other member, to participate. In short, the proximate goal of the rule was to solve a near-term political problem rather than to transform UN governance.

Second, the initial earmarked resources within UNDP were supplemental to the core budget, not a replacement or substitute for unrestricted funds. When making his announcement to the General Assembly the representative of the Netherlands stated "the additional contribution for special industrial services would be given on the understanding that it should indeed be supplementary—not a substitute ..."[48] The Office of Legal Affairs statement on the issue repeatedly refers to the Netherlands' contribution and the anticipated contributions for special industrial services from other donors as "additional" to regular resources.[49] The view applied beyond the Netherlands' case. A few years later, in response to a concern that increased voluntary contributions might be used as an excuse to hold down assessed contributions, both the UN's evaluative arm, the Joint Inspections Unit, and the Advisory Committee on Administrative and Budgetary Questions (ACABQ or Fifth Committee) expressed "doubts concerning the validity" of the concern. They did so on the basis that "in the last analysis, the fact that individual Member States make voluntary contributions [to] particular activities reflects their feeling that those activities are inadequately funded from the regular budget."[50] Implicit in this view was that the member states engaged in earmarking funds were not opposed to unrestricted contributions, they simply wanted to strengthen particular areas of UN work. It is likely that this view rested in large part on the particular donor states involved at the time.

That the donor states engaged in early earmarks were considered "benign" points to the third condition that facilitated change without fanfare. The Netherlands, along with states that quickly followed in earmarking contributions to UNDP, were ardent UN supporters whose size and political interests made their proposals less subject to concern or suspicion. The Netherlands, Sweden, Norway, and Denmark (the latter three all Nordic Council members who would have been aware of earlier earmark proposals made within their group), provided a higher proportion of their aid through multilateral channels relative to the so-called

---

[48] UN Juridical Yearbook 1966, 234.
[49] UN Juridical Yearbook 1966, 235, 236.
[50] Macy 1972; United Nations General Assembly 1972b, 1–2.

"big four" donors (the United States, United Kingdom, France, and West Germany).[51] For example, in the mid-1960s the United Kingdom provided between 8 and 10 percent of its aid multilaterally, with the rest delivered through bilateral channels.[52] By contrast, the proportion of aid delivered multilaterally by Scandinavian states hovered around 50 percent.[53] A report by the Swedish Institute of International Affairs described Sweden's increased involvement with UN technical assistance programs as having "idealistic motives."[54] More than supporters of multilateral aid in general, they were supporters of the UN in particular. While multilateral aid from the US and UK favored the World Bank, the early earmark states channeled a higher proportion of their multilateral aid through the UN. For instance, Norway actually delivered more money annually to UNDP than to the World Bank's IDA (e.g., 108.3 million Nkr versus 92.6 million Nkr) in 1968.[55] Sweden, Norway, and the Netherlands all made voluntary contributions to EPTA and the Special Fund at rates higher than their UN mandatory assessment ratios.[56] Far from being suspects in the pursuit of undermining UN principles, these were the states that had "sought to build up" the United Nations "by authorizing it to undertake as many joint technical aid projects as were practicable."[57]

Beyond their status as UN supporters, the relatively small size of the early earmark states likely increased the chance that their proposals were perceived as innocuous. Perhaps equally important, their behavior and practices were perceived as less consequential to institutional change. A paper from the Overseas Development Institute reflecting on which states might lead an initiative to strengthen multilateral aid mechanisms offers insight on this latter issue. The paper notes that the United States has "already tried and failed" to strengthen the system, "largely because American efforts in the direction raise the suspicion that the USA is presuming on its power as a leading nation of the non-Communist world," and "suspicion" that the US "is motivated primarily by a desire to shuffle off some of the burden on to others."[58] By contrast, the ODI paper notes that:

> The British aid programme is large enough for a British initiative in this field to carry some weight with other donors, *an advantage not possessed by some other strong supporters of a cooperative approach, such as Sweden or the Netherlands.*[59]

---

[51] Cohen 1969, 44; Markensten 1970, 95–96; Reinton 1970, 118. On the Netherlands, van Geet 1972, 80.
[52] Overseas Development Institute 1968, 31.
[53] Overseas Development Institute 1968, 31.
[54] Eek 1956, 215. Eek allows that these "idealistic motives" might be supplemented by Sweden's dependence on foreign trade and the interest in good relations with developing states.
[55] Dahl 1970, 88.
[56] Fox 1965, 784.
[57] Fox 1965, 782.
[58] Overseas Development Institute 1968, 32, 35.
[59] Overseas Development Institute 1968, 32.

(...) Among some of the smaller donors, the necessary will does exist, but the necessary power and influence does not.[60]

The line of thinking summarized in the ODI report suggests that while the French, German, and British aid budgets, which along with the US accounted for more than 80 percent of total aid,[61] were perceived capable of affecting change, other states were not. The behavior of smaller donors—those who would become the early earmark states—were not perceived as likely to affect change or the behavior of other donors.[62]

The absence of political interference in UN aid programs also made them unlikely targets of skepticism relative to the main Cold War protagonists. The well-known political interests of the UN's largest contributor, the United States (responsible for 55 percent of total aid), made its proposals subject to suspicion regarding ulterior motives (oftentimes correctly). By this time other member states were aware of US frustrations regarding UN projects in Cuba and of its informal efforts to delay such projects.[63] In a counterfactual world in which permissive earmark rules were prompted by a US announcement of earmarked funds, it is likely they would have prompted more skepticism. A similar proposal from the Soviet Union too would undoubtedly have raised concerns given its political interests and history of leveraging EPTA and the Special Fund to fulfill bilateral purposes.[64] The political interests and past behavior of the early earmark states stood in contrast to those of the US and Soviet Union. They were not only ardent UN supporters, but their own bilateral aid programs also generally placed fewer restrictions on how recipients used aid relative to their larger European counterparts and to the United States. Aid from Sweden and the Netherlands was formally "untied,"[65] although in both cases aid often came with formal or informal procurement restrictions.[66] This was in an era in which bilateral aid was increasingly "double tied," with both procurement and project restrictions.[67] In this way the early earmark states were generally less restrictive in their bilateral programs than other donors. In the Swedish case, the commitment to untie aid was a principled one that it hoped to

---

[60] Overseas Development Institute 1968, 35. Emphasis added.

[61] Overseas Development Institute 1968, 12.

[62] Overseas Development Institute 1968, 32, 35.

[63] E.g., LBJ Archives, Austin, TX. Outgoing Telegram. Department of State. Action: USUN New York; Amembassy PARIS NESCO 4697; Amembassy ROME FODAG 2119. Special Fund Projects for Cuba. March 10, 1965. 7:24 p.m.; LBJ Archives, Austin, TX. Incoming Telegram. Department of State. Confidential. From: New York. Action: SECSTATE 3039. Subject: Cuba-EPTA. Reference: USUN's A-983. February 2, 1965.

[64] See Chapter 4, pp. 135–137.

[65] Bilateral aid agencies in the 1960s used the term "tying" aid to describe restrictions placed on how aid was used by recipients or earmarks for projects. Aid is often referred to as "tied" or "untied" or "non-tied."

[66] Markensten 1970, 95–98; van Geet 1972, 83–84.

[67] Clifford 1966.

promote "to make the idea [of untied aid] more generally accepted."[68] These were not the states one would suspect of a motive to bilateralize the UN's multilateral system. Indeed, even their bilateral aid programs appeared less self-interested than most.

Coming into View: Early Indications of Transformational Potential

There are two separate issues to consider when evaluating when the transformational potential of earmarked funding came into full view. The first is whether and when voluntary, earmarked contributions were understood to undermine multilateralism. On this issue, we can arrive at the conclusion that it was understood, at least by those member states engaged in the practice and by some working at the various development funds accepting earmarked funds, by the late 1960s. But the evidence simultaneously demonstrates that in general, the practice of earmarking continued to fly under the radar of many throughout this period. In his report on trust funds in 1972, Robert Macy noted that none of the relevant governing bodies—the General Assembly, the Economic and Social Council, or the UN's Administrative Committee on Coordination—had held discussions on trust funds, and as such had not collectively discussed their merits or disadvantages.[69]

The second matter in assessing when transformational potential came into view is whether and when there was recognition that the bilateral element of earmarked resources could overwhelm money controlled by multilateral bodies. The evidence indicates this realization happened much later. Low visibility on this latter issue can be understood in part by the United States' absence from the early single donor trust fund scene. Since US funding remained predominant in the late 1960s and since the United States did not earmark funds, it was easy to imagine that earmarked funding would continue to be practiced by small and medium-sized donors and would lack the capacity to fully transform UN decision-making.

Early Trends and Concerns

Prior to 1965, trust funds were in limited use at the United Nations. A full accounting of trust funds placed the total dollar amount in 1960 at an impressive 12 million. But a closer look reveals that this sum included "special accounts" established by the General Assembly to pay for Korean Reconstruction, and the Congo Relief Counterpart Fund, which was established to compensate for unpaid ONUC

[68] Markensten 1970, 95–96.
[69] Macy 1972, 14.

dues. Other "earmarked" funds at the UN in 1960 added up to just $1,183,091, and about a third of that sum came from a Ford Foundation gift for the UN Library.[70] By 1965, the year the UN Office of Legal Affairs suggested a legal remedy to UNDP, allowing it to accept the Netherlands contribution, the use of trust funds was growing. Excluding special accounts for peacekeeping, earmarked funding totaled just over $6 million, with much of the increase from 1960 owing to a consolidated trust fund to pay the overhead costs for Special Fund projects, a series of multi-donor funds to provide emergency assistance, and a $500,000 account to support construction of the United Nations International School.[71] Member states contributed to multi-donor funds for emergency relief, but single-donor trust funds were sponsored by private actors or other international organizations.

After the creative intervention by the Office of Legal Affairs, the pattern of single-donor funds shifted. In contrast to the earlier periods, of the sixteen single-donor funds listed in 1970, only four held funds from non-state actors, with the other twelve funded by member states. Three were funded by Sweden, three by Denmark, two by the Netherlands, and one each from the Federal Republic of Germany, the United Kingdom, Saudi Arabia, and Zambia.[72] The list of multi-donor funds with member states as donors was also growing, and here the UNIDO/UNDP Trust Fund for Special Industrial Services is listed along thirteen other funds, having received $350,881 in 1970.[73]

The rise of trust funds first received attention at the United Nations in 1972 when the UN Joint Inspections Unit issued the "Report on Trust Funds of the United Nations," authored by Robert M. Macy.[74] Macy described the evolution in UN funding away from mandatory assessments to voluntary contributions, followed by the nascent trend toward earmarked contributions as follows:

> Initially this shift took the form largely of annual voluntary contributions by many Member States to finance such organizations as UNHCR, UNDP, UNICEF, and the World Food Programme. More recently, there has been a trend towards voluntary contributions not to UN organizations as such, but to individual projects and programmes included in the regular programme of work and country programmes of these organizations.[75]

---

[70] Macy 1972, Annex A, 1–4.

[71] Macy 1972, Annex A, 4–6.

[72] Macy 1972, Annex A, 8. In addition, a summary of Norwegian Development Assistance in 1970 notes its growing involvement in an "increasing number of assistance projects" (...) "prepared and administered through cooperation between the [Norwegian] director of development assistance and international organizations." These projects at UN agencies are referred to as being characterized by "a combination of multilateral and bilateral elements" (Dahl 1970, 88).

[73] Macy 1972, Annex A, 9. The Special Industrial Services (SIS) Trust Fund established for UNDP became a joint UNIDO-UNDP fund after UNIDO's formal establishment.

[74] Macy was an American Economist who held high posts during the US Marshall Plan effort and The Bureau of the Budget for the Agency for International Development, in addition to his work for the United Nations.

[75] Macy 1972, 2.

A good deal of Macy's report is spent on definitional issues, and on encouraging and ultimately recommending that the UN act to ensure it has a clear and full account of its trust funds, a topic I return to below. The report does not focus primarily on the relationship between earmarked funding and multilateral governance, but it does identify some associated concerns. This is done most explicitly in a section titled "Reduction of collective financial responsibility, fragmentation of program." Among the issues addressed is "that the very widespread use of trust funds necessarily involves a decentralisation of decision-making and hence a lack of that collective responsibility which is one of the corner-stones of the United Nations."[76] Elsewhere, the report notes that trust funds have a multilateral component since they are administered by the UN, but that they are "*bilateral* in that the final selection of projects to be financed is made by the donor Government …"[77]

The donor countries that were now engaged in the practice of earmarking, too, had surely thought of its potential to support bilateral interests, even if this was not their primary motivation. Of historical note is that for many donor countries, bilateral aid agencies were only just being established in the mid-1960s. Their establishment created a need to outline a bilateral development agenda, for some donors for the first time. As the 1960s and 1970s wore on, bilateral development priorities congealed for many donors. At the same time, growing experience in the parallel bilateral and multilateral aid arenas made many in the same group aware that the latter channel was often more cost-effective. Trust funds were undoubtedly attractive in this context.

The increase in the number of single-donor trust funds noted above received special attention in the JIU report. Macy notes:

> … there is at least the potential danger that some of these trust funds are nothing more than a bilateral programme to achieve certain political objectives for the donor country—a common criticism of bilateral programmes. Proper safeguards should be established to prevent acceptance of such trust fund contributions for such purposes.[78]

This early concern about bilateral projects was prompted in part by a trust fund supported by the Netherlands that came on the heels of their contribution for special industrial services. The second Dutch fund earmarked money for West Irian, part of Indonesia and a former Dutch colony.[79] The West Irian trust fund was "developed independently of UNDP activities elsewhere in Indonesia," and was "not coordinated with the rest of the UNDP Headquarters staff nor with the

---

[76] Macy 1972, 16.
[77] Macy 1972, 27. Emphasis original.
[78] Macy 1972, 27.
[79] UN Yearbook 1968, 303–304; Graham 2017, 384.

UNDP Resident Representative in the capital of Indonesia."[80] It appeared as a relatively clear instance in which the Netherlands was running its bilateral policy through the UN without input from other member states.

The JIU report did not dismiss these problems, but Macy simultaneously stated that having studied the trust fund issue, "I am now persuaded they are not of major importance.[81] The Report reached and was commented on by the UN Secretary-General Kurt Waldheim and the Advisory Committee on Advisory and Budgetary Questions (ACABQ) in October of 1972. Like Macy, in his comments Waldheim described the evolution in UN funding to date, and acknowledged the contradiction between trust funds and multilateral governance. He began by noting that over the years "Member states have expressed support for two fundamental principles, that is, (a) the collective responsibility of Member States in the discharge of Charter obligations in the economic and social field, and (b) the process of collective decision-making in determining priorities." (...) Waldheim noted that in creating UNDP and the Capital Development Fund, Member States

> accepted a weakened version of the first principle—the effect that any sizable additional funds, at least for operational activities in the economic and social fields, must henceforth come largely from voluntary contributions rather than through assessed contributions for the regular budget. However, inherent in the acceptance of the idea of multipurpose voluntary funds has been the tacit understanding that decision on the management of such funds, including the important question of sectoral priorities, should be the subject of the second principle—the process of collective intergovernmental decision-making.[82]

Waldheim's language of *tacit understanding* actually undersells the commitment to the second principle, which was explicit and formalized in rules prohibiting donor restrictions on contributions to EPTA, and the UN Special Fund. He went on to acknowledge the potential for trust funds to violate collective intergovernmental decision-making.

> Needless to say, the setting up of single-purpose trust funds financed on a voluntary basis could negate this principle, since it could give the donor countries concerned the right not only to make or withhold voluntary contributions, but also to attempt to influence the decisions taken in the specific field or sector for which the contribution is made. The point can be made, therefore, that the proliferation of single-purpose trust funds is a development which, bearing in mind the above point of view, is unlikely to be welcomed by all Member States.[83]

---

[80] Macy 1972, 9.
[81] Macy 1972, 16.
[82] United Nations General Assembly 1972a. A/8840/Add.1, 2–3.
[83] United Nations General Assembly 1972a. A/8840/Add.1, 3.

But from here, the Secretary-General pivots sharply, emphasizing that trust funds promise "substantially larger" "total resources" for the UN.[84] Further, in response to the single recommendation from the Inspector that directly addresses concerns about bilateral interests, the Secretary-General is dismissive. The Inspector proposed that "proper safeguards be established to cope" with the possibility of "donors gaining special advantages" through the use of trust funds. The S-G dismisses the need for safeguards, noting "the Secretary-General is convinced that he is dealing effectively with such matters. (...) He also hopes, of course, that Governments will continue to exercise all due restraint in the proposals they make."[85]

Like Macy and the Secretary-General, comments from ACABQ alluded to the potential for trouble before concluding there was no problem. On the one hand, ACABQ appeared more favorable to Inspector recommendations calling for greater transparency and safeguards. On the other, the Committee dismissed the concern that trust funds undermine multilateral priorities, arguing that "in the present situation" "there is no set hierarchy of priorities."[86] ACABQ seemed to state that bilateral priorities did not pose a threat to multilateral priorities at the UN, because there were no set multilateral priorities. In December of 1972, ACABQ recommended that the General Assembly defer consideration of the Inspector's report to the 1973 session, which the Assembly did.[87] The ACABQ summary and recommendations reached the General Assembly a year later in December 1973. The recommendation from the Inspector that safeguard procedures be put in place to avoid donors using trust funds for political advantage was not among the ACABQ recommendations. Indeed, although two of the recommendations encouraged increased transparency around the use of trust funds, the problem of bilateral interests was not mentioned or addressed in the report to the Assembly.[88] The Assembly approved the Committee's recommendations and took note of the report with appreciation, endorsing the decision without a vote on December 18, 1973. No discussion of the report is logged in the UN Yearbook and no further action on the matter was taken.[89]

Slow Moving and Invisible

It is fair to say that by 1973, many at the United Nations understood that earmarked resources violated multilateral decision-making. Robert Macy of the Joint

---

[84] United Nations General Assembly 1972a. A/8840/Add.1, 3.
[85] United Nations General Assembly 1972a. A/8840/Add.1, 8.
[86] United Nations General Assembly 1972b. A/8840/Add.2, 2.
[87] United Nations Yearbook 1972, 694.
[88] United Nations General Assembly 1972b. A/8840/Add.2, 5.
[89] United Nations Yearbook 1973, 872.

Inspection Unit, the Secretary-General, and the sixteen members of the ACABQ Committee had described the *potential* for trust funds to undermine UN governance in writing. The extent to which the broader UN membership was cognizant of the issue is difficult to discern; they had received comments on the JIU report, but ACABQ's recommendation to delay its consideration implied it was not an urgent matter. The recommendations they received from the Secretary-General and ACABQ did not mention concerns about donor control. And if they read the comments in full—an unlikely scenario for most member states with small delegations receiving hundreds of documents during an Assembly session—they would have seen the Secretary-General asserting there was little to be concerned about.

The theoretical framework developed in Chapter 2 conceives of institutions transforming slowly, with most of the process taking place under the radar. The JIU report provides evidence of how trust funds had remained somewhat invisible at the UN to that point in 1973. The UN approach to trust funds is described as "ad hoc," rather than formal or systematic.[90] The budget process did not include projections of trust fund expenditures as it did for other types of funding.[91] The Inspector noted that extra-budgetary resources were sometimes included in annexes to budget documents, "but no-one seems to pay much attention to these annexes."[92] Trust funds were mentioned in the section on United Nations programs for technical cooperation, alongside regular budget (mandatory assessments) and UNDP funds. However, prior to 1974, trust funds were lumped in with other extra-budgetary resources, and their location (whether at the UN proper or UNDP) was not identified.[93] Budget numbers for UNDP and UN trust funds were separated starting in 1974, perhaps in response to the JIU Report, but detailed information about individual funds, their size, or their donors, remained absent.[94]

Perhaps of special importance given the inherent challenge that trust funds posed to multilateral governance, the Inspector described a system in which there was no single entity or individual with the authority to review proposed funds on their substantive merits. Macy notes a "total lack of control of trust fund expenditures by the General Assembly."[95] When a proposed trust fund is reviewed in New York, "it is reviewed from the standpoint of UN financial regulations and rules."[96]

---

[90] Macy 1972, 14.
[91] Macy 1972, 14.
[92] Macy 1972, 62.
[93] E.g., United Nations Yearbook 1973, 334. The sum of $12.6 million in 1973 is said to include "activities under United Nations trust funds; projects financed by recipient Governments; the provision of services of associate experts; special education and training programmes for southern Africa; international law programmes; and development and planning projections and (b) UNDP trust funds" (United Nations Yearbook 1973, 334).
[94] E.g., United Nations Yearbook (1974) provides an annotated list of UNDP trust funds under "extrabudgetary operations," but in most cases does not indicate contributor countries, see 410–412. By contrast, contributions to the core budget are clearly indicated (413–414).
[95] Macy 1972, 25.
[96] Macy 1972, 25.

But, "the Secretary-General is not also held responsible for a 'substantive' review in depth, nor is anyone else in the UN Headquarters in New York."[97] In short, the question of who approved the content of proposed trust funds remained opaque, decentralized, and ad hoc.

As in accounts of gradual transformation in domestic institutions, the subterranean nature of gradual change served to facilitate transformation. And while change was slow-moving and remained invisible to many, it also was not yet *big*. Data available from the latter half of the 1970s demonstrates that earmarked allocations for technical cooperation from trust funds were not rising steadily relative to allocations from regular budget resources or unrestricted voluntary contributions at UNDP, and in some years trust fund allocations actually decreased.[98] During the same period, the regular UN budget grew substantially from $169 million in 1970 to $666 million in 1980 and regular budget allocations for technical cooperation increased in some years.[99] Unrestricted contributions to UNDP did not decline, lending credence to the view that earmarked resources were a supplement, and a modest one at that, rather than a substitute.

At this point, on the eve of the Reagan administration, change at the UN had proceeded sufficiently to illustrate a number of the framework's expectations about the nature of change processes. No single incremental change—the establishment of EPTA with voluntary funding rules, the Goldberg reservation, the Office of Legal Affairs articulation of a legal method to accept trust funds at UNDP—accomplished transformation. Nor did the individuals involved in these changes coordinate their actions in a narrow or broad sense. In a narrow sense, they did not explicitly work together, and in a broad sense, they did not appear to see these developments as part of a shared project. The changes to funding rules did not replace or revise Article 17 of the UN Charter, but were layered alongside them. Reinterpretation of Article 17 and the obligations it entailed occurred not through negotiation and revision, but through a reliance on subsequent practice to infer its evolved meaning. More repurposing lay ahead. If in the 1970s it remained reasonable to conceive of earmarked resources as supplemental money offered by friendly member states, the election of US President Ronald Reagan and his appointment of Jeane Kirkpatrick as the US representative to the United Nations, would soon change that. The Reagan administration would lead the Geneva Group to implement a policy of zero real growth across the UN system; Kirkpatrick would alert the US Congress to its ability to employ a "pick and pay" approach at the UN, using permissive earmark rules. In doing so the rules would

---

[97] Macy 1972, 25.

[98] E.g., from 1976 to 1977 UNDP trust fund allocations dropped from $17.3 million to $12.43 million. United Nations Yearbook 1976, 377ff; United Nations Yearbook 1977, 460.

[99] $327 million in constant 1971 dollars. Global Policy Forum, UN Regular Budget Expenditures. https://archive.globalpolicy.org/un-finance/tables-and-charts-on-un-finance/the-un-regular-budget/27466.html.

be repurposed to replace unrestricted contributions. From here the proportion of funding governed by multilateral bodies would shrink quickly.

References

Beckman, Bjorn. 1979. "Aid and Foreign Investment: The Swedish Case." *Cooperation and Conflict* 14(2): 133–148.

Búzás, Zoltán. 2017. "Evading International Law: How Agents Comply with the Letter of the Law but Violate Its Purpose." *European Journal of International Relations* 23(4): 857–883.

Clifford, Juliet. 1966. "The Tying of Aid and the Problem of 'Local Costs.'" *The Journal of Development Studies* 2(2): 153–173.

Cohen, Benjamin I. 1969. "Bilateral Foreign Aid and Multilateral Foreign Aid." Discussion Paper No. 86. http://elischolar.library.yale.edu/egcenter-discussion-paper-series/86.

Dahl, Karl Nandrup. 1970. "Norwegian Development Assistance: Technical Guidelines and Political Leadership." *Cooperation and Conflict* 5(2): 85–94.

Economic and Social Council. 1966. "Summary of Activities." *International Organization* 20(2): 327–365.

Eek, Hilding. 1956. "Swedish Policy in the United Nations." In Sweden and the United Nations: National Studies of International Organization. Report by a Special Study Group of the Swedish Institute of International Affairs. Prepared for the Carnegie Endowment for International Peace, pp. 165–241.

Fox, Annette Baker. 1965. "The Small States of Western Europe in the United Nations." *International Organization* 19(3): 774–786.

Graham, Erin R. 2017. "The Institutional Design of Funding Rules at International Organizations: Explaining the Transformation in Financing the United Nations." *European Journal of International Relations* 23(2): 365–390.

Kaser, Michael. 1966. "The Soviet Ideology of Industrialization: A Review Article." *Journal of Development Studies* 3(1): 63–76.

Macy, Robert M. 1972. "Report on Trust Funds of the United Nations." United Nations Joint Inspections Unit, Geneva. February. JIU/REP/71/1.

Manno, Catherine Senf. 1966. "Selective Weighted Voting in the UN General Assembly: Rationale and Methods." *International Organization* 20(1): 37–62.

Manzer, Ronald A. 1964. "The United Nations Special Fund." *International Organization* 18(4): 766–789.

Markensten, Klas. 1970. "Swedish Foreign Assistance." *Cooperation and Conflict* 5(2): 95–101.

Murphy, Craig. 1983. "What the Third World Wants: An Interpretation of the Development and Meaning of the New International Economic Order Ideology." *International Studies Quarterly* 27(1): 55–76.

Overseas Development Institute. 1968. "Initiatives for Improving Aid." *Development Policy Review* A2(1): 31–43.

Reinton, Per Olav. 1970. "Nordic Aid and the Politics of Inequality." *Cooperation and Conflict* 5(2): 112–124.

Rubinstein, Alvin Z. 1964. *Soviets in International Organizations: Changing Policy toward Developing Countries, 1953–1963.* Princeton, NJ: Princeton University Press.

United Nations Development Programme. 1967. "Harmonization of Administrative and Financial Procedures." DP/DC/67/6.

United Nations General Assembly. 1972a. A/8840/Add.1 October 13, 1972. "Joint Inspections Unit. Report on Trust Funds of the United Nations. Note by the Advisory Committee on Administrative and Budgetary Questions. Comments of the Secretary-General and the Administrator of the United Nations Development Programme (UNDP).

United Nations General Assembly. 1972b. A/8840/Add.2. December 5, 1972. "Joint Inspection Unit. Report on Trust Funds of the United Nations. Report of the Advisory Committee on Administrative and Budgetary Questions at Its Twenty-seventh Session."

van Geet, Dick. 1972. "Netherlands Aid Performance and Development Policy." *Development Policy Review* A5(1): 77–91.

6

Tighten the Screws and Bilateral Contracts

The United Nations development system experienced two trends in the 1980s. On the one hand, it was an era of austerity and disenchantment. The United States, in a pursuit embraced by most Western contributors, effectively halted growth of the mandatory assessments system. In a move that received less attention in the press, the US also halted growth in its voluntary (core) contributions to UN programs, with some facing severe cuts by the decade's end. Belt tightening characterized both the mandatory assessments system and the core (unearmarked) budgets of UN programs. On the other hand, the UN system experienced a financial boon as it became a contract agency to wealthy states. UN programs became home to a multitude of trust funds. European states increasingly sought out the UN as a partner to implement projects that would otherwise be part of bilateral aid agendas. Single-donor trust funds with purposes that aligned with donors' bilateral interests and enhanced their control over UN programming proliferated during this period.

The groundwork that would be used to transform UN funding, and in turn, its governance, was laid in the 1960s. With these parallel moves, enhancing income through single-donor funds, while stifling growth or cutting unrestricted resources, the transformation began in earnest in the 1980s. In contrast to previous eras, donor states were now explicitly focused on egalitarian multilateralism as a problem to be circumvented. Recognizing that formal revision of the UN Charter was not possible, they did so creatively. Permissive earmark rules, initially used to enhance UN activity in underfunded areas, were repurposed by European donors, and later the US, to enhance their control over programming and even to pursue bilateral interests. In the United States, discontent with egalitarian multilateralism was felt throughout the 1970s. But congressional opponents' efforts to curtail commitments and exert influence were mostly ham-handed, led by those who lacked basic knowledge of UN rules. This changed with the selection of Jeane Kirkpatrick as the United States Ambassador to the United Nations. Kirkpatrick articulated and justified limits on mandatory obligations to the UN, reinterpreting Article 17 in a way that proved persuasive to many. This strengthened the shared commitment of the so-called Geneva Group of donors to enforce zero-real growth across the UN system. She simultaneously advocated that the US join European states in their earmarking behavior, effectively advising the US Government to substitute

Transforming International Institutions. Erin R. Graham, Oxford University Press. © Erin R. Graham (2023).
DOI: 10.1093/oso/9780198877936.003.0006

earmarked funds for unrestricted contributions. By reconceptualizing various UN funding modalities as substitutes rather than supplements, Kirkpatrick turned the original logic of permissive earmark rules on its head. Egalitarian multilateralism could be constrained through cuts; activity consistent with US interests could be simultaneously enhanced through earmarks.

This period of change in the UN story illustrates the processes of reinterpretation and repurposing, the latter with an emphasis on state practice, articulated in the theoretical framework. It also illustrates that transformation often occurs gradually through *uncoordinated actions* by various actors over time. Change is uncoordinated in the sense that, for example, the Netherlands or the UN Office of Legal Affairs hardly had the Reagan administration's strategy in mind when they found a way for UNDP to legally establish trust funds. Jeane Kirkpatrick nonetheless utilized opportunities created by their actions two decades later. In the same way, in writing their advisory opinion in the *Certain Expenses* case when the US was a strong proponent of mandatory assessments, the International Court of Justice had little idea their opinion would be used decades later by the US Ambassador to the UN to fashion a legal basis for American withholding. These uncoordinated actions and actors jointly facilitated transformation over time.

This chapter unfolds in three sections. The first focuses on how (mostly) European donors repurposed trust funds for bilateral efforts during the 1980s, providing evidence for the growth of single-donor funds at UNDP, and the various multi-donor funds administered by UNDP, and the UN Environment Program (UNEP). The second and third sections focus primarily on shifts in US policy ushered in by the election of Ronald Reagan. I describe the growing antipathy in the US toward the UN in the 1970s, and how the executive branch had previously managed and suppressed this sentiment. By contrast, the Reagan administration harnessed the frustration and, led by Kirkpatrick, offered paths toward enhanced influence, including the reinterpretation of Article 17 and advocacy for adopting European practice regarding earmarks. The chapter concludes with a discussion of how the UN was well on its path to transformation away from egalitarian multilateralism at the Cold War's end.

Repurposing for Bilateralism

In 1966, the UN Office of Legal Affairs created a pathway for the UNDP administrator, allowing him to accept an earmarked contribution from the Netherlands that would otherwise be illegal under UNDP rules. The following year, the UNDP governing council incorporated this method in its financial rules, allowing the UNDP administrator to establish trust funds so long as they were used for purposes broadly consistent with those of the United Nations. Similar rules were incorporated at most other UN programs.[1] The initial intended purpose of these rules was to supplement unrestricted UN resources, often in areas that provoked disagreement in multilateral bodies. The contribution from the Netherlands that sparked Legal Affairs creativity allowed UNDP to expand its industrial development work with new funding that was otherwise difficult to obtain due to opposition from the United States. These resources were *supplementary* to the unrestricted funds supplied by their contributors. The Netherlands did not substitute earmarked funding in place of its core contribution, and other states subsequently contributed to the Special Industrial Services fund established by the Netherlands' contribution.[2]

When conceived as a supplement, there appeared to be little downside associated with earmarked resources. From the perspective of potential recipients who advocated for greater assistance, there would be more funds available for the purposes they supported. For the UN bureaucracy, whether at UNDP, the specialized agencies, or other UN entities that implemented projects, additional resources were welcome. For donors eager to expand or reinforce UN mandates in particular areas, they were now able to finance that activity without multilateral fights. For donors wary of the same, they were freed from the frustration and associated political costs of providing money for activities they did not support. The policies were not thought of as friendly to donors; rather they were thought of as providing a range of benefits to a range of actors engaged with the UN.

In the decades that followed, permissive earmark rules were repurposed in two ways. The first, discussed in this section, involved donors using trust funds (and sub-trust funds) as a substitute for aid that would traditionally be delivered through bilateral channels. Special industrial services, the substantive area of the Netherlands' fund noted above, could be easily linked to broad multilateral demands and long-standing discussion in UN governing bodies. Industrial development did not lack broad multilateral support, rather it lacked universal support, and the *not universal* contingent included UNDP's largest contributor, the United States. But as time passed, permissive earmark rules were increasingly repurposed to establish trust funds that mirrored bilateral donor agendas rather than the broad, multilateral concerns of UN governing bodies. Chapter 5 covered the earliest instances of single-donor trust funds that served bilateral interests. But at the time (the early 1970s), the UN Joint Inspections Unit and other relevant actors judged this use of trust funds to be the exception rather than the rule and concluded that they did not threaten the multilateral character of the system.

By the mid-1980s, however, UN trust funds were on the rise, and among that group, single-donor trust funds, which often betrayed bilateral origins, were a fast-growing component. Of the trust funds established by the UNDP Administrator

[1] Graham 2017.
[2] See Chapter 5.

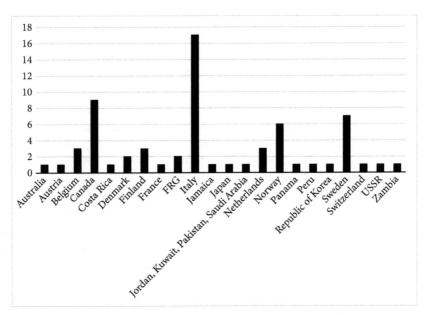

Figure 6.1 Single-Donor Trust Funds Established by the UNDP Administrator, 1981–89.

from 1981–1989,[3] fourteen were open, multi-donor trust funds, seven were funded by private sources, and sixty-five were single-donor funds (see Figure 6.1).[4]

Five of the sixty-five single-donor funds were established by recipient states to fund domestic projects. Three of the donors discussed in Chapter 5 in the group of "early earmark" states (the Netherlands, Norway, and Sweden), were prominent in establishing single-donor trust funds in the 1980s, establishing three, six, and seven funds respectively. Additionally, Canada and especially Italy, stand out, establishing nine and seventeen funds respectively. Belgium and Finland established three funds each. By contrast, the UN's largest contributors of mandatory assessments were not driving the trend. France, Japan, and the Soviet Union each established one fund, alongside two from the Federal Republic of Germany. The United Kingdom and the United States are entirely absent from the list.

The alignment of trust fund purposes with donors' bilateral interests is sometimes evident even from the names of various funds. In 1985, Italy established the "Ethiopia-Italy Programme for Rehabilitation and Development," to aid its former colony. In 1982, the Soviet Union established the "USSR/UNDP Trust fund for the

---

[3] In addition to the categories listed, two funds were established on behalf of UN programs, and a third was established on behalf of the German Catholic Bishop's Association (Bischofliches Hilfswerk Misereor E.V.).

[4] Governing Council of the United Nations Development Programme 1989.

training of specialists from developing countries in the USSR."[5] Some single-donor trust funds with ostensibly broad, generic titles also served country- or region-specific purposes. For example, although not evident from its name, the "Australia Development Assistance Bureau/UNDP Programme Trust Fund," was established to support the Pacific Islands, reflecting Australia's interests in the region.[6]

Although rarely discussed in UN multilateral forums, the contracts governing trust funds demonstrate that donors often exercised incredible control over the nature of funded projects. One example with ample documentation comes from "the Trust Fund for Norwegian Contribution to the Angolan Petroleum Training in Sumbe (Angola)" to which Norway provided $1,895,601 in 1984 and $3 million in total.[7] The Norwegian Agency for Development Cooperation (NORAD) worked with UNDP to establish the fund to finance a Regional Petroleum Training Center for the group known as the Southern African Development Cooperation Conference (SADCC) to train national specialists to work in the petroleum industry.[8] The project was funded by Norway, administered by UNDP, with UNIDO as the executing agency. The Training Center had previously received support from Italy, and an Italian company, COMERINT, had run the school, which at that time ran "a modest set of courses on bilateral aid from Italy."[9] With Norway's $3 million in promised funds, the school was set to undergo an expansion, and competitive bidding on the contract was expected. Norway expressed its position that the Italian firm must continue to run the school. The UNDP Deputy Chief of the Africa bureau traveled to UNIDO headquarters in Vienna to communicate the importance attached to the firm. Documents show that "NORAD which will contribute for US $3,000,000 insists that only one single company will execute the project, that is to say the project will be subcontracted by COMERINT. The position of NORAD is inflexible about this matter."[10] UNIDO was requested "to carry out the project under reference through a contracting agreement with COMERINT (Italy) without calling for proposals, advertising or formal invitations to bid."[11]

Norway's fund to train petroleum workers also provides an example of how bilateral interests can drive project selection. The Norwegian Government owns 67 percent of Statoil (now Equinor), the Norwegian oil company.[12] In 1991, Statoil entered the Angolan market and Angola became "the biggest contributor to its [Statoil's] portfolio outside of Norway,"[13] accounting for some 40 percent of its

[5] United Nations General Assembly 1986, 17.
[6] Governing Council of the United Nations Development Programme 1986a, 3.
[7] United Nations Industrial Development Organization 1986.
[8] United Nations Industrial Development Organization 1986, 2.
[9] United Nations Industrial Development Organization 1986, 30.
[10] United Nations Industrial Development Organization 1986, Annex 2.
[11] United Nations Industrial Development Organization 1986, Annex 2, p. 38.
[12] Statoil was renamed "Equinor" on May 15, 2018. https://www.equinor.com/en/about-us/about-our-name-change.html (accessed February 19, 2021).
[13] "Statoil Briefs Norwegian Police on Angola Payments." Reuters, February 22, 2016. Published in The Maritime Executive. https://maritime-executive.com/article/statoil-briefs-norwegian-police-on

international portfolio.[14] The relationship has endured over time. In 2018, Norwegian Prime Minister Erna Solberg referred to Angola as Norway's "most important partner in Africa," stating that "The petroleum sector is currently the backbone of our business cooperation."[15]

The single-donor trust funds established by the UNDP administrator and shown in Figure 6.1 also include a new trend: donors' practice of earmarking contributions *within* previously established multi-donor trust funds (MDTFs). MDTFs, like the United Nations Trust Fund for Sudano-Sahelian Activities increasingly took on single-donor "sub trust funds."[16] As early as 1985, UNDP clarified in its financial reports that there were three types of contributions to the multi-donor trust funds it administered: unrestricted (core) contributions; those earmarked by recipients for local costs; and those earmarked for "country or project-specific contributions." Figure 6.2 demonstrates the extent to which the large multi-donor trust funds, administered by UNDP, were now subject to and reliant on single-donor earmarks. In 1985, earmarked funds accounted for 8 percent of the resources for the Sudano-Sahelian trust fund, (where cost-sharing contributions were dominant), 23 percent of the resources contributed to the UN Capital Development Fund (UNCDF), and fully 88 percent of the contributions to the United Nations Financing System in Science and Technology Development (UNFSSTD).

Other United Nations programs experienced a similar shift toward earmarked funding in the 1980s. Established in 1973, the UNEP was initially designed to rely entirely on unrestricted voluntary contributions. All member state contributions were pooled in the Environment Fund, which is governed by the UNEP Executive Council in which each state, regardless of size or wealth, is allocated one vote. But by 1978, the UNEP administrator had established its first trust fund for projects to support protection of the marine environment in the coastal areas of Gulf Coast states.[17] In 1979, two new trust funds were added, and by 1981 there were five "main trust funds" that operated at UNEP.[18] This included its first single-donor fund, established with money from the Swedish International Development Agency (SIDA) in 1981.[19] The SIDA-financed trust fund was designed to support training workshops for the pulp and paper industry, which aligned with SIDA's

-angola-payments (accessed March 14, 2023). See also: https://www.cmi.no/events/1432-angola-and-norway-the-perfect-partnership (accessed February 19, 2021).

[14] Gordon and Stenvoll 2007, 38.

[15] "Norway as a consistent partner in Angola." December 3, 2018. Opening speech by Prime Minister Erna Solberg at an Angola/Norwegian trade seminar in Luanda, Angola, December 3, 2018. https://www.regjeringen.no/en/aktuelt/norway-as-a-consistent-partner-in-angola/id2621191/.

[16] This issue, along with the methodological difficulties it poses for identifying earmarked funds, is discussed in Graham and Serdaru 2020, 686.

[17] UN Yearbook 1978, 536. https://www.un.org/en/yearbook

[18] UN Yearbook 1979, 691; UN Yearbook 1981, 820.

[19] UN Yearbook 1981, 820.

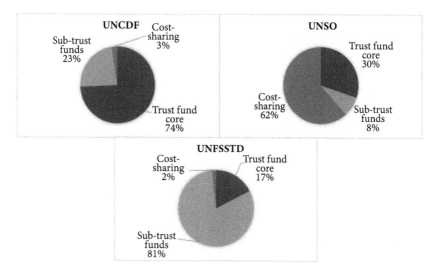

Figure 6.2 Earmarks (Single-Donor Sub-Trust Funds) within Major MDTFs Administered by UNDP.

Note: Governing Council of the United Nations Development Programme. 1986b. "Annual Report of the Administrator for 1985." DP/1986/11/Add.1. Original: English. April 22, 1986. Geneva.

bilateral programs to expand that industry in a number of developing states.[20] In the same year, outside the "main trust funds," UNEP established region-based trust funds for west and central Africa, the Caribbean, and east Asian seas, and extended a pre-existing regional trust fund for Kuwait.[21] By 1985, UNEP trust funds numbered at least fifteen, and by 1987, at least twenty-two.[22] These included single-donor funds[23] financed by the Federal Republic of Germany,[24] Sweden,[25] Finland,[26] Japan,[27] and Norway.[28]

Both at UNDP and elsewhere in the UN development system, the growing number of trust funds, and single-donor trust funds in particular, illustrates an important component of the UN's shift toward reliance on earmarked funding. As states learned how to pursue bilateral programs through the UN, effectively using it as a contract agency, earmarked funding grew. But the trend toward greater reliance on earmarked funding was also contingent on mandatory and unrestricted voluntary contributions *not growing*. While the trend of increased

[20] UN Yearbook 1981, 820; Lang 2002.
[21] UN Yearbook 1981, 833.
[22] UN Yearbook 1985, 798; UN Yearbook 1986, 651; UN Yearbook 1987, 691.
[23] This is not intended as an exhaustive list, but rather is based on best available documentation.
[24] UN Yearbook 1985, 798; Governing Council of the UN Environment Programme 2002, 8.
[25] UN Yearbook 1985, 798; Governing Council of the UN Environment Programme 2002, 6.
[26] UN Yearbook 1986, 652; Governing Council of the UN Environment Programme 2002, 4.
[27] Governing Council of the UN Environment Programme 2002, 8.
[28] Governing Council of the UN Environment Programme 2002, 8.

earmarks was driven primarily by small and medium-sized donors, this latter trend was driven by weakening support from the UN's largest contributors, and especially from the United States. The robustness of mandatory assessments and unrestricted (core) funding had always depended disproportionately on the US. With the election of Ronald Reagan and the selection of Jeane Kirkpatrick as US Ambassador to the United Nations, UN critics found allies in the executive branch and financial support for the UN became precarious.

Broadening Discontent in the United States

The United Nations always found opponents in the United States, but during the 1970s discontent with the Organization became more widespread and mainstream. Decolonization had progressed to a stage where developing states held a majority at the UN and were increasingly organized in their policy positions and statements. Congressman Dante Fascell[29] remarked of the period, "If we are lucky, we can get a resolution on motherhood through the agencies or through the UN General Assembly."[30]

Two issues commanding attention during this period were critical in worsening US views of the United Nations: the New International Economic Order, and the Zionism is racism resolution. The SUNFED proposal in the 1950s, which called for a new grant-based development organization within the UN, foreshadowed developing states' cooperation around the NIEO. Passed by the General Assembly in 1974, "The Declaration on the Establishment of the NIEO" had the express purpose of "eliminat[ing] the widening gap between the developed and the developing countries."[31] The means to achieve this were redistributive. Franczak writes, "Third World supporters hoped to negotiate a redistribution of money and power from the global North—the rich capitalist countries—to the global South— everyone else but the Communist bloc."[32] The NIEO declaration echoed earlier statements on self-determination and development, like those from the Bandung Conference in 1955, but in some ways was more radical.[33] It asserted every state's right to nationalize private companies and regulate transnational corporations.[34] Alongside calls to bring about "sustained improvement in their unsatisfactory

---

[29] Fascell was a member of the Democratic party from the state of Florida.

[30] House of Representatives. "United Nations Finances." Hearing Before the Subcommittees on International Operations and on International Organizations of the Committee on Foreign Affairs. Ninety-Sixth Congress. First Session. June 27, 1979.

[31] UN General Assembly, Resolution 3201 (S-VI) Declaration on the Establishment of a New International Economic Order.

[32] Franczak 2019, 867.

[33] Benjamin 2015, 34–35; see also Fioretos 2020, 76.

[34] United Nations General Assembly, Resolution 3201 (S-VI), 4e and 4g.

terms of trade" and expand development assistance "free of any political or military conditions," the NIEO directly confronted American economic orthodoxy.[35] The NIEO provoked "alarm" and resistance from the United States,[36] alongside the United Kingdom, France, Germany, Japan, Italy, and Canada.[37] Although some in the US foreign policy elite were conciliatory, considering larger aid budgets and increased participation in trade, others saw the NIEO as a fundamental threat to capitalism and liberal democracy, calling for it to be forcefully rebuked.[38] The US worked to undermine unity in the global South and promote unity among the large industrialized economies to resist the NIEO agenda.[39]

The passage of General Assembly resolution 3379, which "determine[d] that Zionism is a form of racism and racial discrimination,"[40] served as a further inflection point and touchstone for anti-UN sentiment in the years to come. UN supporters in Congress lamented that constituents complained loudly about the United Nations, believing it was anti-American and anti-Israel.[41] Senator Javits stated the problem in moderate terms when he said "there is a feeling at this time (...) that there has been a degree of hostility and discrimination shown by the actions of the General Assembly toward Israel (...) for example in the much discussed and condemned anti-Zionist resolution."[42] Tony Hall, the second ranking Democrat on the House Subcommittee on International Organizations remarked about his support for the UN, "I find myself voting against the general feeling of my district."[43]

Taken together, the NIEO and Zionism is racism resolutions reduced US support for the UN to a low ebb. The Congressional Record summary of the UN's World Conference of the International Woman's Year, held in 1975, is indicative of US views and frustrations at the time:

[35] United Nations General Assembly, Resolution 3201 (S-VI), 4j and 4k.
[36] Puchala 1982–1983, 582.
[37] Fioretos 2020, 76.
[38] Sargent 2015; Franczak 2019, 871ff.
[39] Fioretos 2020.
[40] See United Nations Resolution A/RES/3379, November 10, 1975. The resolution passed 72–35, with 32 abstentions.
[41] E.g., Hearings before the Committee on Foreign Relations. United States Senate. Ninety-Fourth Congress. Second Session on the Nomination of Governor William W. Scranton of Pennsylvania to be Representative of the United States to the United Nations, with the Rank of Ambassador and the Future of the United Nations Participation in the United Nations. March 2, 17, 18, and 25, 1976. See especially questions from Senator Percy, p. 13; US Participation in the United Nations and U.N. Reform. Hearings Before the Subcommittee on International Organizations of the Committee on Foreign Affairs. House of Representatives. Ninety-Sixth Congress. First Session. Part I. March 22, 1979.
[42] Hearings before the Committee on Foreign Relations. United States Senate. Ninety-Fourth Congress. Second Session on Nomination of Gov. William W. Scranton of Pennsylvania, to be Representative of the United States to the United Nations with the Rank of Ambassador and the Future of the United Nations Participation in the United Nations. March 2, 17, 18, and 25, 1976. US Government Printing Office. Washington, 1976, p. 20.
[43] United Nations Policy and Major Issues in the 34th U.N. General Assembly. 1979. House of Representatives, Committee on Foreign Affairs. Subcommittee on International Organizations, Washington DC.

attempts to politicize the proceedings were increasing. Substantial majorities voted to condemn Zionism as racism; to give support to the aims of the Charter of Economic Rights and Duties of States (CERDS) against which the United States had voted in the 29th U.N. General Assembly; and to (...) call for a New International Economic Order (NIEO). The U.S. delegation could support none of these resolutions. Nor could it support G-77's Declaration of Mexico, which insisted on linking women's inequality to underdevelopment and called again for a new and just international economic order; it contained a seemingly gratuitous statement of "the inalienable right of nationalization" (without reference to compensation) and made inflammatory references to Zionism.[44]

Both the political and fiduciary concerns about the UN held by the US and much of the West were by now clearly linked to a single source: the UN's egalitarian multilateralism. The General Assembly was often the target of UN opponents' ire, but the complaint now extended to the UN's programs. At UNDP, UNICEF, UNEP, and other UN programs, developing states' numbers advantage was not so overwhelming as in the Assembly, but with each state allocated a single vote, they still enjoyed a majority. In one exchange that laid bare the complaint, Congressman Bill Chappell[45] asked the Deputy Assistant Secretary of State for International Organization Affairs, Roy Douglas Morey, about representation on the UNDP Council, implying the developing states' majority was problematic.[46]

> Mr. Chappell: "What constitutes the membership of this Management Council? The UNDP's Governing Council?"
> Mr. Morey: "The UNDP Governing Council is composed of 48 countries."
> Mr. Chappell: "How many of these are underdeveloped or developing countries?"
> Mr. Morey: "Twenty-one of these are developed countries and 27 are developing countries
> (...)."
> Mr. Chappell: "If they are undeveloped and we are trying to help them get developed, how much expertise can they lend to this Council in showing how these countries ought to develop? If they had the expertise, it seems they would have been able to develop a little bit more themselves."

After pontificating on the inequity of US money being controlled by a developing state majority, Chappell concluded "It seems we are asking welfare recipients to

---

[44] Congressional Record. Proceedings and Debates of the 94th Congress, Second Session—Senate. October 1, 1976, 34801.

[45] Chappell was a member of the Democratic party representing Florida.

[46] Foreign Assistance and Related Agencies Appropriations for 1976. Hearings Before a Subcommittee of the Committee on Appropriations. House of Representatives, 94th Congress. First Session, p. 245.

tell us how much money they want, how much they will receive and how they will spend it."[47] Chappell used stronger language than others, but his core complaint was echoed by the Chair of the Committee, Congressman Otto Passman.[48] After ascertaining that UNICEF provided funding for projects in communist states, Passman asked, "Could you please tell the committee how the U.S. contribution is not channeled to Communist countries if UNICEF does in fact operate in these countries?" Morey replied that the US did not control how its money to UNICEF was spent because it was provided to the general fund controlled by the multilateral Board. He noted, "the majority of the Board members feel that children in need in any country regardless of politics should receive UNICEF assistance."[49]

These complaints about developing states' control due to the UN's egalitarian multilateralism were heightened by dual forces during the second half of the 1970s. The first was Daniel Patrick Moynihan's short-lived but vocal tenure as US Ambassador to the United Nations from June 30, 1975 to February 2, 1976. Moynihan was among the elites in the US who saw the NIEO as a threat to liberal values[50] and he did not pull punches when sharing his view. As *New York Magazine* once put it, "Moynihan flouted conventional rules of diplomacy by regularly denouncing the Third World as undemocratic and tyrannical."[51] Past UN Ambassadors and State Department officials generally downplayed the importance of criticisms lobbed at the US, emphasizing to Congress the importance of making a distinction between rhetoric and policy outcomes. When testifying before the Senate Foreign Relations Committee in 1975, Richard Gardner encouraged Committee members to distinguish between "what is said at the United Nations and what is done by the United Nations" because there were two systems, "a rhetorical system" and "an action system."[52] Moynihan took the opposite approach: he focused on verbal attacks and lopsided votes against the US and with his trademark bravado asserted that the US exerted essentially zero influence at the Organization.[53] In one House Foreign Affairs Hearing, Moynihan explained that although the UN was built on liberal principles, today most of its members were totalitarian states who distorted its purpose, and the US had not pushed back as it should have.[54] His colorful allegations included that at UNESCO "there is no single American even at the assistant

---

[47] Foreign Assistance and Related Agencies Appropriations for 1976, 250.

[48] Passman was a member of the Democratic party, representing Louisiana.

[49] Foreign Assistance and Related Agencies Appropriations for 1976, 288.

[50] Franczak 2019, 876.

[51] Dorothy Rabinowitz, "Reagan's 'Heroine' at the UN." *New York Magazine*, July 20, 1981.

[52] The United States and the United Nations: Hearings Before the Committee on Foreign Relations, United States Senate, Ninety-Fourth Congress, First Session, 1975. Prepared statement by Richard N. Gardner, p. 82.

[53] Moynihan's view of the UN is articulated in *A Dangerous Place*, his monograph about his time spent as UN Ambassador.

[54] US Participation in the United Nations and UN Reform. Hearings Before the Subcommittee on International Organizations of the Committee on Foreign Affairs. House of Representatives. Ninety-Sixth Congress. First Session. Part I. March 22, 1979.

director general level. We don't even have a typist in the Office of the Director General," and "that for some time now it has been quite clear that the Soviets have been placing KGB agents in the Secretariat."[55]

Media coverage of the United Nations in the US was a second factor that heightened negative perceptions by disproportionately covering controversy rather than accomplishments. Margaret Mead explained American alienation from the UN partly as a function of the press. She noted that UN headquarters in New York had an "unfortunate practice" "of treating the press of the United States as if they were the press from some distant country," and characterized *The New York Times* coverage of the UN, which typically played an important role in disseminating information about international affairs, as "extraordinarily uneven."[56] Much of the US press coverage that did exist was negative and even misleading. A series of articles written by *Washington Post* reporter Ronald Kessler were premised on fundamental misunderstandings about the structure and operation of the UN system, and were particularly damaging. The series, which depicted the UN as dominated by the Third World, also took aim at UN finances. The UN was experiencing a budget crisis, but Kessler's articles implied the crisis was manufactured. One headline read: "UN System Claiming Deficits Has $1.4 Billion in Bank."[57] Another article, "Contracts at United Nations Awarded Without Bidding," asserted that contracts were subject to political interference and implied that the company hired to clean UN headquarters in New York was fraudulent.[58] A third article criticized UN investment practices, accusing the Organization of "forfeiting millions of dollars" by keeping its money in accounts with low interest rates when better terms were available.[59]

The House Foreign Affairs Committee called hearings on UN finances on the heels of the series.[60] In response, the State Department issued a sixty-five-page point-by-point rebuttal of the *Washington Post* articles to the Committee.[61] Among the revelations that emerged from the House Hearings was the inadequate knowledge of Congress, even among those on the Subcommittee for International

---

[55] Ibid., 9–11.

[56] Hearings before the Committee on Foreign Relations. United States Senate. Ninety-Fourth Congress. Second Session on Nomination of Gov. William W. Scranton of Pennsylvania, to be Representative of the United States to the United Nations with the Rank of Ambassador and the Future of the United Nations Participation in the United Nations. March 2, 17, 18, and 25, 1976. US Government Printing Office. Washington, 1976, p. 39.

[57] Headline from the *Washington Post*, June 17, 1979. Byline: Ronald Kessler.

[58] Appeared in the *Washington Post*, June 18, 1979. Byline: Ronald Kessler.

[59] "U.N. Accounts Lose Millions in Interest." *The Washington Post*, June 18, 1979. Byline: Ronald Kessler.

[60] "House Panel Calls Hearings on U.N. Banking Practices." *The Washington Post*, June 19, 1979.

[61] United Nations Finances. Hearings Before the Subcommittee on International Operations and International Organizations of the Committee on Foreign Affairs, House of Representatives, Ninety-Sixth Congress. First Session. June 27, 1979. See appendix 2, State Department Response to Washington Post Articles by Ronald Kessler.

Organization Affairs, about how UN funding worked. On perhaps the most significant charge made in the Kessler series, that the UN held vast reserves and could cover its budget deficit, Marion Creekmore, then Deputy Assistant Secretary for Economic and Social Affairs in the Bureau of International Organization Affairs at State, explained:

(...) the UN system has been accused of amassing large financial bank reserves well beyond its ordinary needs. Charges of this sort (...) are misleading and unfair. Any complete and fair look at the UN's financial practices would lead one to the conclusion that it is generally a well-managed institution. (...) These charges do not take into account the following facts: 1. Many UN agencies and programs are responsible for administering special trust funds for one or several nations. These funds, which by their nature are held in special accounts as a trust, can in no way be considered as part of the operating capital of a UN body. If a UN agency were to try to use these funds for its operating expenses, it would be violating the trust and the terms under which the situation was made. They should not, then, be viewed as available funds.[62]

The existence of earmarked contributions to trust funds and their associated constraints appeared to be new information to the Subcommittee. Following Creekmore's detailed answer on why the UN did not have authority to transfer money from earmarked trust funds to pay UN administrative costs, Congressman Don Bonker[63] the chair of the Subcommittee on International Organizations, again asked "What about trust funds, Mr. Creekmore?" Creekmore again explained "(...) These are funds that serve special purposes and have conditions attached to them. The funds belonged to the government or governments that put them there."[64]

Creekmore also refuted the facts of the *Washington Post* article on the contract for cleaning UN headquarters, and explained to the Subcommittee that the UN often could not take advantage of the most competitive interest rates. He explained that some states required their UN contributions to be held in national banks until the UN needed the money (e.g., Japan) and others supplied funds in non-convertible currencies that could not be invested.[65] More surprisingly, the Committee's questions about UN investments give the appearance that they were

[62] United Nations Finances. Hearings Before the Subcommittee on International Operations and International Organizations of the Committee on Foreign Affairs, House of Representatives, Ninety-Sixth Congress. First Session. June 27, 1979, p. 58. See also pp. 41–42.
[63] Bonker was member of the Democratic party and a representative from Washington State.
[64] United Nations Finances. Hearings Before the Subcommittee on International Operations and International Organizations of the Committee on Foreign Affairs 1979, 73.
[65] United Nations Finances. Hearings Before the Subcommittee on International Operations and International Organizations of the Committee on Foreign Affairs 1979, 31.

unaware that the US itself did not provide cash to the UN to cover its voluntary contributions.[66] As Creekmore explained:

> We [the United States] make our larger voluntary contributions by letters of credit, which the organizations are not supposed to draw upon until expenditures within the organization are actually required. In this way, the U.S. delays its actual transfer of funds from the Treasury to the Organization. The international organization, therefore, earns no interest on US contributions paid in this manner.[67]

On a factual basis, the State Department discredited the articles that appeared in the *Post*, but the accusations cast suspicion on the UN's fiscal competence and continued to inform questions from Congress in subsequent hearings. Assistant Secretary of State Maynes noted to the House Foreign Affairs Committee in 1979: "The *Washington Post* series on UN financial management, though discredited in its major conclusions by testimony from the US General Accounting Office, has nevertheless focused attention on the need to push for adjustments to existing procedures."[68]

Rising antipathy toward the UN in the latter half of the 1970s is also seen in bills introduced to limit US contributions. Most were focused specifically on rectifying the mismatch between egalitarian voting rules and mandatory assessments based on capacity to pay. A series of House Resolutions were put forward to limit US contributions to the United States' share of the world population, implying UN dues should be allocated based on population size rather than GDP and other economic indicators used in the capacity to pay formula.[69] Others insisted that UN dues should simply be divided equally across the member states, or established a formula to gradually reduce the US assessment over time.[70] Reflecting anger about anti-Israel bias in the General Assembly and other UN forums, another series of bills called for the end of contributions to the Committee on the Exercise

---

[66] United Nations Finances. Hearings Before the Subcommittee on International Operations and International Organizations of the Committee on Foreign Affairs 1979, see pp. 31, 32, and 35.

[67] United Nations Finances. Hearings Before the Subcommittee on International Operations and International Organizations of the Committee on Foreign Affairs 1979, 51.

[68] "U.S. Policy and Major Issues in the 24th U.N. General Assembly." House of Representatives, Committee on Foreign Affairs. Subcommittee on International Organizations. Tuesday, September 13, 1979. Washington, DC. Prepared Statement of Hon. Charles William Maynes, Assistant Secretary of State for International Organization Affairs.

[69] In the 95th Congress, see. H.R. 147 (John Ashbrook (OH-17); H.R. 371 (Barry Goldwater, CA-20); H.R. 506 (Kenneth Robinson (VA-7); H.R. 973, Carlos Moorhead (CA-22); H.R. 1910 (Joe Waggoner Jr. (LA-4); HR 2064, Joseph Gaydos (PA-20); H.R. 3644, Philip Crane (IL-12); H.R. 4689 (Matthew Rinaldo (NJ-12); H.R. 5337, Jack Kemp (NY-38); H.R. 6553, Philip Crane (IL-12) with four co-sponsors; H.R. 8512, Manuel Lujan, Jr. (NM-1).

[70] In the 95th Congress, see H.R. 891; John Flynt Jr. (GA-6); S. 1507, Dewey Bartlett (OK).

of Inalienable Rights of the Palestinian People and the Special Unit on Palestinian Rights.[71] The last of these, titled "A bill to amend the Foreign Assistance
Act of 1961 to provide a reduction of the United States contribution to the United
Nations" was introduced by Abner Mikva, an Illinois Democrat, and enjoyed
sixteen co-sponsors.

The bills introduced during this period reflect the UN's diminished standing in
the Congress and the widespread nature of Congressional opposition to the UN's
egalitarian multilateralism, but they mostly died in Committee. A crucial exception came from conservative Republicans in the Senate, led by Jesse Helms, who
in 1978 succeeded in attaching a provision to the State Department appropriations bill that prohibited US assessments to the UN or its specialized agencies from
being used for technical assistance.[72] For those with knowledge of the history of US
policy at the UN, the irony would have been clear. Technical assistance had only
found its way into the regular budget in the late 1940s with United States' support.[73]
The Soviet Union had vigorously and consistently opposed it, and the Europeans
were lukewarm on the issue at best. But just as the Congress lacked knowledge of
UN trust funds and investment options, most did not know this history. Indeed,
in debates surrounding the Helms amendment, Congressman Robert Bauman,
Republican of Maryland, supported the amendment on the false premise that:
"(...) from the beginning [of the UN], the understanding of the United States was
that these agencies would be financed by voluntary contributions of the members
for the most part."[74]

When the Helms amendment prohibiting the use of US contributions was
passed in September of 1978, *The New York Times* described it as having "caught
the congressional leadership by surprise."[75] The amendment ostensibly withheld
$27 million in assessments to the UN and its specialized agencies, based on the US
estimate of the portion of its contribution that went toward technical assistance. Its
supporters "argued that the concerned organizations [the UN and its specialized
agencies] could and would accept the conditional funds."[76] But this, too, reflected
ignorance about basic UN rules. In reality, neither the UN nor the specialized
agencies could accept conditional funds. In an update to the House Foreign Affairs
Committee on UN reform in 1979, the State Department explained:

---

[71] In the 95th Congress, see H.R. 10842, Joseph Minish (NJ-11); H.R. 11190, Abner Mikva (IL-10);
H.R. 11747, Abner Mikva (IL-10).
[72] See, "U.S. Makes Payments on Money Owed U.N." *The New York Times.* Saturday, September 1,
1979 (no author); Graham Hovey, "Carter Suffers Two Foreign Aid Defeats in House." *The New York
Times,* April 6, 1979.
[73] See Chapter 3, p. 127.
[74] Meagher 1983, 113–114.
[75] Graham Hovey, "Carter Suffers Two Foreign Aid Defeats in House." *The New York Times,* April 6,
1979.
[76] Meagher 1983, 113.

the appropriations bill now precludes any payment of U.S. assessed contributions to the UN agencies because we are unable to ensure that no part of such a payment would be used for technical assistance. The organic statute of each agency refers to the budget as a whole and makes no provision for earmarking within, or attaching conditions to, assessed contributions to the regular budget. Further the agency heads do not have the right to earmark assessed contributions in such a manner as to prevent their being used to finance any specific agency or program.[77]

Key figures in the Carter administration, including US Ambassador to the UN Andrew Young, and Assistant Secretary of State for International Organization Affairs, Charles Maynes, pushed back against Congressional skepticism about the UN's worth. Maynes debunked misinformation about the United Nations, reported in the press, and argued against those in Congress making claims that the US had lost all influence in UN forums. Young argued strongly against the efficacy of withholding assessments as a means to enact UN reforms, stating: "We cannot reform the UN by wreaking havoc on its system and by participating in an emotional campaign on how badly it functions. Reforms will not spring from dissatisfaction but from constructive approaches."[78] He similarly opposed linking US bilateral aid to UN General Assembly votes, arguing it would draw anger rather than constructive engagement.[79] Efforts by the Carter administration succeeded in keeping Helms's restriction out of the bill in 1979 and the US was once again able to pay its dues at the end of August of that year.[80]

These early efforts by UN opponents failed in part because they were pursued with little knowledge about the UN system and how it worked. They did not know enough to address the problem creatively. Actors best positioned to tap into rule permissiveness are typically those with deep knowledge of the rule system and an understanding of relevant players.[81] Lacking knowledge of this sort, these early efforts were successful only in signaling displeasure, but not in exerting US influence at the UN, or in enacting change in UN rules. For instance, the assertion that the UN would accept funds with conditions made sense only if one did not

---

[77] US Participation in the United Nations and U.N. Reform. Hearing Before the Subcommittee on International Organizations of the Committee on Foreign Affairs. House of Representatives. 96th Congress, First Session. Part II. Peacekeeping and Dispute Settlement. June 14, 1979, p. 27.

[78] US Participation in the United Nations and U.N. Reform. Hearings Before the Subcommittee on International Organizations of the Committee on Foreign Affairs. House of Representatives. Ninety-Sixth Congress. First Session. Part I. March 22, 1979, p. 8.

[79] Nomination of Hon. Andrew Young as US Representative to UN: hearing before the Committee on Foreign Relations, United States Senate, Ninety-Fifth Congress, First Session, on the nomination of Congressman Andrew Young to be the United States Representative to the United Nations, with the rank of Ambassador, and representative in the Security Council of the United Nations. January 25, 1977, p. 39.

[80] Graham Hovey, "Carter Suffers Two Foreign Aid Defeats in House." *The New York Times*, April 6, 1979; "U.S. Makes Payments on Money Owed U.N." *The New York Times*, September 1, 1979 (no author).

[81] Adler-Nissen and Pouliot 2014; Cornut 2018; Búzás and Graham 2020.

know UN rules or viewed it as a corrupt, fraudulent organization. Those who did possess knowledge about the UN—both at State and other executive agencies, and long-time members of the Foreign Relations Committee—remained support-ive of the United Nations. But the underlying discontent did not dissipate. And soon, UN opponents would have an ambassador who was both knowledgeable and sympathetic to their cause.

Kirkpatrick Enters the Frame

Jeane Kirkpatrick's appointment as US Ambassador to the United Nations in 1981 marked an important turning point in US policy toward the UN.[82] In some ways, her rhetoric on the UN echoed Moynihan's. Her public statements and addresses often drew attention to anti-Israel rhetoric in the Assembly and underlined the isolation of the United States. In one address before B'nai B'rith International in Toronto, Kirkpatrick cited "over 150 anti-Israel resolutions" in the General Assem-bly, Security Council, and the Commission on Human Rights, and called the UN's anti-Israel campaign "obsessive."[83] Kirkpatrick's predecessors (save Moynihan), had downplayed these resolutions, with Andrew Young recently having argued they were merely a means for weaker powers to annoy the United States. By con-trast, Kirkpatrick depicted the UN's "automatic majority" as anti-Semitic, referring to the UN as "deeply implicated in an assault against the very state which serves, more than any other, as a haven for the survivors of Nazi persecution."[84] She regularly reminded her audience that waning US influence at the UN was not a function of the Reagan administration but had been "deteriorating for years."[85] Sharing Moynihan's skillful incorporation of dry humor in political rhetoric, she built on a line from a speech he gave in 1976, when he lamented, "In the past year we were frequently reduced to voting in a bloc which, with variations, consisted of ourselves, Chile and the Dominican Republic." Kirkpatrick then quipped, "Since then we have lost Chile and the Dominican Republic."[86]

Statements from Kirkpatrick about anti-American or anti-Israel sentiment were often accompanied by reminders that egalitarian multilateralism empowered countries that did not pay the UN's bills to dictate its policies. A detailed account of the campaign to expel Israel from the United Nations was followed by a reminder

---

[82] Kirkpatrick was a Columbia-trained political scientist and diplomat, and the first woman in the US to be appointed UN Ambassador.

[83] Jeane Kirkpatrick with Allan Gerson, "An Unrelenting Assault." Address before B'nai B'rith International, Toronto, Canada, October 18, 1982. In Kirkpatrick 1988, 10–11.

[84] Kirkpatrick 1988, 10.

[85] Jeane Kirkpatrick, "Standing Alone." Address before the Arizona State University, Tempe, Arizona, October 23, 1981, in Kirkpatrick 1988, 193.

[86] Kirkpatrick 1988, 194.

that "the 86 countries which decided Israel is not a 'peace-loving state'"[87] collectively contribute "only 22 and three quarters percent of the total UN budget. This is
less than what the US contributes alone."[88] This highlights another pattern in Kirkpatrick's statements, which repeatedly underlined the gap between US funding
and the proportion paid by developing states in the "automatic majority." To wit:
"effective control over the budget is exercised by a solid majority whose members
(88 countries) pay less than two percent of the budget."[89]

Kirkpatrick did not think the US should get out of the United Nations, that
position was too extreme. But like UN opponents, she viewed the egalitarian
multilateralism of the Assembly as a fundamental problem. In contrast to earlier
instances of change that paved the way for the UN's transformation analyzed in
this book, the changes pursued by the Congress in the 1980s, and by Kirkpatrick
in particular, were *intended* to undermine egalitarian multilateralism. Proponents
were not necessarily confident that their actions would transform the system, but
it was clear from this point that they would welcome such a transformation and
that their policies aimed to move the UN system in that direction.

Kirkpatrick emerged as well positioned to bring these changes about. The tenure
of most US ambassadors between 1960 and 1980 had been short. Kirkpatrick, by
contrast, served more than four years between 1981 and 1985.[90] During this period
she learned how the United Nations worked, how it received funding, and studied
the history of US policy on Article 17. Some of the lessons Kirkpatrick absorbed
echoed views held by Moynihan, Young, and senior members of the Senate Foreign
Relations Committee, which focused on the United States' need to "work harder
at the politics of the UN."[91] Like her predecessors, she believed that the US should
constructively engage but also defend itself, rather than withdraw or sit aloof. But
she also brought new strategies to alter US policy with regard to both mandatory
dues and voluntary contributions. The first involved *reinterpreting* Article 17 to
limit US obligations. The second involved *repurposing* permissive earmark rules
to constrain the UN and channel it in directions more favorable to US interests.
In pursuing these strategies, Kirkpatrick handed UN critics in Congress the tools
they needed to exert influence and to accelerate insipid trends caused by smaller
contributors' earmarking behavior.

[87] This language is significant since UN membership is open to all peace-loving states. A General
Assembly resolution declaring Israel not a peace-loving state, passed 86 to 21, with 34 abstentions,
Kirkpatrick 1988, 13.

[88] Jeane Kirkpatrick with Allan Gerson, "An Unrelenting Assault." Address before B'nai B'rith
International, Toronto, Canada, October 18, 1982 in Kirkpatrick 1988, 13–14.

[89] "Getting a Grip on the Budget." With Harvey Feldman. Human Rights and International Organization Subcommittee of the House Foreign Affairs Committee, October 3, 1983 in Kirkpatrick 1988,
267.

[90] Kirkpatrick's tenure ran from February 4, 1981 to April 1, 1985.

[91] Jeane Kirkpatrick, "Standing Alone." Address before the Arizona State University, Tempe, Arizona,
October 23, 1981, in Kirkpatrick 1988, 202.

Reinterpreting Article 17

Previous US attempts to withhold mandatory assessments from the United Nations had been opposed by the State Department on the grounds that paying UN dues was a treaty obligation. As Zoller writes, as late as 1978, "the Legal Adviser of the Department of State had concluded in a memorandum of law that Article 17 of the UN Charter 'impose[s] a legal obligation on members to pay the amount assessed to them by the General Assembly.'"[92] An exchange between Senator Jesse Helms and Charles Maynes in 1980 over withholding mandatory dues on technical assistance illustrates the typical State Department defense. First, Helms frames mandatory dues that pay for technical assistance as a tax on Americans, and Maynes pushes back.

> Senator Helms: "Do you consider the provisions of technical assistance through mandatory assessment to be in fact, an international tax? Isn't that what it really is?"
>
> Assistant Secretary Maynes: "I think it is shared costs for international cooperation, Senator Helms." (...)[93]
>
> Helms then continues to press Maynes on whether he thinks the US should really pay *all* of its assessment. Maynes replies by arguing that it should, and offers a strong defense of US influence at UN organizations.
>
> Assistant Secretary Maynes: "I am saying that we ought to meet the obligations of membership, that's right."
>
> Senator Helms: "One hundred percent?"
>
> Assistant Secretary Maynes: "If we believe in the organization, yes, we should meet the obligation. (...) You are making the assumption, Senator, that we are unable to shape the policies of these organizations in any circumstance, and I would argue that is not true. We have great influence. We attempt to use it. We don't always get what we want. But I would argue, on balance, we come out far ahead in all of these organizations, and that should guide the congressional response, I would hope."[94]

This was a standard State Department response, that mandatory assessments to the UN were a treaty obligation and that responsible member states paid their dues and lived up to their obligations. But as the US Ambassador to the UN, Kirkpatrick offered an alternative view. In one House Foreign Affairs hearing she stated:

---

[92] Zoller 1987, 610.

[93] Department of State Authorization Act, Fiscal Years 1980 and 1981. Hearing before the Committee on Foreign Relations, United States Senate, Ninety-Sixth Congress. Second Session on S. 2444 A Bill to Amend the Department of State Authorization Act, Fiscal Years 1980 and 1981 to Provide Additional Authorization for Fiscal Year 1980 and for Other Purposes AND S. 2445, A Bill to Provide Additional Authorization for Fiscal Year 1981 and for Other Purposes. March 25, 1980, p. 28.

[94] Department of State Authorization Act, Fiscal Years 1980 and 1981, 28.

Although this is a controversial subject, I desire to make clear that I do not believe the US treaty obligation to contribute 25% of the assessed budget is absolute. It is sometimes argued that as signatories to the treaty we assume an absolute legal obligation to pay the assessed share of the budget. It seems to me, after consultation and on reflection, that this obligation is real, substantial and serious, but also that it is not absolute."[95]

Distinguishing herself from UN opponents in Congress for whom not wanting to pay was reason enough to withhold assessments, Kirkpatrick offered a set of legal arguments to support the position that the obligation was "not absolute." The first step in her argument relied on precedent. She resurrected the statement made by UN Ambassador Arthur Goldberg at the conclusion of the Article 19 crisis in 1965. The so-called "Goldberg Reservation" was articulated in response to the General Assembly's decision *not* to invoke Article 19, which would have suspended the Soviet Union's vote in the General Assembly due to their failure to pay UN assessments.[96] The failure of the General Assembly to invoke Article 19 was a diplomatic failure for the United States, and to save face Goldberg stated that the US would reserve the right to make an exception to its obligation "if, in our view, strong and compelling reasons exist to do so."[97]

The language of "strong and compelling reasons" is subject to interpretation. But Kirkpatrick implied such reasons included instances where "the purposes for which they [funds] are being spent are not consistent with the goals of the Charter."[98] Her position was strengthened by consulting Arthur Goldberg himself. Goldberg had been an ardent UN supporter as Ambassador, but had more recently become concerned that the General Assembly and some of the specialized agencies "have been taking actions in violation of the UN Charter."[99] When Kirkpatrick consulted Goldberg, he replied, "there can be no question that under the 'Goldberg Reservation' the United States reserves the right to withhold assessments for UN activities, which in our opinion, do not serve our national purpose."[100]

[95] "Getting a Grip on the Budget." With Harvey Feldman. Human Rights and International Organizations Subcommittee of the House Foreign Affairs Committee. October 3, 1983 in Kirkpatrick 1988, 268.
[96] On the Goldberg Reservation, see Chapter 4.
[97] Arthur Goldberg, 1965. "Statement by Ambassador Goldberg, US Representative to the United Nations, as Delivered in the Special Committee on Peacekeeping Operations," August 16, 1965. International Legal Materials, 1000–03.
[98] "U.S. Financial and Political Involvement in the United Nations: Hearing before the Committee on Governmental Affairs," United States Senate, Ninety-Ninth Congress, First Session, May 7, 1985. Washington, U.S. G.P.O., p. 15; See Gerson 2000, 63–64.
[99] The United States and the United Nations: hearings before the Committee on Foreign Relations, United States Senate, Ninety-Fourth Congress, First Session. 1975, p. 12.
[100] "Getting a Grip on the Budget." With Harvey Feldman. Human Rights and International Organizations Subcommittee of the House Foreign Affairs Committee. October 3, 1983 in Kirkpatrick 1988, 269.

As a second step, Kirkpatrick's position relied on subsequent practice, though without referring to it as such. She pointed out that thirty UN member states withheld portions of their assessed contributions and that they incurred no penalties for doing so. Further, these countries did so "as a matter of announced policy."[101] In a later hearing, Kirkpatrick reminded the Congress that "selective withholding [of mandatory assessments] is *consistent with the practice of other nations*."[102] During the 1980s these were not only small, poor states that could not pay, but also the Soviet Union (owing more than $40 million), France (owing $4.2 million), and the German Democratic Republic ($3.6 million owed).[103] The fact that big and small states regularly withheld UN assessments without consequence led some to conclude that Article 17 might no longer be regarded as binding.[104] In this view the "tolerance for breaches of Article 17(2)"[105] indicated that the obligation to pay UN dues had fallen into desuetude,[106] modifying Article 17 as a result. Consistent with this view, Henry Schermers wrote that "the toleration of too many violations may lead to *a tacit revision of the constitution*."[107]

As Kirkpatrick admitted, this was a controversial position, especially when measured against past US policy. After all, "in the past the Administration used to come up to the Hill and fight amendments that would violate our legal obligations to the UN."[108] Nelson (1985) questioned the idea that the General Assembly's failure to invoke Article 19 weakened Article 17, writing that "neither logic nor practice (except possibly in the context of "Goldberg") demands that Article 17 is solely and utterly dependent for its survival on the support given it by the sanction under Article 19."[109] Others echo this view, arguing that Article 17 remained binding and pointing to the United States' *"emphatic"*[110] position supporting its binding nature during the *Certain Expenses* case.[111] In a similar vein, Zoller's analysis undercut Kirkpatrick's argument based on subsequent practice by citing the United States' consistent complaints and disapproval of other states' withholdings. According to the VCLT, subsequent practice should be taken into account when it indicates the agreement of states parties. On Zoller's reading, the United States'

---

[101] Kirkpatrick 1988, 268.

[102] Quoted in Zoller 1987, 615. Emphasis added. From hearing: US Policy in the United Nations: Hearings and Markup Before the House Comm. on Foreign Affairs and its Subcomms. on Human Rights and International Organizations, and on International Operations, Ninety-Ninth Congress, First Session. 58 (1985).

[103] Estimated cumulative withholdings to the Regular Budget are from 1985. See Nelson 1986, 980–981.

[104] E.g., Franck 1985, 259. Franck later moderated his position, see Alvarez 1991, 255, fn. 101.

[105] Zoller 1987, 614. Note: Zoller does not find a basis for withholding based on subsequent practice under treaty law but rather based on international institutional law.

[106] Franck 1985, 259.

[107] Cited in Zoller 1987, 615, emphasis added. Original cite: Schermers, International Institutional Law.

[108] Zoller 1987, 613, fn 18 citing Margaret E. Galey.

[109] Nelson 1986, 981.

[110] Galey 1988, 248.

[111] E.g., Scharf 2000.

disapproval of others meant that as a practice, withholding did not demonstrate such an agreement.[112]

But while most believed that large-scale withholding violated Article 17, many saw legal space for Kirkpatrick's position on withholding when a sound argument could be made that a specific set of activities included in the regular budget were *ultra vires* (unlawful).[113] A test of this argument came when the Reagan administration used the *ultra vires* justification to withhold the portion of its assessment that would be allocated for the Preparatory Commission for the Law of the Sea, which had been included in the UN's regular budget. In a statement on December 30, 1982, President Reagan stated "it is not a proper expense of the United Nations within the meaning of its own Charter, as the Law of the Sea Preparatory Commission is legally independent of and distinct from the U.N. It is not a subsidiary organ and not answerable to that body (...)."[114] According to some legal analysis, the position of the Reagan administration was consistent with the *Certain Expenses* decision, which had determined ONUC and UNEF constituted "expenses" of the Organization, in part because they "arose from activities of [the UN's] principal and subsidiary organs."[115] The work of the Preparatory Commission for the Law of the Sea, by contrast, did not.

Other legal scholars disagreed that treaty law provided legal justification for withholding but found justification in international institutional law.[116] The most thorough analysis of the issue came from Elisabeth Zoller, who argued that international institutional law "must be supplemented with established practices or rules tailored to the needs of the system."[117] According to Zoller, the pattern of withholding of assessments by large powers (e.g., the USSR, France, the United States) represented an established practice by the minority to reject the "corporate will" of the majority in the United Nations. A dissenting opinion from Judge Andro Gros, in the ICJ's influential *Namibia* decision, usefully illustrates the issue when he stated, "For if a minority of States which are not in agreement with a proposed decision are to be bound, however they vote, and whatever their reservations may be, the General Assembly would be a federal parliament."[118] Applied to the context of withholding, the Gros opinion suggested that if there were no grounds for

[112] Zoller 1987, 616–617. Zoller concludes that such a "shaky practice" is not legally meaningful (617).
[113] On *ultra vires* acts of IOs see Cannizzaro and Palchetti 2011.
[114] "Statement on the Withholding of United States Funds From the Law of the Sea Preparatory Commission." President Ronald W. Reagan (December 30, 1982). https://www.reaganlibrary.gov/archives/speech/statement-withholding-united-states-funds-law-sea-preparatory-commission (accessed January 25, 2021.)
[115] Hynes 1982–1983, 487; Franck 1985, 259–60.
[116] The body of law pertaining to international organizations.
[117] Zoller 1987, 630.
[118] Legal Consequences for States of the Continued Presence of South Africa in Namibia (South West Africa) Notwithstanding Security Council Resolution 276 (1970), Advisory Opinion, 1971 International Court of Justice. 16 (June 21). Dissenting Opinion of Judge Andro Gros.

the US or others to withhold assessments when they disagreed with the budget, the Assembly was effectively a parliament. On the same grounds, Zoller concludes that "The truth is that withholding, like reservations, has been 'necessitated through the need' to keep the Organization from turning into 'a super-State.'"[119] In general, legal analysis of the Reagan administration's position found that state practice pointed toward an interpretation of Article 17 that provided space for targeted withholding (i.e., for the amount associated with the unlawful act).[120] Indeed, Alvarez writes that "The *ultra vires* exception to the duty to pay, rationalized on the grounds of preventing the tyranny of the majority, has won general, if sometimes grudging, acceptance."[121]

One cannot confidently state that Article 17 was modified through subsequent practice or the interpretive acts that followed, few make that claim. But one can say that the reach and binding character of Article 17 were muddied, and that limits to its reach now rested on serious legal arguments. This had important effects. First, the Zoller reading of states' obligations under Article 17 could be used to legitimize a number of withholdings by wealthy states that voted against UN regular budget resolutions that had passed with majority support. This extended to prior objections by Senator Helms and others who opposed the inclusion of technical assistance in the regular budget and wanted to withhold the amount associated with those activities. In short, the legitimation of selective withholding that that reinterpretation provided, served as a reminder to the Assembly that it was in fact not a parliament and that the UN could not indefinitely undergo budgetary expansion by ignoring the views of the minority.

In the same way, the reinterpretation added a sense of legitimacy to efforts of the Geneva Group to curtail regular budget growth at the UN. Beginning in April of 1981, the Geneva Group agreed that the budgets of the UN and its Specialized Agencies should be kept to zero-real growth for the first half of the 1980s.[122] The US and the USSR also coordinated on UN funding policy based on their shared interest in controlling budget growth.[123] Geneva Group members regularly voted against, or abstained from, regular budget votes that did not adhere to zero-growth. Alongside the US and USSR, "no votes" came from the United Kingdom, Japan, and West Germany.[124] In 1985, the Geneva Group announced in a joint policy statement that their zero-real growth effort would continue for the second half

[119] Zoller 1987, 631.
[120] Nelson 1986, 981. Gerson 2000, especially 64–65.
[121] Alvarez 1991, 257–258.
[122] State Department Bulletin, January/June 1985, 178; "Getting a Grip on the Budget." With Harvey Feldman. Human Rights and International Organization Subcommittee of the House Foreign Affairs Committee, October 3, 1983, p. 266 in Kirkpatrick 1988.
[123] Kirkpatrick 1988, 266.
[124] Kirkpatrick 1988, 267.

of the 1980s with an increased focus on improved management, cost effectiveness, and lowering personnel costs.[125]

The reinterpretation of Article 17 effectively sealed off the regular budget as a path to growth for the foreseeable future. This was a significant shift from previous decades when the regular budget had expanded at a fairly rapid pace.[126] The General Assembly could still incorporate activities that major contributors disapproved of in the regular budget, but they did so with the knowledge that withholding should be expected. To avoid withholding, the General Assembly's majority would need to take contributors' position into account. Over time, an understanding of this sort emerged. No rules were formally revised or amended, but the Assembly became more circumspect in its appropriations, implicitly mindful of contributors' interpretation of their obligations, and a norm of consensus decision-making emerged, governing the budget.[127]

This change through reinterpretation is consistent with the theoretical framework and it is worth noting how change did *not* occur, that is, through formal rule revision or replacement. The failure to revise relevant UN rules was not for lack of trying on the part of the United States and its allies. Wary of the expanding size of the Assembly and its control over financial matters, the issue of a possible "associate [UN] membership" for newly independent small island states had been raised in 1967.[128] In 1970, the UK and the US proposed a costless membership, that is, one in which states could join without paying assessments.[129] The tradeoff for these alternative memberships would be that states lacked full voting rights. Both efforts were doomed to fail, given developing states' interest in maintaining and extending their voting power in the General Assembly, and were quietly set aside by their proponents. In 1975, Harold Stassen, at that time the last living member of the US delegation to the San Francisco conference, spoke of the need to introduce weighted voting at the UN for some matters.[130] The Kassebaum-Soloman amendment of 1986 pursued this goal using coercion, withholding 20 percent of the US assessment to induce the General Assembly to adopt weighted voting rules, like those used at the World Bank and the International Monetary Fund, to govern budget votes. Each of these direct efforts to revise the egalitarian multilateralism of the Assembly failed. Status quo voting rules enjoyed support from too many stakeholders to be revised even in the face of US withholding.

[125] State Department Bulletin, 1985, January/June, p. 178.
[126] See: Global Policy Forum, UN Regular Budget Expenditures. https://archive.globalpolicy.org/un-finance/tables-and-charts-on-un-finance/the-un-regular-budget/27466.html (accessed December 8, 2021).
[127] Peterson 2006, 3. This norm was broken in 2008 when the US voted against the regular budget in the Fifth Committee, "breaking with recent tradition of consensus on budgets" (Crook 2008, 355).
[128] Franck 1985, 255–256.
[129] Ibid.
[130] The United States and the United Nations: hearings before the Committee on Foreign Relations, United States Senate, Ninety-Fourth Congress, First Session. 1975, p. 4.

The meaning of rules evolved through reinterpretation based on state practice and legal reasoning rather than formal renegotiation and revision. With the
regular budget off limits as a path to UN expansion, the UN could only grow
through voluntary contributions. Here the second strategic move from Ambassador Kirkpatrick emerged: she encouraged the Congress to pick and choose
which UN voluntary program to support, and to join European states in more
readily earmarking voluntary contributions to the UN.

"Pick and Pay"

Voluntary programs at the UN had always been vulnerable to a "pick and pay"
approach. Early in the UN's history, the fact that paying for development programs
was voluntary reflected that some member states, and likely an important one, did
not want to pay. It was the Soviet Union that provided the impetus for voluntary funding. When the Expanded Program on Technical Assistance (EPTA) was
established in 1949, the USSR did not contribute funds. By the mid-1960s, the US
sometimes served as that relevant, reluctant, member state. But surprisingly, the
US did not wield its voluntary contributions as weapons very often. Congressional
attempts to influence or express dissatisfaction with the UN were often ineffective,
reflecting inadequate knowledge of where and how the US could exert influence.
Kirkpatrick's diagnosis of the problem of egalitarian multilateralism was the same,
but her answer to the question of how the US could best wrest control away from
multilateral bodies was different.

In addition to Kirkpatrick's arguments regarding Article 17, she advocated two
other policies. In their early days, voluntary contributions, and later earmarked
voluntary contributions, had been used by friendly donors to empower the UN
to get new operational work off the ground. By contrast, Kirkpatrick sought to use
these tools to shape the existing system to reflect US interests. Previous UN Ambassadors defended the UN system by focusing on programs favored by Americans,
like UNICEF or UNDP. Kirkpatrick did the same, but she went a step further by
advocating that the US use its financial might to reward its favored programs and
punish others.

> I would encourage the Congress in its desire to exercise greater control over the
> U.S. contributions and expenditures to distinguish between UN operations and
> programs which U.S. taxpayers support and those they do not. We should set
> priorities and make choices in ways that favor programs which are consistent
> with our values, and that favor agencies which pursue the purposes for which
> they were established. We should penalize those which, because of polarization
> and/or inefficiency, have strayed from their legitimate purposes and tasks.[131]

[131] Kirkpatrick 1988, 269–270.

Kirkpatrick's statement made clear the goal was to use financial levers to constrain the UN and channel its activities toward those deemed "consistent with our values." More than simply provide unrestricted contributions to preferred agencies, she emphasized earmarked contributions as an effective way to achieve this goal:

> ...since our voluntary contributions exceed our assessed contributions and there are no binding restraints regarding such contributions, I recommend that if Congress is concerned principally about economy, it makes sense to start there [voluntary contributions], and afterward to move agency by agency through assessed contributions. In this regard I would like to respectfully suggest to this committee, as I have done in the past in testimony before other Congressional committees, *that the U.S. consider adopting the practice of many other large voluntary contributors of earmarking our funds to specific agencies and for specific projects.*[132]

The rationale of Kirkpatrick's earmarking arguments—like her Article 17 position—was the long-standing practice of other UN member states, in this case, the UN's other Western donors. But Kirkpatrick's approach also turned the original logic of permissive earmark rules on its head. Permissive earmark rules could be repurposed to constrain the UN rather than to empower it in new areas. Earmarked contributions could be a substitute for money that would otherwise be provided through regular or unrestricted voluntary contributions. As a substitute, earmarked contributions would rise and unrestricted contributions would decline, reducing the resources controlled by egalitarian multilateralism in UN governing bodies. This accords with substitution thinking from the State Department at the time, which emphasized that contributions to UNDP should be treated as a substitute for the technical assistance program in the regular budget that the US was working to eliminate.[133]

The implementation of Kirkpatrick's advice was uneven, but significant. The Reagan administration typically presented UNDP and UNICEF as well-run programs that were consistent with US interests, but other UN programs faced significant cuts. Among the early and prominent cuts were those to the UN Population Fund (UNFPA). The US Congress had been a strong supporter of establishing UNFPA in 1968, when it encouraged the Nixon administration to support family planning programs through the UN in response to rising concerns about population growth.[134] In UNFPA's first year, the US contributed $1.7 million, or

<hr>

[132] Kirkpatrick 1988, 270, emphasis added; see also State Department Bulletin, 1983 July/December, p. 86.

[133] State Department Bulletin, January/June 1983, 181.

[134] "The U.N. Population Fund: Background and the U.S. Funding Debate." Congressional Research Service Report. December 16, 2004–July 15, 2010. https://www.everycrsreport.com/reports/RL32703.html.

75 percent of all contributions. As more states contributed to the effort, the proportion of US funds declined, but it remained the largest UNFPA donor. Well into the Reagan years in 1984, the US contributed $38.2 million or 27.5 percent of all UNFPA funds, the highest proportion it had paid since 1977.[135] That same year, however, Reagan announced what became known as the "Mexico City Policy." Reflecting the position of his white evangelical political base, Reagan outlined new eligibility restrictions on organizations that received US contributions for family planning. Among them was the requirement NGOs receiving US funding could not actively promote or perform abortions.

In 1985, the United States Agency for International Development (USAID) informed Rafael Salas, the Executive Director of UNFPA, that it would withhold $10 million of the US pledge for fiscal year 1985. The allegation that UNFPA participated in "coercive abortion or involuntary sterilization activities in China" was used to justify withholding.[136] USAID had cleared UNFPA of participation in such programs on multiple occasions and other donors defended the program. Canada supported UNFPA, and directly countered US allegations. Canada indicated that its support "for UNFPA's China Program should be underlined," and that Canada "found no evidence of UNFPA's involvement in coercive activities and in fact concluded that UNFPA is a moderating influence on such tendencies."[137] Despite the defense, the US did not reverse course, cutting all funds to UNFPA in 1986, a practice that continued throughout the Reagan administration and the subsequent presidency of George H.W. Bush.[138]

Other components of the UN development system faced cuts as well. The Bush administration's request for the UN Capital Development Fund (UNCDF), never a favorite in the United States, fell to a low of $1.5 million in 1990[139] and continued to decline.[140] In some later years, as in 2005, US contributions to the UNCDF were entirely absent.[141] Although the US continued to support the World Food Program through food commodities and transport subsidies, it made no funding request to

---

[135] "The U.N. Population Fund: Background and the U.S. Funding Debate." Congressional Research Service Report. December 16, 2004–July 15, 2010.

[136] "The U.N. Population Fund: Background and the U.S. Funding Debate." Congressional Research Service Report. December 16, 2004–July 15, 2010.

[137] "The U.N. Population Fund: Background and the U.S. Funding Debate." Congressional Research Service Report. December 16, 2004–July 15, 2010.

[138] Foreign Relations of the United States, 1981–1988. Volume XLI, Global Issues II. 300. Editorial Note.

[139] "Foreign Operations, export financing, and related programs appropriations for fiscal year 1990: hearings before a subcommittee on the Committee on Appropriations, United States Senate, One Hundred First Congress, First Session, on H.R.2939/H.R.3743. An Act Making Appropriations for Foreign Operations, Export Financing, and Related Programs for the Fiscal Year Ending September 30, 1990, and for Other Purposes." Part 1 (Pages 1–1097).

[140] In 2018, UNCDF contributions from the US Government totaled $1 million ($500k core, $500k non-core). http://uncdf.org/contributions-to-uncdf (accessed February 22, 2020).

[141] In the mid-2000s, the US contribution to UNCDF fell to between $200,000 (2004) to $321,4500 in 2006. In 2005, the US made no contribution. Core and Non-Core UNCDF contributions available at http://uncdf.org/contributions-to-uncdf.

Congress in 1990 (down from $980,000 in FY 1989) to support the administrative costs of the WFP. Questioned about the cut, the Bush administration pointed to budget constraints and argued that "other countries, which do not have commodities to contribute, should meet WFP's cash requirements for administrative costs."[142]

At UNEP, the small Environment Fund had grown steadily during the 1970s, in large part on the strength of US contributions. Throughout that decade US contributions were more than twice the size of the second largest contributor (the USSR) and more than three times the size of the third largest (Germany or Canada depending on the year).[143] But beginning in the 1980s, when the State Department described UNDP and UNICEF programs as being of "generally high quality," UNEP received only "acceptable" marks for efficiency and effectiveness.[144] Its contributions diminished despite the increased prominence of environmental issues. After reaching $10 million in 1977, US support declined during the 1980s, and did not exceed $10 million again until 1990. Contributions from other major donors were mostly stagnant during the same period (see Figure 6.3).[145] This meant that while UNEP trust funds and trust fund income were rising with financial support from donors like Sweden, Finland, and Germany, unrestricted contributions to the Environment Fund were stagnant, due in large part to a shift toward frozen or declining contributions from the United States.

Even programs long favored in the United States endured declining US support in the latter half of the 1980s. US contributions to UNDP had either increased or held steady every year since the program's inception in 1966. This trend held up during the first term of Reagan's presidency, when contributions to the main (unrestricted) UNDP account reached a peak of $165 million in 1985. But a precipitous decline began in 1986, when contributions dropped to just under $138 million, and in 1987 to $104 million.[146] US funding hovered around that mark in subsequent years ($105 million in 1990, $109 million in 1991).[147] The Reagan

[142] "Foreign Operations, export financing, and related programs appropriations for fiscal year 1990: hearings before a subcommittee on the Committee on Appropriations, United States Senate, One Hundred First Congress, First Session, on H.R.2939/H.R.3743. An Act Making Appropriations for Foreign Operations, Export Financing, and Related Programs for the Fiscal Year Ending September 30, 1990, and for Other Purposes." Part 1 (Pages 1–1097).

[143] See UNEP's "Check Your Contributions" tool, which shows individual member states' contributions to the Environment Fund throughout UNEP's history: https://www.unep.org/about-un-environment/funding-and-partnerships/check-your-contributions (accessed December 7, 2021).

[144] "Foreign Operations, export financing, and related programs appropriations for fiscal year 1990: hearings before a subcommittee on the Committee on Appropriations, United States Senate, One Hundred First Congress, First Session, on H.R.2939/H.R.3743. An Act Making Appropriations for Foreign Operations, Export Financing, and Related Programs for the Fiscal Year Ending September 30, 1990, and for Other Purposes." Part 1 (Pages 1–1097), 537.

[145] Contributions to the Environment Fund, 1973–2020 are available from UNEP at: https://www.unep.org/about-un-environment/funding-and-partnerships/check-your-contributions   (accessed February 25, 2021).

[146] United States Department of State 1988, 138.

[147] United States Department of State 1993, 14.

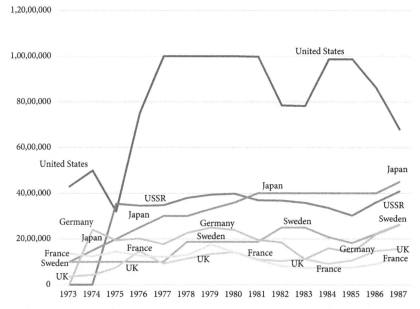

Figure 6.3 Contributions to the UNEP Environment Fund by Major Donors, 1973–87.

Note: Contributions to the Environment Fund, 1973–2020 are available from UNEP at: https://www.unep.org/about-un-environment/funding-and-partnerships/check-your-contributions (accessed February 25, 2021).

and Bush administrations did not directly criticize UNDP in making these cuts. On the contrary, they often praised the program's work, explaining their declining requests as a function of budget constraints. But the effect was similar to the UNEP case. In the past, US contributions had spurred growth in unrestricted voluntary contributions. Now, with the UN's other large donors driving growth in earmarked funding, the US stepped back from its outsized role in providing unrestricted funds. This constrained egalitarian multilateralism by reducing the resources controlled by governing bodies and accelerated the UN's growing dependence on earmarked funds governed by contracts negotiated by the UN agency and the donor state.

The extent to which the US directly contributed to growing trust fund income during the 1980s was limited. In general, the US did not follow other donors in establishing single-donor funds that effectively treated the UN as a contract agency for bilateral aid. According to UNDP documents that list trust funds administered during the 1980s, the US never established a single-donor fund in that period or in the prior decades. There is even evidence that the US opposed the proliferation of country-specific and single-donor trust funds at the UN during the Reagan administration.[148] The US instrumental use of trust funds during this period was distinct and often focused on burden-sharing. The aim was to support and sometimes initiate the establishment of multi-donor trust funds that aligned with US interests. The goal was not primarily about delivering *US* aid, it was about using MDTFs, and by extension the UN architecture, to mobilize other donors to support causes that aligned with US interests. A few examples from across issue areas illustrate this practice. In 1981, the US supported a General Assembly resolution to convert a country-specific trust fund for Chilean victims of human rights abuse into a more general trust fund for victims of torture to provide psychological and medical support to victims and their families.[149] The Soviet Union opposed the new fund, while the United States' position was that it "supplements US bilateral human rights efforts."[150] In 1990, the US was among eighteen states that supported the fund, providing about 10 percent ($100,000) of annual contributions.[151]

Support for the UN Afghanistan Emergency Trust Fund, established in 1988, provides an example with direct ties to US security interests.[152] In 1988, the Bush administration was reducing core contributions across UN programs, but the administration found room for a new appropriations request in the international organizations & programs (IO&P) account: $16 million for the UN Afghan Emergency Fund. Then Ambassador to the UN Tom Pickering called the US contribution "a significant component of our overall Afghan strategy. It will allow us to influence the development of relief efforts and encourage contributions from other donor nations."[153] He explained, "We will continue our bilateral cross-border humanitarian assistance, but the enormity of the problem and the demands for expertise, experience and funds compel an international response. The UN

---

[148] Foreign Relations of The United States, 1981–1988. Volume XLI, Global Issues II. 39. Telegram from the Mission to the United Nations Department of State. Geneva. January 6, 1981. Subject: UN Human Rights Commission: U.S. Interests, Objectives and Strategy for the 37th Session, February 2–March 31, 1981.

[149] Foreign Relations of The United States, 1981–1988. Volume XLI, Global Issues II. 39. Telegram from the Mission to the United Nations Department of State. Geneva. January 6, 1981; Foreign Relations of The United States, 1981–1988. Volume XLI, Global Issues II. 47. Telegram from the Mission to the United Nations to the Department of State. Geneva, March 18, 1981. 1732. Subject: United Nations Human Rights Commission. Final Report on the Thirty-Seventh Session.

[150] "Foreign Operations, export financing, and related programs appropriations for fiscal year 1990: hearings before a subcommittee on the Committee on Appropriations, United States Senate, One Hundred First Congress, First Session, on H.R.2939/H.R.3743. An Act Making Appropriations for Foreign Operations, Export Financing, and Related Programs for the Fiscal Year Ending September 30, 1990, and for Other Purposes." Part 1 (Pages 1–1097).

[151] "Foreign Operations, export financing, and related programs appropriations for fiscal year 1990: hearings before a subcommittee on the Committee on Appropriations, United States Senate, One Hundred First Congress, First Session, on H.R.2939/H.R.3743; UN Yearbook 1991, 556.

[152] UN Yearbook 1988, 396.

[153] "Foreign Operations, export financing, and related programs appropriations for fiscal year 1990: hearings before a subcommittee on the Committee on Appropriations, United States Senate, One Hundred First Congress, First Session, on H.R.2939/H.R.3743. An Act Making Appropriations for Foreign Operations, Export Financing, and Related Programs for the Fiscal Year Ending September 30, 1990, and for Other Purposes." Part 1 (Pages 1–1097).

and its technical and development agencies, if fully and effectively managed and coordinated, have the capacity to lead this effort."[154]

In other instances, the twin pillars of the Kirkpatrick strategy emerge in a single UN program. At UNIDO, the US regularly withheld a portion of its mandatory assessment. Unlike at the UN proper, where allegations of *ultra vires* acts accompanied withholding, State Department documents list "an appropriation shortfall" as the only reason for not paying in full.[155] During the same period, the US began earmarking voluntary contributions to the UNIDO Investment Promotion Office in Washington, DC. "The Washington IPS [Investment Promotion Services] office matches U.S. business organizations with industrial investment opportunities in developing countries, resulting in joint ventures between the two parties." This office was effectively a single-donor project, as the US noted that for FY 1990 "our voluntary contribution" is the "sole funding source" for this account.[156]

In retrospect, the UNIDO example was a harbinger for future US behavior. Over time, the United States continued to negotiate reductions in its mandatory assessments across the UN system, and reduced its unrestricted contributions to most UN programs while increasing earmarked funding. The US limited its contributions that would be controlled by multilateral bodies, and increased contributions to earmarked funds that aligned with its bilateral interests. Nowhere is this more apparent than at UNDP. Since 2012, the United States has contributed $80 million to the UN core account, less than half of its 1985 contribution, and on par with contribution levels from 1970. At the same time, the US contribution to UNDP has grown to $252 million ($172 million in earmarked contributions). Between 2012 and 2016, approximately 75 percent of the total US contribution to UNDP was earmarked for projects in Iraq and Afghanistan,[157] reflecting US security interests in the region.

Taking Stock

The 1990s are often identified as the decade that earmarking trends began at the United Nations. But the decline of egalitarian multilateral control of UN resources was well underway by 1990. This chapter showed that increased reliance on earmarked resources was caused not only by increased earmarking behavior, but

---

[154] Foreign Operations, export financing, and related programs appropriations for fiscal year 1990: hearings before a subcommittee on the Committee on Appropriations, United States Senate, One Hundred First Congress, First Session, on H.R.2939/H.R.3743, 516.

[155] United States Department of State 1988, xiv, fn 7.

[156] "Foreign Operations, export financing, and related programs appropriations for fiscal year 1990: hearings before a subcommittee on the Committee on Appropriations, United States Senate, One Hundred First Congress, First Session, on H.R.2939/H.R.3743.

[157] "United States and UNDP: A Partnership that Advances U.S. Interests." UNDP. https://www.undp.org/sites/g/files/zskgke326/files/funding/PDF/UNDP_PG_US_Brochure.pdf (accessed March 14, 2023).

also by reduced support for the mandatory assessments system, and for unrestricted voluntary resources to UN programs. Like in earlier instances of change, processes of reinterpretation and repurposing are central to understanding how UN institutions developed. Severe limits to the mandatory assessments system cut off a previously reliable path of budget growth. To achieve this, the Reagan administration offered a creative reinterpretation of the UN Charter's Article 17 obligations. Relying on a combination of state practice and prior decisions by the International Court of Justice, elites created space for member states to withhold assessments if they determined the majority acted in violation of the Charter.

During the Reagan years, the US not only championed the zero-growth policy embraced by other net-contributor countries to halt budget growth stemming from mandatory assessments, but also halted growth in the unrestricted voluntary contributions made to the UN development system. The shift in US policy occurred alongside European states' creative repurposing of permissive earmark rules as tools to allow them to redirect bilateral aid through the United Nations. This repurposing is illustrated by the rise of single-donor trust funds at UNDP and other UN programs and is especially evident in the trend of establishing sub- (single-donor) trust funds within multi-donor funds like the UNCDF. On the US side, Ambassador Jeane Kirkpatrick learned from the Europeans and creatively adapted their practices to pursue US interests across UN funding modalities, in the context of Article 17, cuts to unrestricted funds, and in the utilization of trust funds.

The joint pursuit of these strategies—capping mandatory assessments and unrestricted voluntary contributions on the one hand, alongside a willingness to increase trust fund money on the other—accelerated the United Nations journey away from egalitarian, multilateral control over resources. The system that would emerge was complex; a rump of unrestricted core resources to UN programs remained governed by multilateral bodies but the majority of resources would be governed by a multitude of contracts between donor agencies and UN administrators. Without any revision to the United Nations Charter—not to the General Assembly's allocation of voting rights, its authority over the budget, or member states' obligation to pay "expenses of the Organization,"—United Nations' funding, and in turn its governance, was transformed.

References

Adler-Nissen, Rebecca, and Vincent Pouliot. 2014. "Power in Practice: Negotiating the International Intervention in Libya." *European Journal of International Relations* 20(4): 889–911.

Allen, Karen. 2005. "A Formidable Task for Torture's Healers." *SAIS Review of International Affairs* 25(1): 153–154.

Alvarez, Jose E. 1991. "Legal Remedies and the United Nations' à la Carte Problem." *Michigan Journal of International Law* 12(2): 229–311.

Benjamin, Bret. 2015. "Bookend to Bandung: The New International Economic Order and the Antinomies of the Bandung Era." *Humanity: An International Journal of Human Rights, Humanitarianism, and Development* 6(1): 33–46.

Búzás, Zoltán I., and Erin R. Graham. 2020. "Emergent Flexibility in Institutional Development: How International Rules Really Change." *International Studies Quarterly* 64(4): 821–833.

Cannizzaro, Enzo, and Paolo Palchetti. 2011. "*Ultra Vires* Acts of International Organizations." In *Research Handbook on the Law of International Organizations*. Edited by Jan Klabbers. Cheltenham, UK: Edward Elgar Publishers, 365–397.

Cornut, Jeremie. 2018. "Diplomacy, Agency, and the Logic of Improvisation and Virtuosity in Practice." *European Journal of International Relations* 24(3): 712–736.

Crook, John R. 2008. "United States Votes Against UN Budget: Breaking Recent Tradition of Consensus on Budgets." *American Journal of International Law* 102(2): 355–356.

Fioretos, Orefeo. 2020. "Rhetorical Appeals and Strategic Cooperation in the Rise and Fall of the New International Economic Order." *Global Policy* 11(S3): 73–82.

Franck, Thomas. 1985. *Nation Against Nation: What Happened to the U.N. Dream and What the U.S. Can Do About It.* Oxford, UK: Oxford University Press.

Franczak, Michael. 2019. "Losing the Battle, Winning the War: Neoconservatives versus the New International Economic Order, 1974–82." *Diplomatic History* 43(5): 867–889.

Galey, Margaret E. 1988. "Reforming the Regime for Financing the United Nations." *Howard Law Journal* 31(4): 543–574.

Gerson, Allan. 2000. "Multilateralism À La Carte: The Consequences of Unilateral 'Pick and Pay' Approaches." *European Journal of International Law* 11(1): 61–66.

Gordon, Richard, and Thomas Stenvoll. 2007. "Statoil: A Case Study in Political Entrepreneurship." *Case Study Series, The Changing Role of National Oil Companies in International Markets. Energy Forum.* James A Baker III Institute for Public Policy, Rice University. https://www.bakerinstitute.org/media/files/page/9ffcb110/noc_statoil_gordon_stenvoll.pdf (accessed February 19, 2020).

Governing Council of the United Nations Development Programme. 1985. *Other Matters. Financial Structure of the UNDP-Administered System.* Report of the Administrator. DP/1985/64. June 13, 1985. New York.

Governing Council of the United Nations Development Programme. 1986a. *Financial, Budgetary and Administrative Matters. Trust Funds Established by the Administrator in 1985.* Report of the Administrator. DP/1986/61.Add.3. Original: English. April 19, 1986. Geneva.

Governing Council of the United Nations Development Programme. 1986b. *Annual Report of the Administrator for 1985.* DP/1986/11/Add.1. Original: English. April 22, 1986. Geneva.

Governing Council of the United Nations Development Programme. 1987. *Financial, Budgetary and Administrative Matters. Annual Review of the Financial Situation, 1986. Net Flow of Contributions by Donor and Recipient Governments.* Report of the Administrator. DP/1987/54/Add.1. April 21, 1987. New York.

Governing Council of the United Nations Development Programme. 1989. "*Financial, Budgetary and Administrative Matters. Trust Funds Established by the Administrator in 1988*. Report of the Administrator. Addendum. Summary Financial Information for All Trust Funds established by the Administrator since 1981. DP/1989/57/Add.1. May 4, 1989. New York. http://web.undp.org/execbrd/archives/sessions/gc/36th-1989/DP-1989-57-Add1.pdf.

Governing Council of the United Nations Environment Programme. 2002. *Trust Funds Administered by the United Nations Environment Programme: Programmatic Descriptions and Expenditures for 2001–2002, 2002–2003, 2003–2004.* Annex 1. Programmatic Descriptions of Active Trust Funds Administered by UNEP. UNEP/GC.22/INF/8. November 26, 2002. file:///Users/erg49/Downloads/UNEP_GC_22_INF_8-EN.pdf

Graham, Erin R. 2017. "The Institutional Design of Funding Rules at International Organizations: Explaining the Transformation in Financing the United Nations." *European Journal of International Relations* 23(2): 365–390.

Graham, Erin R. and Alexandria Serdaru. 2020. "Power, Control, and the Logic of Substitution in Institutional Design: The Case of International Climate Finance." *International Organization* 74(4): 671–706.

Hynes, Patrick J. 1982–1983. "United Nations Financing of the Law of the Sea Preparatory Commission: May the United States Withhold Payment." *Fordham International Law Journal* 6(3): 472–500.

Kirkpatrick, Jeane. 1988. *Legitimacy and Force: State Papers and Current Perspectives. Volume II: National and International Dimensions.* Oxfordshire, UK: Routledge Press.

Lang, Chris. 2002. "The Pulp Invasion: The International Pulp and Paper Industry in the Mekong Region." *WRM (World Rainforest Movement) Bulletin* 58: May.

Meagher, Robert F. 1983. "United States Financing of the United Nations." In *The U.S., the U.N., and the Management of Global Change.* Edited by Toby Trister Gati. New York and London: New York University Press.

Nelson, Richard W. 1986. "International Law and U.S. Withholding of Payments to International Organizations." *American Journal of International Law* 80(4): 973–983.

Peterson, M.J. 2006. The UN General Assembly. New York, NY: Routledge Press, Global Institutions Series.

Puchala, Donald J. 1982–1983. "American Interests and the United Nations." *Political Science Quarterly* 97(4): 571–588.

Sargent, Daniel J. 2015. "North/South: The United States Responds to the New International Economic Order." *Humanity: An International Journal of Human Rights, Humanitarianism, and Development* 6(1): 201–216.

Scharf, Michael P. 2000. "Dead Beat Dead End: A Critique of the New U.S. Plan for Payment of U.N. Arrears." *New England International and Comparative Law Annual* 6: 5–8.

United Nations General Assembly. 1986. *United Nations Development Programme. Financial Report and Audited Financial Statements for the Year Ended 31 December 1985 and the Board of Auditors.* Official Records. General Assembly Forty-first Session. Supplement No. 5A A/41/5/Add.1.

United Nations Industrial Development Organization 1986. *Assistance to the Petroleum Training Centre (PTC) Sumbe, People's Republic of Angola.* DP/RAF/83/002. Preliminary Draft Report by Youri Samohin, UNIDO Consultant. February 9–March 23, 1986. #15494.

United States Department of State. 1988. *Thirty-Sixth Annual United States Contributions to International Organizations. Report to the Congress for Fiscal Year 1987.* Department of State Publication 9666. Bureau of International Organization Affairs. Released September 1988.

United States Department of State. 1993. *Fortieth Annual United States Contributions to International Organizations. Report to the Congress for Fiscal Year 1991.* Department of State Publication 10003. Bureau of International Organization Affairs. Released July 1993.

Zoller, Elisabeth. 1987. "The Corporate Will of the United Nations and the Rights of the Minority." *American Journal of International Law* 81(3): 610–634.

7

Conclusion

What Is the UN and Where Is It Going?

Trends that characterized United Nations financing in the 1980s persisted in subsequent decades. Mandatory and core funding continued their long plateau, and reliance on earmarked funding accelerated. The UN development system expanded as a function of this acceleration. In some ways, the UN's twenty-first century trajectory looked miraculous. In the 1980s, the Geneva Group supported an agenda of "zero real growth" for all UN institutions alongside a requirement that "any new program initiatives be financed within existing resource levels."[1] States central to the UN's fiscal health expressed grave doubts about its usefulness and frustration with its costs. Jeane Kirkpatrick described the US position at the UN as "essentially impotent, without influence, heavily outvoted, and isolated."[2] Australia warned its fellow UN members that "the resources Australia can provide to the UN are not without limit" (...) "As long as the costs of multilateralism continue to rise so steeply and so freely, we will have to make difficult choices: whether or not we should continue membership of all UN agencies, for example."[3] A 1987 analysis by the Overseas Development Institute (ODI) represents the prevailing pessimism, when it notes, "some observers have doubted whether the UN system could survive into the twenty-first century."[4]

Policy institutes like ODI were joined by international relations scholars in diagnosing a "crisis of multilateralism" in the 1980s, which broadly referred to the West's tendency to turn away from multilateral cooperation toward either bilateral alternatives or isolationism.[5] Developing states similarly criticized their wealthy counterparts for their "apparent retreat from multilateralism."[6]

In retrospect, reports of the UN's death were greatly exaggerated. In the wake of expectations that wealthy states would turn away from the UN, they instead put more money into the system. Between 1995 and 2010, the UN Development

---

[1] Alvarez 1991, 249, Supra note 8. For details on the policy, see John R. Bolton, "The Concept of the 'Unitary UN,'" Address before the Geneva group consultative level meeting in Geneva on June 29, 1989.

[2] Richard Bernstein, "The U.N. Versus the U.S." *The New York Times*, January 22, 1984.

[3] "Australia Warns UN to Cut Waste." *The Sydney Morning Herald*, October 10, 1987.

[4] Overseas Development Institute. Briefing Paper. "The UN and the Future of Multilateralism." October 1987.

[5] Cox 1992; Kahler 1992.

[6] Neel Patri, "Asian Nations Criticize Lack of Multilateralism." *Journal of Commerce*, March 17, 1987.

Transforming International Institutions. Erin R. Graham, Oxford University Press. © Erin R. Graham (2023).
DOI: 10.1093/oso/9780198877936.003.0007

Program budget grew by more than 250 percent in real terms.[7] The irony of the "crisis in multilateralism" diagnosis, is that it rightly characterized the outcome (a retreat from multilateralism was underway) without comprehending the UN's transformation. Whether inside Turtle Bay or the academy, the conflation of inter-governmental organizations with *multilateral* organizations was pervasive. With this taken-for-granted understanding, a retreat from multilateralism necessarily meant working *outside* the UN and other international organizations. The confla-tion rendered what was actually happening harder to see. Multilateralism was in retreat *inside* the UN.

Consistent with the definition of transformation offered in Chapter 2, funding rules and the behavioral patterns those rules enabled, reorganized the relation-ships between member states and UN programs, and between the member states themselves. Earmarked funding renders the hard work of multilateral coopera-tion unnecessary. Individual member states or groups of like-minded member states contract directly with a UN program to establish a fund on their preferred issue, without dealing with the more egalitarian, multilateral, and messy pro-cess of working through intergovernmental bodies. The center of gravity shifts away from collective decision-making among diverse formal bodies of member states, toward individual donor decisions. It simultaneously reorders accountabil-ity relationships between member states and UN operational entities. In early UN development programs, the multilateral body was the primary locus of author-ity, jointly responsibly for holding UN bureaucratic entities accountable. In the contemporary system, UN programs and funds are subject to a plethora of accountability relationships with individual donors and small "minilateral" groups of donors, each with their own set of expectations and requirements.[8] Direct con-tracts between donors and UN entities dominate; the multilateral bodies are no longer primary.

Beginning around the year 2000, UN programs and evaluation offices began to formally indicate that the rise in earmarked funds was marginalizing multilateral governing bodies (Table 7.1). The realization was described in remarkably similar terms across UN programs. The World Food Program (WFP) noted in 2000 that earmarked funding made it "very difficult" for WFP to meet program obligations set by its Executive Board. Specifically, the cumulative effect of donors' individual earmarks meant that WFP violated requirements set by its multilateral Executive Board to prioritize least-developed countries and low-income, food-deficit coun-tries.[9] A multi-program evaluation by the United Nations Joint Inspection Unit found that at UNEP, UNDP, UN-HABITAT, and the UN Office for Humanitarian

---

[7] UN General Assembly/ECOSOC 2012, 20.
[8] On accountability and earmarked funding, see Graham 2015; on "minilateral" groups and ear-marked funding, see Graham 2017, 20–22.
[9] Executive Board of the World Food Program 2000, 20.

Assistance (OCHA), the effect was to undermine need-based allocation arrangements set by their respective multilateral councils. Simply put, some areas received more funding than needed and others went without.[10] At OCHA, earmarked funding "created an imbalance (...) with some activities generously funded and others experiencing severe funding shortfalls."[11] At UN-HABITAT, earmarks "created an imbalance between funds received and the approved work program (...)."[12] At UNDP, earmarked funding created a "problem that some sectors are over funded; earmarking prevents staff from distributing funds to underfunded areas." At UNEP, the allocation of funds "diverged from the priorities set for the Environment Fund by the Governing Council."[13]

By the early 2010s, the idea that earmarks undermined multilateral governance by decentralizing resource allocation was increasingly understood to apply across the UN development system. In addition to the UN Joint Inspection Unit concluding as much in 2007, the General Assembly and Economic and Social Council acknowledged the situation in 2012, noting that core resources were "central to ensuring independence, neutrality and [the UN's] role as a trusted partner" (...) whereas "restricted aid in the form of non-core resources (...) is often seen as potentially distorting program priorities by limiting the proportion of funding that is directly regulated by intergovernmental bodies."[14] In 2010, the OECD wrote:

> The widespread use of earmarked funding has brought about a "bilateralisation" of multilateral organisations. First through voluntary contributions and later through earmarked contributions, some individual bilateral donors have gained more influence to shape the priorities and sizes of multilateral organisations' budgets, bypassing "purely multilateral" governance whereby decisions are made by all members according to collectively endorsed rules.[15]

The OECD further demonstrated that bilateralization was more pronounced at the United Nations relative to other international organizations, including the World Bank.[16] In 2013, the Danish Foreign Ministry concluded that earmarked funds were usually "designed and implemented outside the organisation's formal governing systems, and imitate the agendas of individual donors rather than express the organisations' mandates and strategic priorities."[17] Despite efforts to rebalance funding toward core resources across UN programs, these trends did not

---

[10] Yusef et al. 2007.
[11] Yusef et al. 2007, 13.
[12] Yusef et al. 2007, 13.
[13] Yusef et al. 2007, 13.
[14] UNGA and ECOSOC 2012., A/67/94; E/2012/80.13, p. 12.
[15] Cited and summarized in Tortora and Steensen 2014b, 10.
[16] Tortora and Steensen 2014b, 10.
[17] DANIDA 2013, iii.

Table 7.1 Effects of Earmarked Funding (Selected United Nations Programs).

Agency/Program	Statement	Source/Doc
UNDP Evaluation Office	"A major reason for non-delivery of planned outputs is the under resourcing of projects due to the earmarked nature of funds." Although "most country programmes are successful in mobilizing more resources than the expectations reflected in the country programme," this masks the problem that some sectors are overfunded; earmarking prevents staff from distributing funds to underfunded areas (UNDP 2013, 4).	UNDP/2013/17
UNEP	"There has been a proliferation of trust funds; the allocation of these funds among the sub-programmes has diverged from the priorities set for the Environment Fund by the Governing Council" (Yusef et al. 2007, 13).	JIU/REP/2007/1
UN-HABITAT	"Earmarking has created an imbalance between funds received and the approved work programme, with some programs overfunded and others only partially implemented" (Yusef et al. 2007, 13).	JIU/REP/2007/1
UNHCR	"UNHCR remains concerned about the increasing level of tightly earmarked contributions," which increased from 47% to 65% in 2013. "We remain especially grateful to those donors who give the vast majority of their funds unearmarked. I cannot stress enough how important these contributions are for the Office as they allow us to fund new emergencies and under-resourced operations or forgotten crises for which no specific contributions are received" (UNHCR 2014).	UNHCR. 2014. Remarks from Daniel Endres, Director, Division of External Relations
UNICEF	"The larger the earmarked other resources component in total resources, the greater the tendency for UNICEF to become a contractor rather than a partner, and the less influence it has on assigning income to strategic objectives" (Yusef et al. 2007, 13).	JIU/REP/2007/1
UN OCHA	"Earmarking has created an imbalance in overall funding, with some activities generously funded and others experiencing severe funding shortfalls" (Yusef et al. 2007, 13).	JIU/REP/2007/1
WFP	"WFP's governing body requires that development resources be prioritized to least developed countries and low-income, food-deficit countries with a minimum of 50 percent of resources dedicated to LDCs" and "no more than 10 percent of all resources" for countries outside the LIFDC/LDC category. "The trend away from true multilateral contributions, combined with the increasing conditionality of resources, places WFP in a serious dilemma. Despite the existence of this clearly defined policy of the Executive Board, donors often choose (…) to designate the use of their development resources to particular countries or categories. (…) It further restricts WFP's flexibility, making it very difficult for WFP to meet program obligations."	WFP/EB.3/2000/3-B

Table 7.1 *Continued*

Agency/Program	Statement	Source/Doc
UN system-wide	"Core resources are central to ensuring the independence, neutrality and role as a trusted partner in a rapidly changing development cooperation landscape. Restricted aid in the form of non-core resources, on the other hand, is often seen as potentially distorting programme priorities by limiting the proportion of funding that is directly regulated by intergovernmental bodies and processes" (UN General Assembly and ECOSOC 2012, 12).	ECOSOC. E/2013/87. UNGA 1A/68/97.
UN system-wide	"Although there are wide variations, non-core contributions continue to cause serious problems for the organizations included in this analysis. Activities to which funds are earmarked are often, although not always, designed and implemented outside the organisations' formal governing systems and imitate the agendas of individual donors rather than express the organisations' mandates and strategic priorities" (DANIDA 2013, iii).	Foreign Ministry of Denmark (DANIDA) 2013.
UN system-wide	"Conditionalities attached to voluntary contributions have reduced the flexibility of the funding and inhibited secretariats of the organizations in their efforts to deliver mandated programs. There is evidence that earmarking can lead to the distortion of programme priorities, which has been a major concern of Inspectors" (Yusef et al. 2007, iii).	JIU/REP/2007/1

subside. In 2017, over 80 percent of all voluntary contributions to development-related activities at the United Nations were not directly controlled by multilateral governing bodies.[18] Even when assessed contributions were taken into account, 73 percent of all money for development-related activities in 2017 was earmarked.[19] The United Nations Funding Compact of 2019, which aimed to rebalance funding toward core resources stated simply of earmarked funds: "Ultimately, they compromise the multilateral nature of [the] United Nations (...)".[20] What started as incremental tinkering with the UN funding system to achieve altogether different aims had, over many years, transformed United Nations governance.

Implications for Institutional Design and Change

The United Nations' development over time holds a number of implications for understanding institutional design and change. The UN story illustrates the value of the theoretical framework put forward in Chapter 2. The assumptions that institutional architects experience a decision-making environment characterized by genuine uncertainty, that rules are permissive, and that actors are capable of creativity, provide the foundation of the book's framework. The first implication for design and change is to take seriously the idea that institutional architects' medium- and long-range visibility is low. If institutional designers do their jobs properly, they will engage in a process that accords with cost-benefit analysis that is central to rationalist arguments. The UN case demonstrates that even when such a process occurs, designers will fail to anticipate future developments, and often important ones. UN architects did not comprehend the pace of decolonization and its membership effects, and they did not anticipate the UN would possess major economic development and peacekeeping components. If they had, it is very likely that the United States, the Soviet Union, and the United Kingdom would have designed UN funding rules differently. In particular, they would not have written a general rule indicating members were obligated to pay the "expenses of the Organization" based on a formula of capacity to pay. What is most striking about each of these developments is how quickly they emerged after the UN's founding. Yet they were largely unforeseen during the negotiation process.

Visibility issues do not subside once a particular institutional design is in place. A world in which rules are permissive and agents are creative is unpredictable. Anticipating the downstream effects of changes—even changes that appear small and technical in nature—can be difficult. The UN case shows how changes taken to achieve one purpose can be subsequently repurposed to achieve another. It

---

[18] UN General Assembly 2019, 4.
[19] UN General Assembly 2019, 4.
[20] UN General Assembly 2019, 3.

demonstrates that rules written with a certain understanding and set of expectations about implementation can be reinterpreted later to pursue distinct ends. All of this reinforces Pierson's 2004 plea to social scientists: "Rather than assuming relative efficiency as an explanation, we have to go back and look."[21]

The decentralized, uncoordinated nature of gradual transformation at the UN similarly points to the need to investigate intentionality rather than assuming it. At any moment in time, the expectation that actors intend the rules they create is a reasonable one, but it is less reasonable to assume the same after considerable time has passed and rules may have been subject to reinterpretation and repurposing. Diplomats, lawyers, and others who become enmeshed in the process of institutional design and change may intend their piece, without intending the outcomes they make possible or set in motion. We can say with confidence that the UN Office of Legal Affairs intended to repurpose financial regulations from the UN Secretary-General's office to allow UNDP to legally accept an earmarked contribution from the Netherlands. But to argue they intended to undercut UN multilateral bodies—the downstream outcome of their creativity some twenty-five years later—is a much harder case. Instead, Legal Affairs was merely doing its job well, accommodating a request from the new UNDP Executive Director, who himself was motivated to accept (rather than refuse) a supplemental contribution from an important donor. Only later were rules prompted by Legal Affairs advice used by states to substitute earmarked contributions for core funds. This is a longitudinal example of Wendt's cautionary note that "there will always be *some* intentionality in the process by which institutions are created. However, this does not mean we can automatically conclude that institutions are intended."[22]

The book adds to a growing body of empirical work that demonstrates how gradual transformation processes first articulated by scholars of American and comparative development are relevant to the international realm. Beyond that, it illuminates how distinctive characteristics of international law provide for specific varieties of more general processes of conversion and layering. Interpretive strategies enumerated in the VCLT, especially that focused on subsequent practice, have been key to the UN's development. Interpretations of the UN Charter's Article 17 that pertains to UN member states' financial obligations, broadened and then narrowed over time in response to arguments about how states *behaved* and what that behavior signaled about the meaning of Charter obligations. In the UN's evolution, actors as diverse as the International Court of Justice and US Ambassador Jeane Kirkpatrick relied explicitly on subsequent practice in interpreting the UN Charter. While customary law is often described as "what states do," the revelation that state practice similarly endows treaty law with meaning and can contribute to altering meaning over time is less acknowledged in IR scholarship.

---

[21] Pierson 2004, 47.
[22] Wendt 2001, 1036.

The UN's transformation provides not one, but many instances in which rules evolved through layering and conversion processes on the way to reorganizing the relationships central to UN governance. Consistent with international law scholarship, the book lends credence to the idea that change in international rules and organizations *often* occurs through these pathways.[23] Buga puts it this way, because amendment processes for large multilateral treaties are often "infeasible," "Complex treaty regimes are therefore often more prone to subsequent development through mechanisms other than formal amendment."[24] If this is the case, identification strategies that rely on formal amendment and revision or rule replacement to code change will miss much, if not most, of the change that international rules experience over time.

This challenge can be addressed in a number of ways. First, narrow identification strategies should explicitly acknowledge their limits. As a field of study, international relations should not reproduce the idea that change through amendment or replacement is the only way rules change. Nor should revision and replacement be understood to constitute all formal change. This is a key takeaway of the study. The Vienna Convention on the Law of the Treaties provides a formal, codified set of interpretive tools. These tools, including subsequent practice, can produce substantial reinterpretations and modification over time. These constitute changes *in the rules themselves*. Consistent and explicit acknowledgment that revision and replacement are only a subset of the means through which rules change will help to expand IR scholars' understanding of institutional development.

Second, for those with an interest in investigating change beyond the traditional conception of revise or replace, the book suggests that longitudinal case analysis is necessary. Part of this lies in the fact that the importance of a given alteration—for instance, an added rule or new interpretation—often takes time to emerge. In the context of complex rule systems, like those that undergird international organizations, it also points to distinct empirical strategies to identify change. The first is to treat more rules as if they have the potential to affect broader institutional change. In the UN case, change was "hidden" in part because the rules associated with multilateralism that govern representation and voting did not change. Broadening the scope to think about how other rules, like those governing funding, affect governance makes us more likely to succeed in identifying significant developments.

A related strategy is to treat rule hierarchy as an empirical question with an answer that may evolve over time. For instance, UN Charter rules that pertain to funding (Articles 17 and 19) are treaty law. Beyond identifying whether any revision to Article 17 and 19 occurred, one might look to other Charter rules that could affect their scope, or perhaps to the interpretation of treaty law governing funding

---

[23] For similar statements in political science, see Thelen 2004, 35; Pouliot 2021, 2.
[24] Buga 2018, 4.

at other international organizations. But in the UN's transformation, ICJ interpretation of Article 17 relied on soft law—in this case non-binding General Assembly resolutions conceived as subsequent practice. Further, the marginalization of Article 17 was caused by voluntary funding regulations that lack legal force adopted at various UN programs over time. Both examples suggest that despite soft laws' lesser legal status, it can be as consequential to understanding transformation as its hard law counterpart.

This consequential nature is in part a function of the means of interpretation outlined in the VCLT. International law scholarship recognizes subsequent practice and subsequent agreements as especially important in the interpretation of long-standing treaties.[25] Subsequent agreements most often refer to subsequent treaties that offer conflicting obligations or goals. For instance, many contemplate how the interaction of environmental and trade treaties has affected and will affect their meaning.[26] Human rights law may be read in light of humanitarian law, with states' obligations under the European Convention on Human Rights being read through the lens of the Geneva Convention.[27] Subsequent practice widens the scope of behavior relevant to interpreting obligations further. With these means of interpretation in mind it is difficult to ignore rules' permissive nature or interpreters' room for creativity.[28] Scholars of international institutional development should be aware of the VCLT interpretive toolkit and seek to identify change via these pathways.

How to Think about the UN

The evolution in UN funding and governance should alter perceptions and conceptions of the UN system. Various aspects of the United Nations are regularly depicted as immovable. Its personnel system is "sclerotic,"[29] its high-level appointment process is "sticky,"[30] the Security Council design is "path dependent," "locked-in," and long-sought reforms appear impossible.[31] These characterizations may be true, but to infer that the UN system does not change based on a few sclerotic parts would be to misunderstand the whole. The story of the UN's evolution in financing and governance evokes a system resistant to straightforward attempts

[25] International Law Commission 2007; Nolte 2013.

[26] Eckersley 2004; Dong and Walley 2008, 4–5; Lewis 2014.

[27] Búzás and Graham 2020, 828–831.

[28] As the International Law Commission has noted, the application of VCLT rules of interpretation is "widely acknowledged to be 'more an art than a science'" (Nolte 2013, 2).

[29] Anthony Banbury, "I Love the U.N., but It is Failing." *The New York Times*, March 18, 2016.

[30] Megan Roberts, "Help Wanted: Staffing the Next Secretary-General's United Nations." Council on Foreign Relations. *The Internationalist* blog, April 2, 2016.

[31] Hosli and Dörfler 2019; Thibault 2020, "The UN Security Council Isn't Working. Will It Ever Be Completely Reformed?" *The Conversation*. https://theconversation.com/the-un-security-council-isnt-working-will-it-ever-be-completely-reformed-141109.

at revision but susceptible to more subtle modes of change. The sheer scope of the transformation in funding and governance is enough to warrant attention, but the broader conclusion about how the UN changes is buttressed by other recent studies. In particular, Pouliot demonstrates how important changes have occurred in procedures of the UN Security Council and in the process of selecting the UN Secretary-General.[32] The process of change involves experimentation and emergent practices rather than formal rule revision.[33] Like in the evolution of funding and governance, these modes of change emerge when straightforward revision through formal amendment processes is blocked.[34] In short, and consistent with the book's framework, institutions can remain dynamic even when formal rules appear frozen on the page.

If one implication of the book is that the UN is a dynamic system rather than a static one, how do we make sense of this particular evolution? The egalitarian multilateralism of the United Nations has long been celebrated and criticized. From its proponents, the UN is lauded as the "parliament of the world," from its critics it is derided as hopelessly detached from power realities. How should the crowding out of egalitarian multilateralism alter our conceptions of what the UN system *is*? What are the strengths of the new status quo and how should it be criticized? How does it reshape conceptions of what and who the various programs—UNDP, UNEP, UNICEF, and others—are as actors in world politics?

One possibility is to understand the rhetorical and operational roles of the UN to operate under distinct governance systems. Egalitarian multilateralism remains primary to the rhetorical voice of the UN, which is not unimportant. Whether in the General Assembly or executive bodies of UN programs, voice, representation, and voting remain egalitarian in nature. On the operational side, that is to say, UN-funded work in the field, governance via bilateral contract is predominant. Egalitarian multilateralism is not extinct in this realm, but its operation governs a minority of funds. One might think of this as a form of organized hypocrisy, in which "conflicting material and normative pressures" result in inconsistent rhetoric and action.[35] As the operational arms of the UN expanded over the twentieth century, the persistence of its representation and voting rules was path dependent; the majority had a stake in status quo rules. But consistent with the book's framework, the rules' close association with the UN systems' foundational norms of sovereign equality, multilateralism, and arguably democracy, undoubtedly played an important role as well.[36] By contrast, at the founding and through much of the UN's history, funding rules were not understood as essential to the

---

[32] Pouliot 2020, 2021.
[33] Pouliot 2020, 2021 theorize and illustrate the divergence between the resistance of the UN Security Council rules to formal revision and its tendency to innovate and change via semi-formal practices.
[34] E.g., Pouliot 2021, 1–2.
[35] Lipson 2007, 6.
[36] Grigorescu 2015.

production of multilateralism. This detachment made them more responsive to various material pressures. The characterizations and complaints from various corners of the UN (Table 7.1) center on what scholars of organized hypocrisy would characterize as decoupling,[37] in this case, the divergence of that which is produced by voting rules that reflect normative principles, and funding rules that are now more reflective of material pressures.

The concept of a layered text, as deployed by Tulis,[38] provides a related but distinct conception of how to think about UN governance. Here the layers are not merely individual rules, but principles of governance. The first layer is that formed during the Dumbarton Oaks negotiations and San Francisco conference. It is embodied in representation and voting rules of the General Assembly, Economic and Social Council, and replicated across the United Nations development system in its programs and funds. It is a set of rules and norms that emphasize the equality of UN member states, the primacy of collective decision-making to set policy, and that circumscribe the use of money as a tool for influence. These rules provide the foundational layer of egalitarian multilateralism with which the UN system outside the Security Council is so closely associated. The second layer is that formed by funding rules that emerged in the 1960s and were replicated and normalized across UN programs in subsequent decades.[39] It is a set of rules that facilitates individual decisions and control, and allows influence commensurate with financial contributions. These rules and practices produce governance via bilateral contract. To use Tulis's language, applied in the distinct context of the American presidency, the second layer "can be viewed as superimposed upon" the first. The second layer facilitates a mode of governance that is not only distinct from the original layer, but explicitly proscribed by it. Not only do bodies like the General Assembly and executive boards of UN programs eschew unilateral decision-making, early UN development work was wary of and sought to curb bilateral donor interests from infecting UN aid.

Both the conceptions of organized hypocrisy and layered text capture the tension and contradiction at the heart of the contemporary UN. The advantage of thinking of UN governance as a layered text lies in its attention to time and sequence. The internal contradictions are a function not only of contradictory normative and material pressures, but to distinct pressures and demands that emerged at different moments in time. Consistent with studies of political development in domestic contexts, the UN's evolution reveals that institutions "are not created or recreated at all at once, in accordance with a single ordering principle; they are created instead of different times, in light of different experiences, and often for quite contrary purposes."[40]

---

[37] Meyer and Rowan 1977; Lipson 2007.
[38] Tulis 1987, 17.
[39] For the precise year that each UN program adopted permissive earmark rules, see Graham 2017.
[40] Orren and Skowronek 2004, 112.

Despite the UN's transformation, standard critiques and praise of the UN in the public sphere have remained static.[41] This stems in part from the nature of layered governance and subterranean change: the foundational principle of egalitarian multilateralism and the rules that produce it were not formally or publicly rejected. What is more, in this particular case, the rules that produce egalitarian multilateralism remain visible, active, and widely known, while the funding rules and practices that undercut egalitarian multilateralism are less visible and remain less known. What critiques of the UN require reevaluation in light of its transformation? Perhaps the first is the idea that the UN is perpetually on the brink of irrelevance.[42] Whether the Security Council has failed to act, or the Human Rights Council eschews investigations to protect rights-violators, or member states fail to pay their dues, commentators are quick to suggest the UN does not matter. Without saying so, these characterizations ignore the UN development system altogether. Earmarked funding has allowed that system to compete and expand amidst a crowded global governance architecture. The common perception that the UN is on the brink of irrelevance belies the fact that its development system delivers more aid each year than the World Bank Group or the European Commission.[43]

Changes in financing and governance also require that we revisit the assumption that developing states exert influence such that "real-world" power asymmetries are not reflected in decision-making. My research reveals that prior to the rise of earmarked funding, multilateral bodies *did* exert strong influence over project and resource allocation decisions. Try as it might, the US could not simply buy votes to block projects to assist Cuba, for example. In a world dominated by earmarked funds, smaller states—developing or otherwise—only exert that sort of influence over a small portion of total funds. The rest will reflect the interests of donors as they choose to fund projects and countries aligned with their bilateral interests. These interests are not inherently problematic, but they do reflect the national interest rather than the global. For some, developing states' equal standing in UN forums is an asset, improving its legitimacy by incorporating diverse voices, especially from the Global South. For others, it is a drawback that fails to recognize the need to satisfy those who pay the bills. Both groups' ideas about the UN need updating. The first should evaluate the mismatch between developing states'

---

[41] Outside the development policy and scholarly circles, the UN's transformation has received little attention in popular media. For exceptions, see "Last Week Tonight with John Oliver," October 19, 2020. https://www.youtube.com/watch?v=7g0Jh4h5E1E; Graham, Erin R. "Ignore the Old Complaints about UN Funding. Here Are Some New Ones." *Washington Post (Monkey Cage)*, September 30, 2015. https://www.washingtonpost.com/news/monkey-cage/wp/2015/09/30/ignore-the-old-complaints-about-u-n-funding-here-are-some-new-ones/.

[42] E.g., "A Wounded U.N." *New York Times Editorial Board*, January 2, 2004. https://www.nytimes.com/2004/01/02/opinion/a-wounded-united-nations.html?searchResultPosition=23.

[43] E.g., United Nations 2017 Report of the Secretary-General QCPR Funding Analysis. https://undocs.org/E/2017/4 (see p. 6).

influence in multilateral forums, and the extent to which multilateral decisions actually govern UN program work in the field. That is, they should consider the extent to which the UN's egalitarianism is superficial. The second should consider the extent to which the rise of earmarked funds, alongside a range of reforms aimed at improving transparency in financing, address long-standing qualms raised by OECD states. With donors specifying the use of funds at the project level with the option to set reporting and evaluation requirements, the suggestion that donor interests are not attended to is misleading at best.

This all raises the question of how to think about UN bureaucracies as actors in world politics. The reputation is hardly favorable. As earlier chapters show, historically, popular media depicts UN bureaucracies as bloated—with too many staff, who make too much money, and print too much paper.[44] It is not unusual for mass media to paint it as corrupt.[45] These depictions of the UN as at best sluggish and at worst prone to fraud shape public opinion, with individuals in donor countries reporting that these concerns lead them to prefer bilateral aid.[46]

Scholarly work on IO bureaucracies often sets up a dichotomy between IO bureaucracies as tools of powerful state interests, or alternatively as runaway actors pursuing their own autonomous agenda.[47] From the perspective of delegation theory, autonomous behavior—sometimes conflated with dysfunctional behavior—is more likely when member states sitting in multilateral governing bodies disagree about policy or performance. Disagreement can prevent action to provide clear guidance or exert control, leaving the IO bureaucracy with considerable room to pursue its own interests.[48]

UN agencies' heavy reliance on earmarked funding lends itself to two potential models. The first places emphasis on bilateral donor interests. Consistent with a nuanced realist view of international institutions, IO bureaucracies are used by powerful states to further bilateral interests.[49] This does not imply that assistance delivered by the UN does not benefit recipients. Rather, it suggests that resource allocation across substantive priorities and countries will reflect the preferences and geostrategic interests of important donors. The web of bilateral contracts between donors and UN programs suggests that wealthy states have found a work-around for situations in which multilateral disagreement would otherwise facilitate bureaucratic autonomy. Individual donors—especially those with deep pockets—can exert significant control unilaterally when disagreement among member states would otherwise prevent collective action by multilateral

---

[44] E.g., "Reforming the United Nations." *The New York Times*, February 7, 1996. https://www.nytimes.com/1996/02/07/opinion/reforming-the-united-nations.html?searchResultPosition=26.

[45] See Bayram and Graham 2022.

[46] Bayram and Graham 2022.

[47] E.g., Barnett and Finnemore 2004; Copelovitch 2010; Gutner and Thompson 2010.

[48] Nielson and Tierney 2003; Copelovitch 2010.

[49] Krasner 1991; Gruber 2000; Kim 2010; Kaya 2015; Graham and Serdaru 2020.

bodies. This interpretation undermines perceptions of UN proponents that the system is primarily concerned with needs-based allocation and developing states' welfare. It simultaneously undermines UN critics who make claims that the UN is unresponsive to wealthy states' concerns.

In the first interpretation, UN bureaucracies are effectively empty vessels, if not devoid of their own normative and programmatic commitments, at least over-whelmed by wealthy states' agendas. A second interpretation of UN agencies' heavy reliance on earmarked funding views the bureaucracies less as tools of the power-ful and more as actors who channel wealthy states' (and other actors') resources toward their own agendas. Rather than merely react to donors' demands, they seek out good-fit donors for their own priorities. They possess strong resource mobi-lization departments, are nimble in response to changing trends in the funding landscape, and increasingly communicate their strengths and successes to the pub-lic.[50] The opt-in nature of earmarked funding means that substantive priorities do not have to appeal to all or even most member states or major donors. Rather, knowledgeable of the preferences of individual donors, staff can make targeted appeals to those best positioned to give.

In this view, the IO "brand," is less associated with intergovernmentalism and member states and more with the organization itself. In this model, the primary way in which a member state participates in UNICEF, for example, is through funding the UNICEF programs it most values, rather than trying to dictate its pro-gram portfolio through a multilateral body. Further, in the role of donor, states are joined by non-state actors (e.g., NGOs, private corporations, philanthropic organizations), and by individuals across the globe who cumulatively provide sub-stantial contributions. The opt-in nature of funding and the diversity of funders, begins to blur the distinction between intergovernmental and non-governmental organizations.

Determining what model of IO bureaucracy accurately represents the myriad programs of the UN development system and other international organizations is a question for future inquiry. Some are surely more reactive to donors' preferences, while others are more entrepreneurial in building their brand. This work makes clear that the funding landscape shapes possibilities for what IO bureaucracies can be in new ways that are worthy of consideration.

Possible Funding Futures at the UN

Nearly all United Nations programs have encouraged member states to supply a greater share of their contributions as core, unearmarked funding. OECD reports

---

[50] Ecker-Ehrhardt 2018.

from the Development Assistance Committee (DAC) have repeatedly recommended that donor states reduce earmarked contributions in favor of core contributions to the UN system and other international organizations. The OECD notes that "while earmarked funding can help meet specific needs (e.g., humanitarian crises) (...) it can also make co-ordination and coherence of the international development cooperation system more difficult."[51] There are multiple reasons why these overtures and recommendations have had only limited effect. For contributor countries, earmarking is now the norm and has been for some time. Path-dependent dynamics are in play; contributor countries have a stake in the status quo and earmarking practices are now embedded in the procedures of the domestic agencies of donor states. But UN programs and funds, and even some number of recipients, share a stake in the status quo. With a number of donors effectively running bilateral aid agendas through the UN, saying "no" to earmarked funding almost surely means that overall UN program budgets will contract. In short, UN programs would like donor states to reverse earmark trends by substituting core aid for earmarked aid. Instead, some donors are likely to substitute earmarked aid with bilateral aid, or perhaps not to substitute at all. Confronting the challenge of earmarked funding very likely involves a tradeoff between the reassertion of multilateralism (and greater coherence in UN aid delivery) and a reduction in funds delivered through the United Nations.

Efforts to Roll Back Earmarked Funding

Although the details of UN program efforts to roll back earmarked funding across the UN vary, most have involved simply requesting that member states limit earmarks (see Table 7.2). The World Food Program's funding strategy in 2000 called on WFP to "inform donors of the ramifications of excessive conditions and advocate for their eventual elimination."[52] Most programs have not gone so far as to advocate elimination, instead setting goals to rebalance in favor of core funds in more or less precise terms. UNDP has taken this route. In 2015, when approximately 76 percent of UNDP resources were tightly earmarked, the Executive Board set a goal to reduce that number to around 55 percent.[53] UNEP made a similar effort, but focused on increasing mandatory contributions in addition to voluntary funds without restrictions. In 2012, the General Assembly and UNEP Governing Council agreed on a strategy "to provide secure, stable, adequate, and increased financial resources."[54] The strategy includes "A shift towards increased

---

[51] Tortora and Steensen 2014a, 1.
[52] Executive Board of the World Food Program 2000, 4.
[53] UN Secretary-General 2015.
[54] UNEP 2014, 1.

un-earmarked funding" as its first principle.[55] In addition, UNEP made a budget request for $47.7 million to the General Assembly for 2014–15, up from $14.2 million in 2012–13.[56] This UNEP-focused effort followed a system-wide plea to donors from the General Assembly in 2009, urging "donor countries and other countries in a position to do so to substantially increase their voluntary contributions to the core/regular budgets of the United Nations development system (...)."[57]

Missing in these various requests were incentives to motivate changes in funding behavior. The need for incentives is implied in a 2013 report from UN-Women that called for the adoption of new budget methods with an eye toward "providing incentives to increase core funding."[58] In practice, however, these incentives were largely absent and the effects of early efforts were limited. The United Nations Funding Compact,[59] adopted in 2019, begins by noting that the UN system continues to face "a rising share of tightly earmarked funds for specific activities" and asserts that a "fundamental shift in behavior is required."[60] The Compact is based on the argument that earmarked funding causes incoherence and fragmentation in aid delivery and is an obstacle to achieving the UN's Sustainable Development Goals (SDGs). Its underlying logic is that if donor states' legitimate concerns about the UN development system are addressed—related to transparency and accountability—those states will be more willing to provide higher levels of core funding. The Compact sets up such a bargain: UN programs commit to a series of reforms and donor states commit to providing higher proportions of core funds.

In the Compact, the UN recognizes that it needs to supply "greater transparency and clarity on what the United Nations does with the resources it has been entrusted with, and what is achieved with these resources (...)."[61] Member states commit to bring the core share of voluntary funding for development-related activities to a level of at least 30 percent by 2023, from a baseline of 19.2 percent in 2017.[62] The Compact also seeks to improve the "quality" of earmarked contributions and for member states to commit to increasing contributions to various multi-donor funds relative to single-donor funds or project-specific funds.[63] In turn, specific indicators are set to track improved transparency and accountability at UNDS, where varying degrees of improvement are needed. For instance, UNDS already does well in regular surveys of recipient governments on the question of

---

[55] UNEP 2014, 1.
[56] Governing Council of UNEP 2013, 13.
[57] Yusef et al. 2007, 15.
[58] Executive Board of the United Nations Entity for Gender Equality and the Empowerment of Women 2013, 1.
[59] UN General Assembly 2019.
[60] UN General Assembly 2019, 3.
[61] UN General Assembly 2019, 7.
[62] UN General Assembly 2019, 10.
[63] UN General Assembly 2019, 7.

Table 7.2 UN Programs Encourage Donors to Reverse Earmarking Trends

UN Program	Recommendation	Source
UN System (General)	"Executive heads should develop, or continue to develop, flexible funding modalities, thematic funding and pooled funding, for the consideration and approval of the legislative bodies" (JIU 2007, 11).	JIU/REP/2007/1
UN System (General)	"Notes with concern the continuing imbalance between core and non- core resources received by the operational activities for development of the United Nations system and the potential negative impact of non- core funding on the coordination and effectiveness of operational activities (...) Urges donor countries and other countries in a position to do so to substantially increase their voluntary contributions to the core/regular budgets of the United Nations development system, in particular its funds, programmes, and specialized agencies (...)" (GA 2009)	A/RES/63/311
UN Development Program (UNDP)	UNDP has established a policy that "calls for a shift from a high proportion of tightly earmarked non-core resources (currently 76 percent of total resources) towards a higher proportion of core and minimally earmarked non-core resources (target of around 55%), thereby providing more flexible and predictable funding for development."	UNSG Report. Development Cooperation Policy Branch, 2015.
UN Environment Program (UNEP)	"Encourages Governments to the extent feasible to move towards contributions to the Environment Fund in preference to contributions to earmarked trust funds, with a view to enhancing the role of the Governing Council in determining the programme of work and priorities of the United Nations Environment Program" (Governing Council of UNEP, 13).	Governing Council of the UNEP. UNEP/GC/24/12. 19 February 2007.
World Food Program (WFP)	"While the Programme recognizes that legislative and other constraints often require governments to impose conditions on their contributions, the strategy urges WFP to inform donors of the ramifications of excessive conditions, and to advocate for their eventual elimination" (WFP Secretariat 2000)	WFP/EB.3/2000/3-B

World Food Program (WFP)	"The Board encouraged WFP to seek a greater portion of contributions that are multilateral and predictable, given early in the donor's fiscal year without requirements as to their use." (WFP Executive Board 2005, 6).	WFP/EB.2/2005/14
UN-WOMEN	The Executive Board of the Entity for Gender Equality and the Empowerment of Women adopted new budget methods with an eye toward "providing incentives to increase core funding" (UNWomen Executive Board 2013).	UNWOMEN EB/2013/2
UN Population Fund (UNFPA)	"While UNFPA is grateful for and values the complementarity that non-core resources provide to its work, it continues to advocate for an increase of its regular resources, as they afford neutrality, promote flexibility and enable to organization to respond more effectively to the development needs of countries" (Executive Board of the UNDP, UNFPA and UNOPS 2014, 3). "UNFPA continues to engage the Executive Board members and the wider donor community to increase regular and non-core resources in support of its strategic plan. The resources of UNFPA are deployed in line with the vision and direction of the strategic plan (colloquially known as the 'bullseye') (...) It is in this spirit that UNFPA appeals to the donor community to increase its contributions, particularly its regular resources, to enable the Fund to deliver on its mandate" (Executive Board of the UNDP, UNFPA and UNOPS 2014, 3).	DP/FPA/2014/15

whether governments "agree" that the UN has an improved focus on common results at the country level. The Compact sets a target of 100 percent for 2021 from 85 percent in 2017.[64] But in other areas the targets are ambitious from modest baselines. Just fourteen of thirty-nine UNDS entities published data as per the highest international transparency standards as of 2017. This too, was to be improved to 100 percent by 2021.[65]

Although it is too early to assess the effect of the Funding Compact, preliminary results are modest. A few member states appear to be taking these new commitments seriously. Germany, already the largest core contributor to UNDP since 2017, doubled its core contributions to UNDP in 2020 to €110 million ($124 million).[66] The UNDP press release of the German contribution notes it is consistent with the guidance of the Funding Compact. Belgium, which stands out among donor states for having a core funding policy in place since 2012, appears poised to reaffirm its policy with only minor changes.[67] Between 2017 and 2019 the core share of voluntary funding for development-related activities increased just .2 percent, from 19.4 to 19.6 percent, far from the 30 percent target set for 2021.[68] Overall, half of UNDS entities reported a higher number of contributors to voluntary core resources.[69] More substantial trends may emerge in the years ahead, but the Compact has not spurred a rapid shift in funding patterns.

Possible Pathways to Change

Funding Compact or not, in the near term, the status quo is likely to persist at the United Nations. The UN is disproportionately reliant on earmarked voluntary funding and has been for twenty years. It is by now a highly institutionalized practice, both at the UN and within domestic bureaucracies in contributor states.[70] UN entities have adapted to this environment; they devote substantial staff, energy, and money to resource mobilization efforts. Much of this work occurs around specific appeals, whether for renewable energy projects or a particular country. If international organizations are good at this work, they will continue to attract earmarked funding. If donor governments once did not insist on control over the aid they delivered through IOs, they are certainly used to having it now. It is difficult to give up once in hand. These dynamics mean that a UN with governance

[64] UN General Assembly 2019, 10.

[65] UN General Assembly 2019, 12. The list of commitments made in the Funding Compact is long for both UN entities and member states. These examples are meant to give the reader a sense of the design of the Compact and its mutual commitments.

[66] See   https://www.undp.org/press-releases/covid-19-germany-doubles-its-support-undps-flexible-core-funding (accessed November 29, 2021).

[67] Kingdom of Belgium 2021.

[68] UN General Assembly/ECOSOC 2021, 3.

[69] UN General Assembly/ECOSOC 2021, 3.

[70] Baumann 2021.

via bilateral contract is likely to persist. If this state is not transitory, it makes it all the more important to update our conceptions of what the UN *is* as a system of governance in world politics.

Nevertheless, there are at least two foreseeable pathways for change. The first is straightforward and flows from the Funding Compact. If UN entities meet most of the reforms around financial transparency and effectiveness, perhaps many member states will follow in meeting their commitments to rebalance funding. Most UN entities are capable of implementing necessary reforms and some have already done so. Even in donor communities earmarked aid is viewed as costly in some ways. A recent assessment of Belgium's core funding policy argued in favor of its efficiency, noting the high transaction costs of earmarked funding for both the international organization and the donor.[71] Germany is the second largest contributor to UNDS and its moves to increase core funding could provide leadership for others.

But previous efforts to roll back earmarked funding suggest that without any means to enforce commitments made in the Compact, this path is likely to produce only modest change. It rests on the assumption that genuine concerns about efficiency, reporting, and transparency are the primary cause of donors' choice to earmark. Certainly, at different times and at different UN programs, these concerns have been justified. But such concerns are far from the only driver of earmarked funding. The Funding Compact does not address the control benefits donors accrue by aligning their IO contributions with bilateral aid agendas that reflect geostrategic interests or colonial histories. It does not address the benefits that medium-sized donors that lack a global development apparatus gain from effectively running their bilateral aid through the UN. Further, even when contributor states have access to reliable information about performance that can inform funding choices, they do not always use it.[72] UNICEF has long been regarded as a high-performing UN program and meets transparency and reporting commitments outlined in the Funding Compact,[73] but its share of core funding actually declined from the 2017 baseline of 13 percent to just 11 percent in 2020.[74]

It is difficult to compete with the direct and clear influence that earmarked funding provides donors. Influence as a function of core funding is more difficult to ascertain. For outsized contributors, a large supply of core funding certainly translates into informal influence. We see this in the 1950s and 1960s, when the US often supplied half of all voluntary contributions to UN programs. But examples in Chapter 4 also showed the limits of that influence; multilateral control over contributions meant that UN programs did not always bow to US interests in project selection. Medium-sized contributors are less likely to achieve influence

[71] Kingdom of Belgium 2021, 35–36.
[72] Lall 2021.
[73] UNICEF 2021, 6.
[74] UNICEF 2021, 2.

through the provision of core funding. United Nations officials praise Belgium's core funding policy for strengthening UN programs, but evaluations found it did not enhance Belgium's influence in those programs.[75] If core funding does not provide the same level of influence as the status quo, what might motivate contributor states to change?

One potential path lies in the traditional OECD donors' rising concerns about the influence of others. The UN has long sought to diversify its funding base to include more of its member states as well as private actors. China's increased presence at the UN has motivated considerable discussion. The United Kingdom is reassessing its own role under the rubric of strengthening multilateral organizations.[76] The UK describes multilateral organizations as under attack. The inquiry is motivated as follows:

> Disengagement over contentious issues reduces the effectiveness of multilateral organisations, but far more serious are attempts to bend the purpose of, or even break [multilateral] organisations themselves. We have seen attempts by countries such as China to seize control of strategically important organizations and fundamentally redefine the once universally agreed principles on which they are based. This allows multilateral organisations to be weaponized against the founding principles upon which they were built.[77]

China's financial contributions to the UN have grown steadily since 2013,[78] but most of the increase has come through its obligations under the mandatory assessments system. China is now the second largest contributor to the UN regular budget and the peacekeeping budget.[79] Voluntary contributions from China remain small in relative terms, but the funds it does provide are typically earmarked. As Ruipeng notes, "A large gap remains between China's 'quasi-core funding'—like interagency pooled funds and thematic funds—and the requirements of the UNDS Funding Compact, which has been little discussed in China."[80] Concern that China may gain influence through a substantial increase in earmarked resources may persuade Western contributor states to support formal caps on the proportion of earmarked funding at UN programs. Such a policy may attract developing states with an interest reasserting multilateral control over resource allocation to provide consistent support for strong transparency and reporting requirements. This path would require coordination among the UN's major donors, and in particular, it would require the United States to return to

[75] Kingdom of Belgium 2021, iv.
[76] See https://committees.parliament.uk/work/381/the-uks-role-in-strengthening-multilateral-organisations/publications/.
[77] House of Commons, Foreign Affairs Committee 2021, 3.
[78] Ruipeng 2020.
[79] Peter Yeo, "How Should the US Respond to China at the U.N.?" *Devex*, July 21, 2021.
[80] Ruipeng 2020, 2.

positions it took in the mid-twentieth century when limiting Soviet influence was among its chief aims.

The book's broader argument suggests that these straightforward paths to change may not be the most likely, and other rules and practices may emerge to upend UN funding once more. In the meantime, we must update our conception of UN programs and their governance. The product of a quiet transformation, the UN development system is now a diverse set of organizations, directed and held accountable primarily through a multitude of contracts with bilateral donors and minilateral groups rather than egalitarian multilateralism.[81] With this view in mind, we can better understand the nature of the system, its strengths, and contradictions.

References

Alvarez, Jose. 1991. "Legal Remedies and the United Nations' A La Carte Problem." *Michigan Journal of International Law* 12(2): 229–311.

Barnett, Michael, and Martha Finnemore. 2004. *Rules for the World: International Organizations in Global Politics.* Ithaca, NY: Cornell University Press.

Baumann, Max-Otto. 2021. "How Earmarking Has Become Self-perpetuating in United Nations Development Cooperation." *Development Policy Review* 39: 343–359.

Bayram, A. Burcu, and Erin R. Graham. 2022. "Knowing How to Give: How Funding Knowledge Affects Public Support for Aid Delivery Channels." *Journal of Politics.* 84(4): 1885-2311.

Buga, Irina. 2018. *Modification of Treaties by Subsequent Practice.* Oxford University Press.

Búzás, Zoltán I., and Erin R. Graham. 2020. "Emergent Flexibility in Institutional Development: How International Rules Really Change." *International Studies Quarterly* 64(4): 821–833.

Copelovitch, Mark. 2010. "Master or Servant? Common Agency and the Political Economy of IMF Lending." *International Studies Quarterly* 54(1): 49–77.

Cox, Robert. 1992. "Multilateralism and World Order." *Review of International Studies* 18(2): 161–180.

DANIDA. 2013. "Danish Multilateral Aid Cooperation Analysis: And Assessment of Denmark's Multilateral Engagement in Light of the Right to a Better Life, the Strategy for Danish Development Cooperation." Ministry of Foreign Affairs, Denmark.

Dong, Yan, and John Walley. 2008. "Carbon, Trade Policy, and Carbon Free Trade Areas." National Bureau of Economic Research. Working Paper No. 14431.

Ecker-Ehrhardt, Matthias. 2018. "International Organizations 'Going Public'? An Event History Analysis of Public Communication Reforms 1950–2015." *International Studies Quarterly* 62(4): 723–736.

Eckersley, Robyn. 2004. "The Big Chill: The WTO and Multilateral Environmental Agreements." *Global Environmental Politics* 4(2): 24–50.

---

[81] On contracts with minilateral groups, see Graham 2017.

Executive Board of the United Nations Entity for Gender Equality and the Empowerment of Women. 2013. 2013/2. "Road Map towards an Integrated Budget, Beginning
2014, and Update on Cost Recovery." Resumed first regular session of 2013. February 8.

Executive Board of the World Food Program. 2000. "A Resource Mobilization Strategy for the World Food Programme." WFB/EB.3/2000/3-B. September 4. Executive
Board Third Regular Session. Rome.

Governing Council of UNEP. 2013. "Biennial Programme of Work and Budget for
2014–2015." Nairobi. February 2013. In *Twenty-seventh Session of the Governing
Council/Global Ministerial Environment Forum*.

Graham, Erin R. 2015. "Money and Multilateralism: How Funding Rules Constitutes
IO Governance." *International Theory* 7(1): 162–194.

Graham, Erin R. 2017. "Follow the Money: How Trends in Financing Are Changing
Governance at International Organizations." *Global Policy* 8(S5): 15–25.

Graham, Erin R., and Alexandria Serdaru. 2020. "Power, Control, and the Logic of
Substitution in Institutional Design: The Case of International Climate Finance."
International Organization 74(4): 671–706.

Grigorescu, Alexandru. 2015. *Democratic Intergovernmental Organizations? Normative Pressures and Decision-making Rules*. New York, NY: Cambridge University
Press.

Gruber, Lloyd. 2000. *Ruling the World: Power Politics and the Rise of Supranational
Institutions*. Princeton, NJ: Princeton University Press.

Gutner, Tamar, and Alexander Thompson. 2010. "The Politics of IO Performance: A
Framework." *Review of International Organizations* 5, 227–248.

Hosli, Madeleine, and Thomas Dörfler. 2019. "Why Is Change So Slow? Assessing
Prospects for United Nations Security Council Reform." *Journal of Economic Policy
Reform* 22(1): 35–50.

House of Commons, Foreign Affairs Committee. 2021. "In the Room: The UK's Role
in Multilateral Diplomacy." First Report of Session 2021–2022. HC 199; HC 513 (In
session 2019–2021).

International Law Commission. 2007. "Report of the International Law Commission
on the Work of its 59th Session." (May 7–June 5 and July 9–August 10, 2007). UN
Doc A/62/10, para. 374.

Kahler, Miles. 1992. "Multilateralism with Small and Large Numbers." *International
Organization* 46 (3): 681–708.

Kaya, Ayse. 2015. *Power and Global Economic Institutions*. New York, NY: Cambridge
University Press.

Kim, Soo Yeon. 2010. *Power and the Governance of Global Trade: From the GATT to
the WTO*. Ithaca, NY: Cornell University Press.

Kingdom of Belgium. 2021. "Core Funding: An Evaluation of the Belgian Core Funding Policy of Multilateral Organisations." Federal Public Service, Foreign Affairs,
Foreign Trade and Development Cooperation. April.

Krasner, Stephen. 1991. "Global Communications and National Power: Life on the
Pareto Frontier." *International Organization* 43(3): 336–366.

Lall, Ranjit. 2021. "The Financial Consequences of Rating International Institutions:
Competition, Collaboration, and the Politics of Assessment." *International Studies
Quarterly* 65(2): 343–359.

Lewis, Joanna I. 2014. "The Rise of Renewable Energy Protectionism: Emerging Trade
Conflicts and Implications for Low Carbon Development." *Global Environmental
Politics* 14(4): 10–35.

Lipson, Michael. 2007. "Peacekeeping: Organized Hypocrisy?" *European Journal of International Relations* 13(1): 5–34.

Meyer, John W., and Brian Rowan. 1977. "Institutionalized Organizations: Formal Structure as Myth and Ceremony," *American Journal of Sociology* 83(2): 340–363.

Nielson, Daniel, and Michael Tierney. 2003. "Delegation to International Organizations: Agency Theory and World Bank Environmental Reform." *International Organization* 57(2): 241–276.

Nolte, Georg. 2013. *Treaties and Subsequent Practice.* Oxford, UK: Oxford University Press.

Orren, Karen, and Stephen Skowronek. 2004. *The Search for American Political Development.* Cambridge University Press.

Pierson, Paul. 2004. *Politics in Time: History, Institutions, and Social Analysis.* Princeton, NJ: Princeton University Press.

Pouliot, Vincent. 2020. "Practice Theory Meets Historical Institutionalism." *International Organization.* 74(4): 742–772.

Pouliot, Vincent. 2021. "The Gray Area of Institutional Change: How the Security Council Transforms Its Practices on the Fly." *Journal of Global Security Studies* 6(3): 1–18.

Ruipeng, Mao. 2020. "China's Growing Engagement with the UNDS as an Emerging Nation: Changing Rationales, Funding Preferences, and Future Trends." German Development Institute. Discussion Paper No. 2/2020.

Thelen, Kathleen. 2004. *How Institutions Evolve: The Political Economy of Skills in Germany, Britain, the United States, and Japan.* New York, NY: Cambridge University Press.

Therien, Jean-Philippe, and Vincent Pouliot. 2020. "Global Governance as Patchwork: The Making of Sustainable Development Goals." *Review of International Political Economy* 27(3): 612–636.

Tortora, Piera, and Suzanne Steensen. 2014a. "Bilateral Providers' and Multilateral Organisations' Practices on Earmarked Funding." OECD Development Co-Operation Directorate.

Tortora, Piera, and Suzanne Steensen. 2014b. "Making Earmarked Funding More Effective: Current Practices and a Way Forward." OECD Development Co-operation Directorate.

Tulis, Jeffrey. 1987. *The Rhetorical Presidency.* Princeton, NJ: Princeton University Press.

UNDP. 2013. "Evaluation of the UNDP Strategic Plan, 2008–2013." New York, NY: UN Doc. DP/2013/17 of 5 April 2013.

UN General Assembly. 2019. *Seventy-fourth Session. Operational Activities for Development: Operational Activities for Development of the United Nations System.* Funding Compact, Report of the Secretary-General. GA/ECOSOC A/74/73/Add.1 E/2019/4/Add.1.

UN General Assembly and Economic and Social Council. 2012. *Analysis of Funding for Operational Activities for Development of the United Nations System for 2009.* United Nations. Geneva, Switzerland.

UN General Assembly and Economic and Social Council. 2013. *Analysis of Funding of Operational Activities for Development of the United Nations System for 2011.* A/6897-E/2013/87. June 24, 2013.

UN General Assembly and Economic and Social Council. 2021. *Implementation of General Assembly Resolution 75/233 on the Quadrennial Comprehensive Policy*

Review of Operational Activities for Development of the United Nations System.
Annex: Funding Compact Indicator Table. https://www.un.org/ecosoc/sites/www.
un.org.ecosoc/files/files/en/2021doc/Annex-Table_FundingCompact_Indicators.
pdf.

UN Secretary-General. 2015. *Implementation of General Assembly Resolution 67/226
on the Quadrennial Comprehensive Policy Review of Operational Activities for Development of the United Nations System (QCPR).* Development Cooperation Policy
Branch, Department of Economic and Social Affairs, United Nations.

UNDP. 2013. "Evaluation of the UNDP Strategic Plan, 2008–2013." New York, NY: UN
Doc. DP/2013/17 of 5 April 2013.

UNEP. 2014. *UNEP Funding Strategy: Universal Membership, Global Responsibility.*

UNHCR. 2014. "Update on Funding in 2013 and Requirements for 2014, Daniel
Endres, Director, Division of External Relations." 59th Standing Committee, 4-5
March 2014.

UNICEF. 2021. *Funding Compact: Progress against Member State and entity-specific
commitments related to UNICEF.* United Nations Children's Fund. Executive Board.
Second Regular Session 2021. September 7–10, 2021. UNICEF/2021/EB/12.

Wendt, Alexander. 2001. "Driving with the Rearview Mirror: On the Rational Science
of Institutional Design." *International Organization* 55(4): 1019–1049.

Yusef, Muhammad, Juan Luis Larrabure, and Cihan Terzi. 2007. *Voluntary Contributions in United Nations System Organizations: Impact on Program Delivery and
Resource Mobilization Strategies.* Geneva, Switzerland: UN Joint Inspections Unit.

Index

For the benefit of digital users, indexed terms that span two pages (e.g., 52–53) may, on occasion, appear on only one of those pages.